NIGHT-
MARE

NIGHT-MARE

Uncovering the 56 Strange Personalities of Nancy Lynn Gooch

Emily Peterson and Nancy Lynn Gooch
with **LUCY FREEMAN**

Richardson & Steirman, Inc.
New York • 1987

This book is dedicated to my mother, Nancy Gooch Phipps, and my father, Linley Gooch, for never giving up, and to Deborah R. Kidwell, M.S.W., for the special friendship I cherish.

Nancy Lynn Gooch

Contents

Acknowledgments

We wish to thank Stewart Richardson and Hy Steirman, our publishers, for their help in moulding this book. Mr. Richardson conceived its title and Mr. Steirman, as editor, made valuable contributions as to structure, content and style.

We also want to thank Clinton A. Johnson, M.D., for contributing important information, compiling a chronology of the treatment of Nancy Lynn Gooch, and furnishing valuable transcripts. Our thanks also go to his daughter, Lorraine Johnson Lochner, now in business administration, who typed the transcripts, learning swiftly which voice belonged to which personality, for many would appear unannounced.

Our deepest thanks also to Joel Gotler of The Agency, our literary agent in Los Angeles, and co-agent Jane Dystel of the Edward J. Acton Agency in New York, who had faith in the idea of this book. Thanks, too to Renée Wayne Golden, our lawyer, of Beverly Hills, for her expertise and Lawrence Peterson, psychologist, who contributed support both in the treatment of Nancy and the writing of the book. Last but not least, our thanks to Nancy's mother, Nancy Gooch Phipps, who freely granted interviews and also permission to quote from her writings about her daughter's life.

Emily Peterson
Nancy Lynn Gooch
Lucy Freeman

Introduction

by Clinton A. Johnson, M.D.

This book tells the story of Nancy Lynn Gooch, who suffered from multiple personalities and sought the help of Emily Peterson, her courageous high school teacher, as therapist. It is a tale of determination on both their parts to triumph over the trauma in Nancy's life that was leading her to destroy herself.

The multiple personality is slowly achieving the prominence it has long deserved, after *Sybil* and *The Three Faces of Eve* first informed the public of such disorders of the mind.

The multiple personality is defined by the American Psychiatric Association as a "hysterical neurosis," a "dissociative disorder" in which the person suffers fugues (is unaware of what is happening or where he is—blacks out, so to speak). During this amnesia any one of a number of buried personalities may emerge and engage in behavior foreign to the nature of the "core" personality.

Each personality has a distinctly separate identity, attitude, speech, handwriting, tastes, values and manner of thinking. One authority has mentioned the "totally autonomous existence of the alternates." They, in essence, control the core personality. The work of the therapist centers on reversing this—helping the core personality, in this case, Nancy, become the one in control.

When Emily first met Nancy she was bewildered, wondered how she could possibly rescue Nancy from torment. Then it became a matter of either trying or abandoning Nancy to life in a state mental institution or death at the hands of one of her self-destructive personalities, for there had been several suicide attempts.

In an article by Philip M. Coons, M. D., titled "Multiple Personality: Diagnostic Considerations," almost all of the criteria he presented became evident in Nancy and the alternate personalities as her story unfolded. His relevant observations included: "The personalities may differ from one another in terms of age, sex or sexual orientation. Headaches, hysterical conversion symptoms, drug abuse, suicide attempts, stormy interpersonal relationships and brief psychoses are also common. Suicide is often attempted by wrist slashing and often one personality may attempt to take control by trying to kill another personality only to be rescued by a third personality."

While Nancy was a sophomore at Chaffey High School in Ontario, California, she went into a fugue and was taken in a straitjacket to the Psychiatric Unit of the Los Angeles County General Hospital. She had previously been in hypnotherapy with Harold Gaffney for treatment of her "bleeding ulcers." Harold and his wife, Diane, a social worker, operated a foster home for troubled adolescent girls, now recommended to Nancy's mother as an alternative to a psychiatric hospital.

For five years Nancy lived at the Gaffneys while Emily, as therapist, treated her. I had the privilege of being observer and recorder on tape and in transcripts without being in the direct line of fire. I watched and listened in wonder as Emily worked to develop with Nancy an interaction that went far beyond the exchange of words. It became, in effect, a continual vigorous intervention, often in crisis.

Emily employed principles of confrontation, reward-punishment, approval-disapproval, "cognitive therapy," direct orders and "contracts," all in a consistent structure reinforcing integrity, fulfillment, trust, caring and love. Her recognition of and response to the distress and need of each individual alternate dissolved the fear and anger that seemed to energize the personalities, as the younger ones were able to integrate willingly, almost eagerly.

I hung on breathlessly, trying to keep up with the import of whispered confidences, sudden "switches" in the appearance of personalities, nonverbal clues to their distress, and interim activities of alternates of which Nancy had no memory. With each session I felt increasing admiration of Emily's ability to set up structure—to perceive what was needed and how it could be attained.

Emily discovered early that some personalities had to overcome paralyzing fear, desire for vengeance and suicidal wishes if Nancy was to survive. The fight required Emily to be available twenty-four hours a day, seven days a week if needed in times of crisis, and there were many. Emily also conducted what seemed a neverending search for the childhood horror that precipitated the creation of the alternate personalities.

Sometimes I doubted my senses as sessions took a surprising turn. There were the "helpers" within who aided Emily and the "destroyers" who wanted her out of the picture, since she curtailed both violent and sexual acting-out and forbade drug abuse. The battles that ensued between Emily and furious "destroyer" personalities gradually drained off and defused the anger, assuaging the panic within Nancy so she could use her reason and face reality.

The "re-parenting" function of the Gaffneys and Emily was vital to Nancy's physical survival and to promoting in the personalities a sense of trust that made them accessible. But as Emily became more and more deeply involved in the therapy, and as more alternate personalities came forth, she realized (as did the Gaffneys) that the demands of the dual role of mother and therapist were too much for any one person—even Emily. The wisdom of Nancy and the Gaffneys in enlisting Emily as therapist while Diane retained the maternal role seems to me the primary key to the survival of all concerned.

My regard for these two women, Emily and Diane, goes beyond words. In a time of travail in their own lives, both mustered courage and resources to salvage one whose suffering sharpened their focus on their own pain. Emily realized Nancy's fugues and splits protected her against impending recall of horrors that she unconsciously equated with death. Through Emily's capacity to empathize deeply with another human being in constant torment, she discovered Nancy had to face reality in order to stay alive. With superhuman patience Emily persevered, week after week, year after year, to save Nancy from being destroyed by her pervasive nightmare.

Nancy, too, had a strength, though at first it was hidden, buried deep under her fear, rage and pain. Without that strength she never would have survived the horror of her early life as well as she did.

I view the phenomena of multiple personalities as a vast frontier beckoning more and more pioneers to explore and experience. If the story that follows evokes doubt or disbelief, I can understand. I have come away from sessions saying to myself, "I saw it, I heard it, I feel it, but I still cannot *believe* it!"

CLINTON A. JOHNSON, M.D.
(Former Chief Psychiatrist at California Rehabilitation Center, Department of Corrections facility in Norco, for treatment of narcotic addicts; previously served in the Department of Mental Hygiene as Chief of Child-Parent and Staff Training Clinic and Chief of Professional Education; now pursuing independent study of multiple personality and parapsychology.)

Prologue

Nancy sat quietly on a green wooden bench in Echo Park. A wraith in blue jeans, white shirt, beige sandals. The rays of Southern California sun streamed through the leaves of the maples and palms.

She had walked the mile from home to seek the peace of the spacious park in north Los Angeles. It was a silent Sunday, this March 25, 1973. Only the laughter of the children as they sailed back and forth on the swings stirred the air.

She flipped open her notebook of lined white paper, drew the Number 2 pencil from her shirt pocket. Words formed in her mind, she wrote:

> Evening slips in
> the morning bird sings
> another night lost
> as though it had wings
>
> The face in the mirror
> as always the same
> heartbeat still strong
> in a shell with no name
>
> Whispered secrets too soft
> always so near
> eluding my grasp
> increasing my fear
>
> Eyes of memory
> so quickly dart
> searching in vain
> for a place in the heart
>
> Grief with no blame
> claiming my soul
> running in shame . . .
> with no where to go.

Words served as her savior. That is, when written. Not spoken but placed on the permanence of paper.

She closed the pad, felt sad. The dreams were never fulfilled, destined to remain fantasy. At fifteen, she was alone, had always felt alone, even in the presence of others, especially in the presence of others.

She sighed, stood up, moved slowly to the rose garden near the sidewalk. She inhaled the sublime fragrance of a yellow rose, nothing more regal, more exotic, than a rose of any color.

The streets edging the park were lined with cars of families who brought picnics, stayed for hours as they watched their children romp or fished in the placid lake. She did not give a second thought to the sound of one more car that parked in a space directly behind her.

Suddenly she felt a large, rough masculine hand over her mouth, stifling all sound. Then a sharp knife pressed against her throat, threatening her flesh.

A husky, low voice warned, "Not a sound. Or you'll get hurt."

She turned, saw his face. He was about twenty, dark complexion, Mexican, stocky: His brown-black eyes, hard, mean, stared into her hazel ones. "Get going," he ordered.

He dragged her to the car that had just moved into the empty space. A two-door battered Chevrolet of slimy green. He opened the passenger side, hurled her down on the seat so she could not be glimpsed by anyone, ordered, "Don't move."

He walked around the car to the driver's seat, jumped in. As he drove away from the park, he held the knife to her throat with one hand. She said not a word, dared scarcely breathe.

After twenty minutes he stopped the car. She lay passively until he walked around, pulled her out. He pushed her into a wooded area shielded from the road. He hurled her to the ground, placed his right foot on her chest. He unzipped, stepped out of his blue jeans, he wore no underwear. He kept on his shirt and cowboy boots.

He bent over her, tore open her shirt, pulled off her jeans, tossed them aside. He stared at her slim white body, contrast to his dark one.

Rape on a Sunday, holy day, was not even the Lord's day sacred? she thought. She opened her mouth to protest. He slammed his fist against her nose, she felt blood stream out. He threatened, "Shut up. Or I'll give you the knife." Then he punched her ferociously in the right eye. She winced in agony, not only at the viciousness but the insult to her pride.

He fell on her nakedness, crushed the breath out of her. Her eye felt on fire. She lost consciousness.

When she came to she was back at Echo Park, fully clad. He was carrying her out of the Chevrolet at the very spot he had picked her up. The sky was night-blue, hours had passed. Once again he threw her to the ground, though more gently this time. He threatened, this rapist with the angry eyes, "If you tell anyone, I'll kill you. I know where you live. I've seen you come out of your house. I followed you to the park."

Then he was gone, the terror ended. She pulled herself painfully up from the hard earth. She noticed her notebook, it lay under the yellow rosebush where it had fallen as she felt the knife at her throat. At least the poem was safe, the lines she had prophetically written: "running in shame . . . / with no where to go."

Her head throbbed, her surface flesh hurt all over. Notebook in hand, she walked, wounded, the mile home. What would she tell her mother? Not the truth, never the truth. Her mother must not be hurt by the truth.

She pushed open the door of the house, a comfortable house, a cheerful house, comfortable and cheerful like her mother. She staggered to her mother's room, saw her mother seated on the green taffeta bedspread pinning a pattern on yards of grey silk, the first step in creation of a pants suit.

She caught her own image in the mirror of her mother's dresser. Long brown hair, matted, face black and blue from the punches, one eye almost swollen shut. White shirt bloody, torn and blackened from the dirt on which she had been raped.

She lurched toward her mother, her mother looked up, stared at her for a moment as though she were a stranger. Then dropped the pins she held in her hand. She started to scream hysterically.

"Oh God, Nancy! What happened? Who did this to you?" Her mother's wail of woe.

She said not a word. She was trained to say nothing when bloodied by someone else's cruel hands. Muteness after attack had been instilled in her so early she could not recall the moment.

Maybe someday she would write what she felt. But put it into the sound of words?

Never. That way lay death.

THE UNSPOKEN PLEA

1.   October, 1973

I became aware of a student new to Ontario High when she suddenly stood up. I did not recall her name, she was still just a face in the class.

I thought she was going to ask a question but instead she turned, flew down the aisle. Out the door with the speed of a startled lark.

No one left my class without permission, even for an emergency. I said to my thirty-three students, "Excuse me a moment," went in search of the errant fugitive. No sign of her in the long empty hall. I shrugged my shoulders, made a mental note to speak to her when she reappeared.

I returned to my creative-writing class, which met between ten and eleven each weekday morning. I continued where I left off, explaining character development in the short story and novel. I pointed out, "A writer has to show what a character looks like, how the character feels about the world and how the world feels about the character."

At this point the proctor, who kept an eye out for wandering students among the school's 1,300, opened the door to the classroom. I was about to cite Melville's particular genius in evolving character as well as creating what may be the most intriguing opening of a novel—the three words, "Call me Ishmael."

The proctor walked up to my desk, asked, "Would you come outside for a moment, please, Mrs. Campbell?" He explained, "I need to know if a girl is one of your students."

For the second time in five minutes I excused myself, joined the proctor. We walked out of the mammoth red brick building onto the campus dotted with thick grass and tall trees. I still felt slightly upset by the petite, ethereal girl who left class without permission.

Then I saw her. She was huddled in a corner between the iron gate and the outdoor lockers bolted to the building. As she saw me, she turned sideways, arms folded against her breast, head averted. She shrank back as though to become part of the wall.

The proctor explained to me, "When I asked why she was leaving school at this hour without permission, she started to look real wild. She won't even talk to me. I thought you might know who she is."

"I'm sorry," I said. "I don't remember her name. She's a new student and in the first few weeks of class she hasn't spoken a word."

For the first time I looked intently at the girl. Glimpsed at a distance in the classroom she had seemed no different from the rest of the girls with her long brown hair, slim figure clad in the traditional blue jeans, blouse and sneakers. I guessed she was fifteen, though petite for that age, about five feet tall. Slim almost to the point of anorexia. Her waiflike face exuded a strange vulnerability, I was drawn to her as to a helpless child.

I lost all anger at her leaving class so precipitously. I felt I looked at a cornered soul. To reassure her, I approached her quietly, steadily. I reached out, put my arm around her shoulders.

I asked gently, "What's the matter? Aren't you feeling well?" Thinking she might be on drugs, as many students were.

No response. Not even the shade of a nod.

She obviously was in pain, whether mental or physical or both, I had no way of knowing. I took her hand, pulled her upright, led her away from the wall in the direction of the nurse's office.

She did not resist. As we walked, with my arm still around her shoulder, I kept looking at her lowered head, trying to glimpse more of her face. She seemed to have no awareness of me or the surroundings. Keeping in mind the proctor's description of the girl's "wild look," I reassured her, "Everything's going to be all right." The proctor vanished, left her in my care.

No one in the office looked up, typewriters clicked on, conversations continued. I led the girl down the aisle between desks and into the nurse's private room. I intended to let the nurse take over, return to my class.

But the girl had other plans. As she saw the nurse, she turned, made a sudden dash for the door, a desperate look on her face. But I reached the door first, stood with my back against it, facing her.

She weaved like a football player, trying to find the weakness in my block. She grabbed my arms, attempted to pull me away from the door. I heard our heavy breathing, muted grunts. We were each intent and determined. She trying to escape me, I anticipating her moves.

Finally I put a lock around her with both arms, wrestled her onto the cot. I held her as she continued to struggle lying down. I kept repeating, "It's all right. We want to help you."

The nurse asked, "Will you stay with this girl until I can find out who she is and notify her parents to come and get her? We can't handle her."

As the nurse left, suddenly the girl stopped fighting. I eased my hold. She had said not one word since the proctor and I walked over to her as she huddled against the wall.

I kept trying to reassure her no one wanted to harm her but it was like talking to the deaf and mute. Twenty minutes later the nurse returned, said, "We can't contact the authorities at Reach-Out, where she is staying temporarily. This is an emergency home for teenagers on drugs. She calls herself Penny but her real name is Nancy Lynn Gooch. We'll know more when the Reach-Out supervisor calls us back."

There was no expression on Nancy's face as the nurse talked, she might as well have spoken in Prakrit (Sanskrit is the written language). Nancy looked as though she now had given up trying to escape.

The nurse asked me, "Will you wait it out with us? Will you stay here while I go to lunch, until the Reach-Out call comes in? I'll be glad to bring you back food."

I replied, "I'll be glad to stay if you'll arrange for someone to take over my two afternoon classes. And thank you for the offer of food but I am not hungry."

"I'll see you have replacements at once." Gratitude in her voice.

I looked at the girl who now had a name—Penny. Who had been too terrified to dare speak her name. I wondered how to help ease her distress. I had no experience with youngsters who took drugs, other than seeing them on a high around school.

She had stopped resisting me though I felt she would still try to escape, especially since we were now one to one. I wondered what I could do to lessen her pain.

If I sense someone is hurting I want to hold them close, reassure them, knowing tenderness often eases the psychic wound. I now took her slim body, she could not have weighed more than ninety pounds, in my arms, rocked her, assured her soothingly, "No one wants to harm you, Penny. We all want to help."

She sat quietly on my lap, no longer a "wild" creature. I stroked her hair as I would a frightened child. As I held her the conviction slowly deepened this was a young girl in almost total terror. Too scared to reach out for help from anyone. I sensed I was not dealing with the effect of drugs but a horror even more profound. Not a temporary imbalance of the mind due to heroin or cocaine but a wound or wounds festering for years.

I wanted her to have the courage to step into my world, talk to me. Tell me what monsters haunted her. I wished she would utter one word as symbol of breaking free from whatever fear silenced her tongue.

Perhaps I should concentrate on outer reality, I thought, since her inner one proved so painful. Focus on something in the nurse's office. Something substantial. Why not myself?

"Look at my eyes, Penny. What color are my eyes?"

I repeated this many times, still not the glimmer of a response, she seemed almost a corpse. She stared past me at the wall, mute. I had the strange thought she had done this many times before when confronted by something that terrorized her.

I then asked, "Penny, what color are *your* eyes?"

I repeated this too, over and over, without any indication on her part she had heard it. Then I said, "You have lovely eyes." Expressive, soft hazel eyes set in a face that held the essence of Irish beauty, perhaps her mother was Irish.

She lowered her head to keep me from looking into her eyes. I lifted her head to show her my unusual wedding ring, six alternating silver and gold sections. It proved the one thing on which she seemed able to focus, brought her back momentarily into this world.

It was almost two hours before the nurse returned. She reported, "The authorities at Reach-Out will not take this girl back in her present condition. She had been living with her mother before going to Reach-Out. The supervisor I spoke to said he would call the Pomona Psychiatric Hospital to send an ambulance." Pomona was a neighboring city in the valley.

I looked around that antiseptic office, wondered how much longer we would sit helplessly in it. I sensed Penny, or Nancy, had been just about to talk to me as she studied my ring.

Within fifteen minutes two giant men walked through the open door. They told the nurse they were from Reach-Out. One explained, "We can't be responsible for Nancy in her present condition but we thought we'd come and stay with her until the ambulance picks her up. This can be frightening to a young girl."

The nurse introduced them to me, explained I was Nancy's creative-writing teacher. One of them said, "We've never seen her this way before, Mrs. Campbell."

As I realized they really were going to take her away, I seethed with anger. I thought, Damn it, they can't do this! Don't they see this child needs something right now other than a mental hospital? They've *got* to give me more time. They *can't* take her away from me. I resented also their taking away the energy I needed to focus on helping her, the attention she was so desperately in need of.

I asked the nurse, "May I have more time with Nancy? She seems on the verge of breaking through her private prison. I might be able to prevent her from being taken to a psychiatric hospital."

"We really can't give her any more time," the nurse said. The quiet voice of authority.

I understood, it was three P.M. on a Friday, the school would soon close for the weekend, four hours of the day were enough to devote to one troubled child. In a few minutes the ambulance would arrive and take her off our hands and away from our conscience. I felt hopeless, desperate, as if I too were being dragged away to a mental hospital.

I turned to the girl, took her in my arms, begged, "Penny, *please.* Please speak to me. Otherwise you'll be taken away." Pleaded on, "Just one word. Say just one word."

She could not even give that.

Two white-clad men from an ambulance walked in, approached Penny to take her from my arms. I became aware that whenever a man entered the room the muscles in her right arm would jump, as though in convulsions.

One of the ambulance attendants reached out, grabbed her shoulders. She let out a scream at his touch, I never heard such a sound of terror twisting through the air, as if she were being murdered. I wanted to protect her, fight the man off. But I knew I had no right to try. I could only sit in silence as the two attendants pulled her from my arms. My guts churned, I ached with the tenseness of holding back the wish to fight when I felt in the right.

It took those four tall, husky men almost five minutes to strap a five-foot girl to the gurney. She never stopped screaming in protest. As though on her way to a death cell.

This was the first time I had ever seen anyone "carried off" to a mental hospital. From what I had read of such places, thinking of *The Snake Pit* and *One Flew Over the Cuckoo's Nest*, where patients were either drugged, shocked or lobotomized out of their remaining wits, mental hospitals were places to shun. How could they possibly help a frightened fifteen-year-old, so out of her mind she dared not utter her name?

Even as they strapped her down, she tried to fight them off. She screamed when subdued. She screamed as they wheeled her out of the office.

Then there was silence in the room. The nurse and I stood and looked at each other hopelessly. She finally sighed, said, "Thank you more than I can say, Mrs. Campbell."

I shook my head sadly, felt physically drained though still possessed by a remnant of my anger.

The tragic scene haunted me the entire weekend. I kept thinking, What was Penny's, or rather, Nancy's crime? That she fled my class without permission and would not explain why? That she would not tell her name? That drugs had taken over her senses?

Arriving at school Monday I walked to the nurse's office, asked what had happened at Pomona Psychiatric Hospital. The nurse said only, "Nancy's under observation." I asked again the next day, received the same reply. And again at the end of the week.

I returned to my responsibilities as a teacher. But at odd moments Nancy's screams sounded in memory. And as the hunted expression on her winsome face flashed to mind, my fury at the men who seized her, strapped her down, flooded back full force.

Part of my anger rose from the painful thought an innocent young girl could be trapped into submission by authorities under the guise of giving help. Reach-Out refused to come to her aid even though it specialized in caring for troubled adolescents.

I wondered whether Pomona Psychiatric Hospital would prove any better. Was there any place in the valley, or in the state of California, perhaps even in the nation, that could ease the torment in this girl's eyes?

2. November, 1973

Three weeks passed, I gave up asking the school authorities about Nancy's fate. On a drizzly, cold November morning I arrived at school, steered my red Fiat coupe into its familiar parking place. As I entered the campus, out of the corner of my eye I saw almost a replica of the scene I witnessed after Nancy fled my class.

As before, she was huddled between the iron gate and the outdoor lockers. But now it was cold and damp and her arms were bare. She wore no sweater, no jacket to protect against rain or wind. She was shivering as I walked up to her, took off my navy-blue cloth coat, placed it around her shoulders.

I put out my hand. She took it. I led her into my classroom, removed the coat, rubbed her frail shoulders. Neither of us had said a word.

She spoke, the first time I heard her voice except in screams though I had spent four hours with her. It was soft, appealing.

"Thank you, Mrs. Campbell, for everything you did for me that day in the nurse's office."

"You're very welcome, Nancy," I replied. "I've thought of you a great deal. Worried about you. No one seemed to know what was wrong."

She went on in that low voice, "I know this is going to sound funny but I don't remember anything that happened the day they took me away. I only know what you did for me because the Reach-Out people told me. I came here today because I wanted to tell you how much I appreciate it."

"I'm glad you're all right now," I said.

She seemed to want to speak on. I suggested, "This first period in the morning is usually my time for preparation. But why don't you stay and talk for a while?"

"I'd like that," she said.

I drew up a chair for her, sat at my desk. I faced stacks of papers to grade but they could wait. My emotions were involved in something more important at the moment.

I asked, "Why do you call yourself Penny when your name on the school records is Nancy Gooch?"

"The therapists at Reach-Out called me Penny to remind me of how much I was worth." She sounded bitter. "Apparently therapy there consists of rubbing your worthlessness in your face to help you improve."

I felt furious, to further break down the sense of worth in someone already low in self-esteem is destructive treatment.

I asked, "How old are you, Nancy?"

"I'll be sixteen on the eleventh of this month. Born on Armistice Day. For the past two years I've been in and out of hospitals for physical problems. I've had severe bleeding ulcers. The doctors say that's strange for someone my age."

She added, as though ashamed, "I've also been in hospitals to get off drugs, though I don't remember taking any." And then, "They took me to a psychiatric hospital after I tried to commit suicide."

I was right about her, her terror ran deep, far beyond the average adolescent's so-called natural rebellion against parents and society. She was telling me that at times she did not want to stay alive. That the burden of being human was too torturous to bear.

I asked, "Where did you live before Reach-Out?"

"With my mother. She's divorced and my five-year-old brother, Timmy, and I live with her. She works hard to support us. I often babysit with Timmy. I also work part-time as a babysitter to help mother out." She grimaced at the word *babysitter,* as if it were a loathsome task.

She looked at me, silent for the moment, as though wondering if she dare confide a secret. Then said, "I seem to go through what doctors call 'lost time.' Did you ever hear of that expression?"

"No." I felt puzzled.

"I can't remember what I've done—sometimes for many hours. Doctors also call it a 'fugue' state. I start off in one place, then six or seven hours later find myself in a different spot and don't know how I reached it. Or what happened during those vanished hours."

Silence, then further confession. "Until I was seven, I thought everyone went through lost time. That it was a natural state. One day, talking to some friends, I realized I was different from other children. And I've tried hard to conceal it."

"Were you in a fugue state that day in the nurse's office?"

"Yes. I don't remember one moment of those hours. I came to when we reached Pomona Psychiatric Hospital."

"How long did you stay there?" I asked.

"I'm still there. They haven't decided what to do with me. They want to keep me for a while."

"Do they know you're here?"

"No." She looked sheepish.

"You left the hospital without permission?" I felt alarmed.

She confessed, "I don't know how I got here. I had another fugue state. I came out of it when you put your coat around me and led me into the school."

"I think you should call the hospital and let them know you're okay," I said.

I was astounded to think she had walked ten miles or more in the cold and rain though unaware of a single step. I felt mystified at the thought she could not remember leaving the hospital or my helping her the day she fled my class.

The time for students to arrive was closing in. I said, "Class will be gathering soon. I want to thank you, Nancy, for coming all that distance to thank me. Is there anything I can do for you before you leave?"

She stood up. "Just tell me where I can phone the hospital to come get me."

I led her to the principal's office, left her with his secretary who said she would arrange for the hospital to pick up Nancy. The secretary showed Nancy to a chair where she could wait in comfort.

I asked Nancy, "Would you like my coat to keep you warm?"

"No, thank you, Mrs. Campbell. I'll be warm in the car."

"I hope to see you again," I said. "Please feel free to call me whenever you need me."

"I will," she said.

I took a piece of white paper from the pad on the secretary's desk, wrote my phone number, handed it to her. "You can reach me here in the evenings. Or on weekends."

For the first time I saw a slight smile on that sensitive, wan face. As though thanking me for the hours I spent with her when she was in agony, even though she had not been aware of me.

I returned to my classroom, to prepare for the first surge of students. I taught five classes daily, including creative writing to juniors and seniors (all in one class), and four others for freshmen and sophomores. These were general English classes that included the reading of literature, writing and grammar.

Mine was not a typical classroom. It occupied a corner, the wall common with the outside one of solid red brick. Two other walls at right angles to the brick wall were almost completely covered with chalkboard except for the one with a door that lead into the hall. The fourth wall had windows and a door leading into the next classroom. I contributed several bookcases, now containing mostly reference and textbooks, all the classics stolen, which I did not mind, it meant some students cared enough to want to read and keep them.

Posters on the walls encouraged students to think positively. One showed birds in flight with the words: "They can because they think they can." (We cannot explain how a bird is able to fly.) Another, with the photo of a young woman in a forest setting, held Hermann Hesse's lines:

Within you
There is a stillness
And sanctuary
To which you can retreat
At any time and be
Yourself.

A third poster, illustrated by a field of flowers, contained a quote from the work of Albert Camus:

In the midst of winter
I finally learned
That there was in me
An invincible summer.

Above my desk a poster bore the advice, along with the photograph of a gorilla: "Be kind to me, I've had a Hard day." There were also photographs of Steinbeck, Faulkner, Melville, authors I admire, with quotations from their books.

That night in the kitchen, as I prepared steak, baked potatoes and asparagus for my husband and two daughters, I thought of Nancy's expression, "lost time." The idea of someone not knowing what he was doing for hours on end, losing consciousness then regaining it in another place, another time, was terrifying. I wondered if the drugs Nancy took caused the fugue states? Certainly not at the age of seven, when she said they first started.

Why had she fled the psychiatric hospital to walk ten miles in bitter cold to see me? Was her visit perhaps a plea for help? The two Reach-Out men told her how I tried to comfort her before the ambulance arrived, of the hours I had spent by her side, sometimes holding her in my arms. Was she asking me to come to her rescue once more?

What could I, a teacher of English literature, possibly do to lessen her pain? The most I could offer was my knowledge of human behavior gleaned from the good and great literature I had read and from a course in child psychology given by a teacher at the nursery school my daughters had attended. Plus a semester in introductory psychology at Mount San Antonio College in Walnut, a nearby city.

I did possess a strong need to help those in trouble, including stray cats I brought home when a little girl, still brought home a stray cat or two. I was also consumed by an indefatigable curiosity about the human mind.

Was not an important part of my life dedicated to the understanding of the tormented mind? It was no accident my favorite authors were Melville, Faulkner and Kafka. Each, in his own artistic way, described the terror, rage and hunger for vengeance that stirs in anyone who was a victim. The wish for revenge exists in all of us to some degree, a survival mechanism. It bursts to the surface of the mind if we feel the least threatened.

Ah, but none of these famous writers had invented a character suffering from "lost time." What would cause a fifteen-year-old girl to be possessed by a "fugue?" What unhappiness had driven her to drugs? How was she being treated at the psychiatric hospital?

She was a pupil of mine if only for a few sessions, I felt protective of her. I often wondered if any of my students would become a writer. There is an old saying that a literature teacher feels gratified if only one student per year uses his creativity. So far, over the years I had taught there were none that I knew of. I wondered if perhaps Nancy had the imagination and skill to become a writer. I sensed she had a dramatic story to tell.

I had to trust her to return if she needed me. I realized her visit was the result of a wish to thank me but even more than that. It was also a request for help. Some part of her, conscious or unconscious, during those four grim hours in the nurse's office, realized how much I wished to ease her pain.

I move slowly but thoughtfully, I have only a few strong convictions but I am true to them. One is that those who suffer emotional damage not be hurt further by so-called rescuers who are ignorant, uncaring or exploitive. I was curious to find out whether Nancy had received help for her obvious suffering and if her helpers understood the depth of her fear.

I wanted somehow to lessen her pain, I did not consciously know all the reasons why. Only that this endearing young woman, who had just turned sixteen, seemed terrified of everyone who peopled her world, real and imagined. It did not seem fair she had to carry such a staggering emotional burden.

She had swiftly become special to me. As though in her I saw part of myself even as I felt a strength she did not possess. I identified deeply with her loneliness, her sadness, her somehow stricken spirit.

If she asked, I would do all I could to help find out what had caused her torment, with the hope of easing it.

3.   *Spring and Summer, 1974*

Four months passed without word from Nancy, I could only hope someone was helping her ease whatever agony she so obviously suffered. Life was difficult enough even for the supposedly serene.

Then one morning she appeared back in my creative-writing class, books underarm, as though she had not been absent for four months. I greeted her warmly, said, "I'm glad you're here. I've wondered how you were. Will you stay a few minutes after class and catch me up on news of you?"

"I'd love to, Mrs. Campbell." A faint flush.

We were alone when class ended and she sat at a desk in the front row, facing me. She said, "I spent the past four months at Pomona Psychiatric Hospital. I'm living temporarily with my father and his wife who have a home in Ontario because my mother still lives in Los Angeles, though she expects to move here soon."

"Did you get help at the hospital?" I asked.

"While I was there I saw Arlo Siegersma, a social worker with a master's degree. He sent me to Theodore Baldick, a psychologist at the Voorman Clinic in nearby Upland. I'm in group therapy with him once a week. I also have a weekly private session with him. Just talking to him puts me at ease."

"It sounds as if you feel much better," I said.

"I do." Cheerfully.

"Tell me more about your family," I suggested.

"My mother divorced when I was five. She remarried briefly, gave birth to Timmy when I was eleven, then divorced again. She now goes with a man she hopes to marry. My father also remarried. I have two older brothers and two older sisters. All of them have left home and are on their own."

This was a rocky parental past for any adolescent, I thought, though hardly different from what occurred in at least fifty percent of American homes today. The "lost time" at the age of seven did not fit into the picture somehow.

I said apologetically after fifteen minutes, "We have to stop now. But please know, Nancy, any time you want to talk, I'm here."

She stood up. "Thank you, Mrs. Campbell."

I walked over to her, hugged her, as I had in the nurse's office. She moved swiftly away and out of the classroom but this time it seemed not flight but a wish to wage whatever battles lay ahead,

She came to class almost every day, though once in a while she was absent for several days. I asked no questions, her marks were high. The other pupils did not seem aware of anything startlingly different in her. She spoke intelligently when called on, she wrote commendable papers though I could only give her a B-plus for her term paper. She said sadly, "That's the lowest grade any English teacher ever gave me, I always got an A." She had written a story about her younger brother, Timmy, it was adequate but lacked detail, there were a few inconsistencies and a lapse in character, I felt. I was yet to see her poetry, which I later admired, along with her eloquent writing about her inner feelings.

Always, underneath, as I spoke to her and listened to her, reverberated the memory of that first day she fled. I had been profoundly affected emotionally by her four silent hours. I felt the same necessity now to protect and ease the pain of this child without understanding as yet what caused her torment.

I trusted her not to run away from the class and she never did again. I felt she was running toward me without knowing exactly what approach to take. She did not easily reveal personal feelings, we kept the relationship fairly scholarly.

She told me she had bleeding ulcers and was in hypnotherapy once a week with Harold Gaffney, a hypnotherapist. He had been recommended by Solomon Friedman, the school counselor, and Dr. Simon Klitenic, who admired Gaffney's work in treating psychosomatic illnesses.

She looked as fragile as the day I met her but seemed in higher spirits. She still wore the school uniform for girls—jeans, matching shirt and sneakers. Her brown hair was longer, falling to her shoulders. Her face bore the same look of innocence, the innocence of the child who wants to trust, who as yet does not know the world is often ugly, sordid, frightening.

She had come originally to my school because it was near Reach-Out where she had lived. Both were in the city of Ontario. But in the fall, when the new term started she transferred as a senior to Montclair High School in Montclair, sister school to Ontario High School, because it was nearer the Gaffneys. They planned to take her into their home in family-care custody, which they were licensed to do. Nancy moved into the Gaffneys on the advice of Dr. Klitenic. She continued to see her psychologist, Theodore Baldick, in group and private sessions.

She visited me occasionally, spoke superficially of what she was doing. She seemed more at ease though I still thought her other-worldly. She was exceptionally close to her mother, loved Timmy as though he were her child. She openly adored her father, had left his home only because she felt she did not fit in with his wife and her three children. Nancy told me she preferred living in Ontario to Los Angeles and that her mother had just found a home near the Gaffneys.

The city of Ontario was a place I found picturesque and comfortable. It lay within San Bernardino County, on the border of Los Angeles County. The valley was originally an orange grove at the foot of Mount San Antonio, part of the San Bernardino mountain range. Today twelve cities cluster in the valley, one of them, Ontario, boasts an international airport and by the year 2000 is expected to be the second largest city in California. Los Angeles, the largest, lies forty miles west. Another forty miles east sits Palm Springs. Our valley is midpoint between these two Hollywood-type cities.

Just beyond Mount San Antonio looms the famous San Andreas Fault. It has been predicted that this fault may one day catapult the southern part of California into the Pacific. There is a gap between the mountains that could either close slowly or crack wide open, causing the earth to separate.

Because there are no trees at Mount San Antonio's 9,000-foot summit, it bears the more popular name Mount Baldy. Cloaked in snow during winter, it boasts some of the most difficult ski runs in Southern California. Snowcrest Lodge, one mile up, is a popular summer and winter restaurant and camping grounds. In summer tourists pour onto the mountain, head for the Angeles National Forest, enclosed by the San Gabriel Range.

From our high school we can see the mountains, their grandeur bestows extra pleasure on my daily work. I hope one day to build a house in a mountainous region even though, or perhaps because, I was born and raised in the special wilderness that is New York.

Euclid Avenue in Ontario is possibly one of the most beautiful thoroughfares in the world, with transitions from country road to downtown shopping malls, to elegant residential avenues. Its six-lane highway is divided by rows of palm trees, maples, pines and poplars. The country road leads to Mount Baldy, in late fall as you drive up the mountain you see a kaleidoscope of colors in the trees, bushes and rocks.

At one thousand feet the scrub oaks give a sunset glow. Up 4,000 feet all foliage is purple. At 8,000 feet there is only the gray of rocks. Along curves in the road some days the valley vista shows only clouds of smog, other days reveals the cities of the valley.

The area is typical suburban Los Angeles. The twelve cities run into one another, call themselves entities but in effect resemble one large community. Most of the cities have old Spanish names—Rancho Cucamonga, Chino, Alta Loma, Fontana—others are American—Claremont, Upland, Montclair, Ontario.

My home in Pomona nestled among hills that were dry and brown in summer when it does not rain but velvety green in winter when the rain descends in torrents at times. Gnarled and twisted scrub oaks dot the hills.

The house, of yellow stucco with white trim, was built in the early 1950s. The interior reflected my love of Scandinavian design in the rosewood dining table and chairs and the walnut wall unit where I placed glassware and crystal vases from Sweden. On the walls I hung prints of Wyeth, Utrillo, Monet, El Greco, Klee. The artist Karl Benjamin loaned me an original abstract, he permitted friends to hang his paintings rather than his storing them. In art I preferred colors of different tones of blue, with deep purple and red. I also liked earth colors with accents of muted blue and green.

The area abounded in trees of an amazing variety—Italian cypresses, maples, oaks, pepper trees, poplars, pines, blue-tip spruce. We could boast two tall walnut trees, one in front of the house, the other in the rear.

Once in a while I would call my mother, now living in Miami, hear her slightly reproachful voice ask when she would next see me. My stepfather died in 1968 and I knew she could not be very happy—was she ever? I asked myself.

As at times I thought of Nancy's life, it awakened my awareness that I, too, was the child of divorced parents. I recalled emotions I had buried since childhood because they were painful. My feelings of abandonment when my father left home as I turned three. The fact my mother always treated me as though I, her only child, were *her* mother, as Nancy's mother seemed to do with Nancy. She would ask Nancy's advice, treated the child Nancy as an adult much of the time, Nancy told me.

Looking back, I believe I did not have much joy in childhood. I grew up in a hurry, the way Nancy did. I was never afraid of my mother but she troubled me, not by what she did, but what she did not do. Such as her failure in large measure to comfort or protect me. I never felt much love from her or for her, though I later realized she did the best she knew how. I knew she was dishonest at times and would string out lies for no purpose other than the sheer pleasure of deception.

When my father left us I recall feeling angry at him for not taking me. I also remember the deep hurt I felt when I was four and a half and my mother sent me away to Sweden with her best friend and her husband. When we returned after a year this childless couple wanted to adopt me but my mother would not allow it.

My mother did encourage me, as I grew older, to study the classics. We lived within walking distance of a branch of the New York Public Library and I would take home seven or eight books a week. I discovered early I could escape "me" by plunging into fascinating worlds created in fiction.

At twenty, in 1952, I fell in love at the traditional first sight with a man eight years older. Three months later we married, took off for Los Angeles where my husband had friends. Mother wrote once a week to make sure I was alive. She imagined once I left her side villains would ax-murder me, possibly a projection of her anger at me for deserting her. I am slow to feel upset but when moved to anger will stand up steadfastly for what I believe my rights. I remember giving up hope I would have a loving mother. To make up for it, I became mother to the world in a sense—to my pupils, to my colleagues. The principal of my school called me everybody's mentor.

I first became interested in counseling because of Beverly Benjamin, a teacher at the nursery school my daughters attended. The school required all mothers to take a course in the raising of a child. Ms. Benjamin helped us understand the deep vulnerability of children, that each child needed love from and constant protection by his parents.

As my daughters grew older I realized I needed intellectual stimulation. I decided to seek a degree at Mount San Antonio College and major in literature so I could teach high school. Because of household duties it took eight years to get through the four-year program.

After sixteen years of marriage my husband and I faced marital troubles. We sought a marriage counselor. With daughters at college we did not want to face living in disharmony. My husband could not see me as a separate person, wanting my own life apart from home and children.

When the marriage counselor suggested each of us change our attitudes toward one another, my husband said, "There's nothing wrong with *me*. Emily will have to change." At that moment I knew the marriage was doomed.

I decided to wait it out as I was unconsciously waiting for Nancy to call on me for further help. At times not so unconsciously as I wondered how she felt, what she was doing.

The difference in waiting it out for Nancy and for my husband to change was that I had given up on the marriage but not on easing Nancy's distress. I sensed she wanted to change her life of terror but did not know how.

I was not aware of it at the time but Nancy was living an undercover life that would have made the daily soap operas look placid and plebian. I sensed only that beneath her sensitivity and intelligence lay the deep fear and rage that had stirred her screams of protest in the nurse's office.

The exterior of Nancy—oversweet, wishing to please, seemingly logical—hid an emotional Vesuvius waiting to explode.

4. *Fall, 1974 to April, 1975*

Nancy continued to visit me several times during her senior year at Montclair High School. She reported her group and private therapy classes were continuing, her marks at school were high. Her voice held new assurance, she sounded less bewildered, a tinge of hope ringed her words.

She had moved into the Gaffneys' home on April 5, 1975. She called me a few weeks later, almost a year and a half after the scene in the nurse's office. I still felt deep interest in what happened to her, as though I had to follow through on those first few hours together.

She said, excitement in her voice, "I've told the Gaffneys how much help you've been to me. They're eager to meet you. When can you visit us?"

"How about three on Saturday?" I suggested. Weekly shopping should be finished by that hour, I had no classes nor did I need to rush away to prepare dinner, as on Sunday.

"The address is 5052 Moreno Street in Montclair," she said. "We'll be waiting for you."

Though I was no authority on mental disturbances, from the start Nancy fascinated me in ways I did not as yet fully understand. As though some need in me responded to a similar need in her. I had ardently wanted to save her from the hands of those four giants who had dragged her off screaming as though she were a vicious animal. At that moment I loathed those men as deeply as she did but felt powerless, unable to persuade them to give me more time with her so she could be set free.

That Saturday it took only ten minutes to reach nearby Montclair. Moreno was a residential street, ample space to park. I pulled into a clearing in front of the Gaffneys' home. A single-story, picture-book house of bright yellow stucco with white trim, the colors of my home. A small jockey hitching post near the front door. A rock garden that included my favorite shades of deep purple bordering a green lawn rimmed by bushes.

A woman in her early forties, I judged, answered the doorbell. She was about five feet ten inches, slim. Her deep blue eyes were riveting, set in a pretty face. Long blond hair flowed behind her ears, then over her shoulders, I was to learn she wore a variety of sophisticated hairstyles. She looked chic, a muted green-and-blue print dress swirled around her knees.

She held out her hand, smiled, said, "I'm Diane Gaffney. Nancy has told us how much support you've given her, Mrs. Campbell."

"I haven't done much except be there when Nancy needed me," I said.

"Perhaps you don't realize how much that has helped her." Then, "Come in and meet Harold."

She led me into a living room the complete opposite in style of the modern exterior, I stepped into the past century. Luxurious rose-red velvet curtains draped across the windows. The same velvet covered a pair of old-fashioned loveseats and a couch. A golden antique clock ticked away on a marble table. The lush furniture, Diane later told me, belonged to a New Orleans bordello in the 1870s, later was transferred to Oklahoma City. Diane's mother bought the furniture for her home in Woodward, Oklahoma, where she lived with her husband, one of the wealthiest oilmen in the state. Diane inherited the exotic furniture, brought it to her Montclair house. It provided a neverending subject of conversation after she confided its whorehouse origin.

In the midst of this splendor I saw a portly man, completely bald, sporting a thin goatee, sitting in a wheelchair. Both legs had been amputated above the knees—he later told me he was victim of Thevinard's disease, an inherited neurological disorder in which the end of each limb kept dying, had to be removed. He was confined to this wheelchair though his illness did not keep him from driving a car or planting a rock garden.

Harold held out his hand, said in a deep voice he used like a musical instrument within a bass range, "Welcome, Emily Campbell. We are so very glad to meet you."

He indicated the red velvet couch. "Please sit down. Will you have tea or coffee?"

"No thank you, Mr. Gaffney," I said. "I'm fine." I settled into the luxury of velvet.

"Please call me Harold." He gestured to his wife, "And my co-worker is Diane."

"Where is Nancy?" I asked, eager to see her in her new locale.

"She's in her room," Diane said. "We wanted to get acquainted with you first."

"I've studied Nancy's case thoroughly," Harold said. "Sol Friedman, who is a friend of mine, likes her very much. He is her counselor this year. He wants to save her from being thrown into a state mental hospital, possibly for the rest of her life. He thinks she has a good chance of rehabilitation if she lives with foster parents who give her a protective atmosphere, a firm home base. We offered to take her in. We find there is something endearing about her."

Indeed there is, I thought, otherwise I would not be sitting in this strange house.

Harold explained, "I have used hypnotherapy, in which I specialize, to help cure Nancy's bleeding ulcers. We think they are psychosomatic. I've had a lot of luck with such cases.

"Doctors, psychologists, even psychiatrists, send me private patients suffering from obesity or impotency or who want to quit smoking and I help them, through hypnosis, to solve these problems."

"When did Nancy's bleeding ulcers start?" I asked.

"We don't know exactly when. About a year ago."

Diane said to me, "Tell us about yourself."

"I'm a teacher of creative writing and English literature with some background in psychology and counseling," I said. "Once I thought I might like to be a psychological counselor. Nancy came to me because it was any port in an emotional storm."

"She needs all of us," Diane said. "Do you know she has tried to take her life several times?"

"I didn't realize that." I wondered if Nancy thought I would refuse to see her if I knew the depths of her desperation.

At that moment Nancy appeared. She walked over to me, took my hand, said warmly, "Thank you for coming, Mrs. Campbell."

I thought what a change there had been from the frightened girl crouching against the high school wall, and the girl who later screamed in agony when the ambulance attendants tried to put her in a strait-jacket.

They showed me the rest of the house. The large dining room, then down the long hall off which there were three bedrooms. Nancy's room boasted an ornate headboard, dresser and copious closet. The bedroom sets were the same dark mahogany as the living- and dining-room furniture. I wondered if they too originated in the St. Louis bordello.

Finally the hypnotherapy room, closed off from the rest of the world. Thick black cotton drapes kept out all light. The wallpaper, when you could see it, pictured a mural of trees and clearings in the woods. Two reclining chairs for patients and four straight chairs for therapists or onlookers.

I thanked the Gaffneys for the tour, said, "I should get back to the house for Saturday chores."

"Will you come soon again?" Harold asked.

"Just call me," I said. "I'm usually available except during school hours."

I kissed Nancy goodbye on the cheek, hugged her warmly, drove slowly away from the yellow stucco house. I wondered what the odds were against Nancy, with her fugue states, addiction to drugs which, she said, she was unaware of taking. And, what I had now learned, an open desperation so deep it drove her at times to suicide attempts.

I would guess the odds were not in her favor. As I neared home I wondered what I could do to help Nancy, it would be a new area to explore. It seemed the challenge of challenges but I rose to challenges. Especially when they applied to the human need.

Teaching was a challenge, trying to reach the minds of pupils whose concentration in these days of heroin and cocaine was not always available. Or pupils who did not take drugs but seemed spiritless when it came to reading the classics or even good modern fiction.

Nancy had told me in several instances doctors had found drugs in her system though she did not remember taking any. How could this happen? I wondered. I believed her so there must be another explanation. At the moment I did not dare think what it might be, beyond awareness her fugue states might have a connection to it.

THE
SILENT
SCREAM

Every so often Nancy dropped in at my school after the last class to keep me up on what happened in her life. She said she enjoyed living at the Gaffneys, planning to graduate from Montclair High School the following June. She was delighted she had been accepted at Chaffey Community College in nearby Alta Loma. She planned to work for her associate of arts degree.

The college also assigned her part-time to their counseling office so she could earn money. She told me, "Some day I'd like to be a counselor and help people in trouble."

My phone rang on Sunday, November 7 as I prepared dinner for the family. Harold Gaffney's stagelike command flowed into my ears: "Emily, you *must* come over this minute and see what we have uncovered!"

Harold had a flair for the dramatic, even his background was dramatic. In the early 1960s he fled New York City when drug dealers put out a contract on him because he had helped so many addicts give up drugs through hypnotherapy. He traveled clear across the country to Southern California, started a new practice there.

To Harold's invitation I replied, "I can't leave just now. There's a roast in the oven. We're eating in about twenty minutes."

"Stop whatever you're doing, Emily!" An order. "Jump into your car. If you miss this, you'll be deprived of the experience of your life."

I knew he would not call on a whim. I respected him, the California Rehabilitation Center of the State Department of Corrections in Norco, which helped drug addicts convicted of crimes, had asked him to treat prisoners. I could ask my eldest daughter to carry on with the meal.

I said, "I'll be there in ten minutes."

As I drove to the yellow, white-trimmed house I thought, What could possibly be so important that Harold orders me to his home on a weekend? He did not sound alarmed but excited.

Diane met me at the door, an exhilarated expression in her eyes. She said, almost a whisper, sharing a secret, "Dr. Clinton Johnson, a well-known psychiatrist, is here and wants to meet you. And we invited a few neighbors to drop in." Then quickly, "But that's not the reason Harold called."

"What *is* the reason?" I still felt a bit aggravated at her husband's abrupt order. I am not one to act impetuously.

She did not answer, led me into the room with the red velvet drapes and the loveseats. I saw a man six feet and three inches tall, with a rugged face, loom over Harold. Diane called out, "Clint, *this* is Emily Campbell!"

The tall man walked slowly toward me, stood by my side, looked down at me with a smile of delight. He said, "I'm so happy to meet you, Emily." Expressive hazel eyes sparkled. I liked Dr. Clinton A. Johnson, psychiatrist, at once.

Harold said, "Clint works in the California state psychiatric system. He knows all about fugue states."

"I've read a lot but that doesn't mean I know a lot. I'm still learning." Clint's warm, measured voice.

I liked him even more for saying this, he was not the stereotype psychiatrist the public sees in cartoons and films. There was instant rapport between us. As I learned more about him, my respect deepened.

Other men and women were talking in loud voices, an afternoon tea party. Diane explained, "Harold asked them to come here for the same reason he asked you."

"For what reason?" I was still mystified.

Then I saw Nancy on the couch, speaking to several of the guests. Harold took me by the hand, wheeled his chair over to Nancy. He said to me, "I want you to meet Sarah." Then to Nancy, "This is Emily Campbell."

I looked at him, astounded. Had he temporarily flipped out?

A strange voice came out of Nancy's mouth. It was Nancy I saw but the sound was not Nancy's. Her voice was breathless, soft, unassuming, sometimes frightened. This voice sounded assured, lower in tone, the cadence slower.

She, whoever "she" was, held out her hand, announced, "My name is Sarah. It's a pleasure to meet you, Mrs. Campbell."

A fine job of acting, I thought, Nancy must have her reason and I will go along with it.

"I'm glad to meet you, too," I said.

The look was different. Gone was Nancy's uniform of blue jeans, white blouse and sneakers. Nancy/Sarah wore a tailored beige suit, matching shoes with two-inch heels, a lime-green silk blouse. The brown hair was combed high on her head, fastened with a comb behind her ears. Her posture was vastly different, she held her head proudly, sat in a poised manner, devoid of the fear and insecurity of the Nancy I knew.

Nancy/Sarah, as I thought of her, talked on to neighbors. Harold turned to me, said in his mellifluous voice, "About an hour and a half ago suddenly Sarah appeared. Diane and I were reading the Sunday paper and she just walked in. Her first words were, 'I am not Nancy. I am Sarah.'"

I looked at him in disbelief. He went on, "She told us she first 'came out'—those were her words—when Nancy was eleven and flunking school. Sarah said she stayed 'out' during the day for the entire year, studying hard, getting all A's. Then she disappeared, 'went inside,' no longer needed. At times over the years she returned to help Nancy when she was in trouble."

I stared at him in silence, finally asked, "Do you really believe this?"

"I believe it, Emily." He sounded convinced. Then excitedly, "Do you know what this means? Nancy is a multiple personality. Ted Baldick has suspected this all along. He told me he has seen evidence of it."

"What does multiple personality mean, Harold?" I asked.

"Different personalities exist inside Nancy. They 'take over' whenever she goes into a fugue state." He nodded in the direction of Nancy/ Sarah. "Sarah, who talks fluently and intelligently, doesn't sound at all like the Nancy we know. She told us she is the caretaker for Nancy and all the others—whoever they may be."

He said admiringly, "Sarah told us she has read all the classics, knows Mozart from Schubert, Picasso from Renoir, admires Gucci bags, speaks French, spends hours in museums, loves escargots. Can you believe it?"

"I'm not sure," I said slowly.

I accepted with skepticism the idea "personae" could inhabit a body. This was returning to the fantasies of the Dark Ages when someone claimed he was "possessed by the devil." I intended to watch Nancy carefully for the slightest slip that would reveal she was playing a part.

Harold said, "Please wait until the guests have gone, Emily. Then you, Clint, Diane and I can talk at length to Sarah." It was now not an order but a plea.

"I'll call home and tell them to have dinner without me." I wanted to hear more of what Nancy/Sarah might reveal.

I phoned my husband, explained I would be late because of unexpected developments. The Gaffney guests soon became hungry, returned to their own homes. Diane, Harold, Clint and I were free to gather around Nancy/Sarah.

Harold asked the first question. "Sarah, tell us when you originally appeared?"

She answered in a low, controlled voice, as though she were the therapist, not the patient. "I came out when Nancy was in sixth grade, getting C's and D's. I took over for a year, studied hard, earned all A's."

"Are there other personalities?" Harold asked.

"There are the twins, Jennifer and John. They were created when Nancy was raped at fifteen. They came out during the rape. John tried to fight off the rapist while Jennifer absorbed Nancy's fear and pain from the rapist's beatings and sexual assault."

I listened in amazement to Nancy's hidden life. Nancy/Sarah was saying that during a rape two and a half years ago Nancy summoned from within two personalities, twins, to help defend herself against a cruel assailant, ward off the psychological and physical pain of the rape.

Nancy/Sarah went on, "John and Jennifer joined a street gang shortly after. The leader was Zurdo—his name in Spanish meant 'left-handed'—he was eighteen. He was slim, five feet nine inches, with black hair and brown eyes. He was not formidable in appearance but in acts. He seemed fairly protective of Jennifer, she felt safe with him. Once in a while they had sex though she did not enjoy it, tolerated it because it was required of her. She was never much on birth control but luckily she didn't get pregnant."

Nancy/Sarah took a few sips of the coffee Diane handed her, continued as we listened, transfixed. "Jennifer was really in love with Andrew, another member of the gang. She and Andrew were the two innocents. He was thin, pale and slight. A Westerner who played the guitar and sang love songs to her. John got into drugs. Pot at the beginning, then smack, then heroin. The gang often used him as courier, what they called 'mule' and 'point man.' He sold drugs supplied by the Mafia."

Nancy/Sarah then spoke directly to me. "It was Jennifer, not Nancy, who came out and fled from your classroom, Mrs. Campbell. It was also Jennifer who ran away from Pomona Psychiatric Hospital that day to thank you for helping her in the nurse's office. She was in real trouble. Just before she met you, she had a tragic experience with the gang. It took place when she and her mother lived in Los Angeles where her mother became a member of the police department for a short while. She wore a uniform, carried a pistol."

We were all mesmerized by now, it sounded like a Pacific coast version of the play *West Side Story*. I learned later the Gaffneys knew much of this part of Nancy's life.

The articulate Nancy/Sarah went on, "Jennifer didn't know it but this gang had been under surveillance by the police for a year. They learned the Mafia controlled it and decided to bust the gang. But they did not know where the trades took place. Then one day they followed Jennifer home from school after authorities there suspected she might be involved with the gang.

"The police, knowing Nancy's mother was a member of their department, warned her they were planning a bust on the gang and intended to use her daughter to lead them to the place where the gang sold drugs. They assured Nancy's mother they would not arrest her daughter.

"One night the police followed Jennifer to the hideout, arrested the gang but let her go. Detectives then warned her mother the Mafia might put out a hit price of ten thousand dollars on Nancy's head when they found out she led police to the hideout. This was obvious because the police had let her go but arrested all the others, some of whom went to prison. This gang was a large dealer of drugs and the raid would scare other gangs, hurting Mafia trade.

"Nancy's mother immediately resigned from the police department, moved to another city. She faced the fact her daughter needed help for deep-seated conflicts. She arranged for Nancy to stay at Reach-Out. I think you all know what has happened to Nancy since then. Including several suicide attempts and hospitalizations."

Diane asked, "Are there other personalities besides John and Jennifer?"

"There's Sherry. She 'came out' shortly after Nancy turned sixteen. She's played an important part in Nancy's life. Not, I am afraid, for the good."

"Can we get in touch with Sherry?" Harold asked.

"I don't think she'll come out on request. She is very independent. She has been through some terrible traumas. She cannot listen to me. She is a self-destructive personality."

Harold asked, "Do the personalities know each other, communicate with each other?"

"Yes," Nancy/Sarah said. "But never with Nancy. They consider her their enemy. They hate her. She doesn't know about them."

Harold, an expression of awe on his face, turned to Clint, asked, "Does this convince you Nancy is a multiple personality?"

"It convinces me," Clint said. "She acts just like the few multiples I have heard about though I have never seen one before. She has fugues and loses time. There was the appearance of Jennifer at Emily's school. And now Sarah."

"And you, Emily, are you convinced?" Harold turned to me.

I am not one to tell a lie. I looked him straight in his penetrating blue eyes, said, "I need to know more."

Harold, not one to give up easily, shot back, "We'll see you get the chance." Then to Clint, "And for you to learn all you want about the multiple personality."

Somehow after this meeting there developed an informal formation of a group that included Diane, Harold, Clint and myself. Harold wanted Clint to be part of the group so that he, as a psychiatrist, could protect us from charges of practicing therapy without a license. Clint, whom Harold and Diane had met at a conference on "Integrity Therapy," sponsored by behavioral psychologist O. Hobart Mowrer in 1966, was fascinated by the fugue state and its causes. He planned to write about Nancy's case for clinical journals, offered to sit in on sessions and tape them. He could not attend every session but would come as often as his work allowed.

Diane said, "You'll like Clint, Emily. He's a very warm, genial man. He studied under the famous Dr. Franz Alexander who brought psychoanalysis to Chicago and the whole western United States. Alexander also wrote a pioneer book on juvenile delinquency and another on what he described as the 'corrective emotional experience' in therapy. That's what we hope to provide for Nancy."

There was nothing official about the group, nobody actually said, "Come join us, Emily." Ambivalent though I felt at the moment about strange personalities taking over Nancy's conscious mind, I knew I was already committed. Had been committed the moment I put my arms around a mute, terrified fifteen-year-old in the school yard. Nancy's appeal was not on the mind level but the feeling level.

She seemed to ask, *Are you there for me? No matter what I do or say or need?* And I answered, *I am here for you, no matter what.* Once I have committed myself a secret stubbornness sets in, it is almost impossible to persuade me to change. I act this way with students, they know exactly how I feel.

I had to admit I was possessed by a growing intrigue. I wanted to learn more about Nancy/Sarah, what she meant to Nancy. Whether Nancy was playacting or controlled by another personality within who could emerge at will.

More important than Harold, Diane and Clint wanting me to help was the fact that Nancy, or the Jennifer part who had returned to thank me, and the Nancy I had seen more frequently during the last two years, were quietly asking for help. I had become very fond of Nancy, she was like a troubled daughter. When Harold informed me authorities in mental hospitals threatened to put Nancy away, perhaps for life, because she was suicidal and sometimes appeared out of her mind, I felt horrified. I thought, This is like murdering someone psychically without giving her a chance to grow stronger.

If the alternatives for Nancy were suicide or life in a mental hospital, I would certainly try to help her in any way I could, even though I knew nothing about multiple personalities. But then neither did Harold or Diane. Before I left that afternoon at the Gaffneys' Clint said he would attend as many sessions as he could to learn from me how to treat a multiple personality. *That* was a laugh, I thought, my teaching a psychiatrist.

For me, it would be a process of discovery, step by step. Perhaps my not knowing much was even an asset, I could explore new paths. All I knew was that Nancy suffered so deeply she had tried to kill herself several times. Nancy/Sarah had revealed other aspects of Nancy—personalities who "came out" at times to protect Nancy but also engaged in destructive behavior.

I felt excited at this new venture into what is perhaps the greatest exploration man can make. Not climbing the highest mountain or diving deep into the unexplored sea. But slowly delving into the depths and rising to the heights of the capacity of the human mind as it strives for survival. Often against great odds.

What could I do for someone who lived controlled by personalities unknown? This was the crucial issue, I had to trust my growing awareness of how best to help Nancy.

I would follow both my head and heart. And I trusted Nancy to help in her way. Nancy/Sarah was proof Nancy was trying.

From then on, every so often I would get calls from the Gaffneys when Nancy would go into a fugue, and I rushed over to calm her down. Or if she tried to run away I comforted her. Thus did I start on the path to helping Nancy uncover the murderous mosaic of a bloody time long submerged in unspeakable memories. Memories lived out in coded expression through her multiple personalities.

I entered a world stranger than science fiction as we decided to start weekly sessions on Thursdays at 7 P.M. To explore what might be causing Nancy's fugue states and what happened during her "lost time."

As homework I read *The Three Faces of Eve* and *Sybil* though they did not tell much about how to treat multiple personalities. Clint reported clinical articles by psychiatrists were scarce on this subject but he would locate them.

I do not know if there was any one moment I finally believed separate personalities did exist within Nancy. I think I became convinced because of the consistency of their appearance, attitude and behavior as well as the different roles each played. I saw unfold before my bewildered eyes a world of apparent magic performed by the human mind as it takes flight from a horror it cannot face.

I never *had* to believe. It did not matter whether Nancy was acting or possessed by spirits or was a "multiple." Her agony was real. She needed someone to help her understand why she lived an eternal nightmare. At this point too many "experts" had treated her with no success, she presented a psychic puzzle they could not solve.

I became curious about the cause of multiple personalities. People who lived within her and came out at certain times to perform acts the "core" personality, as Nancy was called, would never dare. One of the personalities tried to kill her, another took drugs, there were undoubtedly more intent on destroying the mind and body of Nancy Lynn Gooch. I decided to search for a curative process Nancy desperately needed.

My mother died in October and I mourned the loss. I had lived with her until the day I married. We all have to mourn our losses, face our grief, then our fury and hurt and accept the loss. Each loss of a loved one makes us feel abandoned, in extreme cases, annihilated. Life deals small losses from the day we are born, losses we must learn to bear as part of being human.

I wondered if Nancy had been able to mourn and accept the losses of her life, face her grief and anger. The reliving of the hostility and hatred we all suffer in early childhood is a necessary part of every therapy, I learned from my recent readings of the development of the human mind. Had some early trauma interfered with Nancy's capacity to mourn?

One devastating loss would be that of her father when she was five and he left the house, which meant he abandoned her, in her mind. But her loss had to be more wounding than this for such a loss is experienced by children in half the families of the nation but they do not become multiple personalities. Nancy had an exceptionally deep attachment to her father. She wrote when she was fifteen, on June 25, 1973, in a diary she let me see: "Oh, daddy, I wish you still loved me. I wish you were here."

I never gave up hope I could help Nancy face her pain. As I learned in my reading, Dr. Karl Menninger believes that without this feeling of hope in the therapist, a hope the patient senses and absorbs, there is little chance the patient will gain the strength to understand his inner conflicts. I had hope within myself that somehow I would discover the proper way to help Nancy. The hope that had allowed me to embark on new discoveries in my life, to work out ways of alleviating the hurts inflicted by others. And by myself.

Nancy's hope was at low ebb, buried beneath layers of suffering. I trusted I could uncover it. Trusted too that in spite of whatever torment she suffered, she would not give up. I thought of her as special in this way. Possessing the courage to wage war against high emotional odds.

Clint gave professional support to Nancy's treatment not only out of friendship to the Gaffneys but because he was interested in learning more about the causes of the multiples. Diane met Clint when she worked at the California State Rehabilitation Center, she and Harold had become friends with Clint. We all needed each other.

Clint attended about one in every ten sessions, kept telling me, "You are the expert here, you have to lead the way." He might ask an illuminating question of the personality out at the moment or suggest a question I might ask.

Money never became an issue. I never asked for one cent. I wanted to help Nancy become free of the psychic prison sentence she imposed on herself for crime or crimes committed, actual or fantasied. Clint did not charge either, he attended because he wanted to see what emerged in the process of helping Nancy. The Gaffneys were paid by the state as foster parents for Nancy's room and board but not for therapy. Harold and Diane provided Nancy with a comfortable, reassuring home, guaranteeing protection twenty-four hours a day. I learned much from the Gaffneys, including how to perform hypnotherapy.

Harold kept in touch with Theodore Baldick, whom Nancy still saw in group therapy. Harold showed me a letter he wrote Baldick:

It has been, to put it mildly, rather interesting. With one exception, Nancy has gone into a catatonic fugue state every day; always on the sound of a siren. [The Gaffneys lived two blocks from the firehouse.] Last night at 11:20 after Nancy had retired, the fire company went past our house, sirens screaming; we tore into her bedroom, to find her sitting up in bed, rocking, her ears covered; every muscle in her body in a cataleptic state.

We have observed that in her severe withdrawals, it is well nigh impossible to get any response from her. While we know she is receiving, there is absolutely no reaction in any manner, shape or form. It took us more than one hour to talk her out; Diane can fondle her, hold her and caress her with no untoward results. Let me touch her, even tentatively, with a fingertip, and she withdraws violently; notwithstanding the fact that Nancy has me mixed up with God. She worships me.

In any event, Nancy started to abreact violently as she started to come out, crying piteously, "No! No! No!" Questioning as to what was happening was ignored by her. Our experience has been that if she is left alone, she will come out of her fugue spontaneously. To try to move her physically entails a berserk reaction.

A few weeks later Harold showed me another letter he wrote Baldick:

Nancy had a bad fugue Monday night; someone hit the siren right outside the door; I jumped two feet; rushed into Nancy's room and found her in a bad fugue. Except this one was different. She was shivering and shaking and in minor convulsions; in brief, she was reliving withdrawal at Gateways Hospital [one of the hospitals to which she was confined for a short while]. I was working with a client; we got Diane home from City Council via the police. Diane recognized the symptoms; got Nancy into hypnosis, and gave her an *imaginary* fix of heroin in the arm. Nancy got as high as a kite. You may not believe this—*next morning Nancy's arm was swollen and black and blue, with a puncture wound in the arm!* Wednesday, she returned from Group highly agitated; went into another spontaneous fugue, went into withdrawal symptoms again; once more the same routine was repeated. An imaginary fix; a *high* and puncture marks the next morning. We have considered, and ruled out the possibility the lesions were self-inflicted. So, what answer remains? Nancy is producing "stigmata," which is a definite ability with her depth as a hypnotic subject.

Over the years Nancy kept diaries. She allowed me to see some of them. For instance, on Christmas, 1972, when she attended East Los Angeles High School before moving to Ontario, she wrote: "I seem to be losing more and more time." Which meant the personalities were coming out. She was then in first year high school, not yet complaining she felt drugged at times.
There were also the following entries:

January 1, 1973: Today is the first day in the year of 1973. Mom let me drive the car to the end of the street and back. It's so much fun. Timmy is banging on a tin pan with a spoon. Well, here's to a good year. Cheers!!!
January 3, 1973: Mom and Robert [a professor her mother was dating] are talking about marriage. I am babysitting downstairs now.
January 4: Today was odd. I vomited blood first period. Was sent home. [Jennifer, in one of her suicide attempts, had swallowed rust remover; Nancy would find herself at times sitting up in bed at night, gushing out a pint of blood.]
January 6: Sister Susan planning marriage. Plans to live at home. Mom is spending the night with Robert. But decently, of course!
January 28: Dear Diary: I wish you were a real person, so you could talk back to me. I wish I could hide inside of you.
March 10: Mother breaks up with Robert. I feel so lonely.
April 3: I feel something violent inside my stomach, as though I had swallowed poison.
June 25: Dear Diary. I am sick. I am so sick I am scared. I think my brain is bleeding because if I am sad, or cry, I throw up blood. I do not want mom to find out. She would be upset. I wonder if I am dying? I do not want to die. Something is wrong with me but I can't tell anybody.
July 16: I just found out that Shela, who I babysit for, murdered her baby. It gives me the creeps.
August 23: Fuck teachers!! [Later discovered this was in Nancy/John's handwriting.]
Sept. 11: Started another year. Spanish, algebra, safety ed, lab assistant, English, modern dance, drama.

Sept. 28: Stomach hurt. Doctor said I had ulcers.

Nov. 2: Quitting school. I failed at home. I failed at school.

Nov. 11: Well, I'm 16 today.

Nov. 22: Mom is in pretty good spirits. HAPPY THANKSGIVING.

Dec. 8: Nightmare as I woke up in the middle of the night and threw up. During the day I saw my father and his pregnant wife. I put my hand on her stomach and felt the baby kick. I pray to God it's healthy and she's healthy.

Dec. 25: I hate Christmas. I ended up in the park with John, a guy I just met. I was scared but I pretended it was fine. [They had sex.]

Nancy liked to write, along the way she provided me with descriptions of some of her terror-stricken moments. Once, after a school counselor had tested her, Nancy described her feelings as she stayed home for a day:

I walked around the apartment. Restless, edgy. That awful thing [losing time] was going to happen again. I knew it. It always did when I felt this way. Somehow I never expected it, but I was never surprised, either. This time I knew. I didn't want it to happen. It was scary, this knowing ahead of time. I didn't know how to stop it; I wasn't sure of what I was fighting, even.

I had come to understand it as lost time. But this way, approaching, it felt more like doom. The phone rang, and I went to pick it up. But I stopped myself. What if IT happened while I was talking to someone? Would they know? Better not, just to be safe. It could be mom. Or the school nurse, or . . . the school counselor!

She [school counselor] said she would call today. Dear God, please don't let her find out! She would know I was crazy, for sure. She had probably read a lot of books that could make her know those things about people. She was my biggest threat. I got confused at her questions. I was never sure when I left her if I had given my secret away. Those tests . . . I'll bet she could see it! She would KNOW and tell everyone I was crazy. Oh no, no, no . . .

They put people in crazy places when they didn't fit. I knew that. But I wasn't like those people. I don't think so. Was I? If they would just leave me alone, I'd work it out.

I'd remember. I just needed time to think, that's all. How much longer could I hide it from them? Even quitting school didn't help. It had started happening there, too. They said there was a law, I had to keep studying. Until I was sixteen. So they sent a lady here. I managed. But this counselor . . . it was harder with her. I hated her. She wanted to expose me. And I was helpless to fight her, too. I felt sad.

Another time she wrote of her stay in the Medical Center of the University of California at Los Angeles:

These are my impressions, thoughts and experiences of "Life on the Mental Ward." Ha-Ha. Let's see, first off I'll start with the good, at least I know I won't get writers cramp.

PRO. It is a relatively secure environment, people are around you *all* the time. You know what is expected of you, everything you do is scheduled. You have lots of time to relax and do nothing, 9/10 of the day, in fact. Very little is asked of you—you are not considered a responsible person or you wouldn't be here. If you are not happy with the outside world, you can just forget about it—this is a great hiding place, I'm sure no one would ever find you. You can really improve your ping-pong game. You will never need ashtrays when you leave here—you've probably made 30 identical ones.

CON. I hate it here. I hate the bare halls. I hate the programmed patients. I hate the programmed nurses. I hate being awakened at 6:30 in the morning just to do nothing. I hate occupational therapy and the ridiculousness of it all. I hate the forever ongoing hours. I hate being on the 5th floor overlooking a beautiful campus and not being able to see it through the mesh wires on the windows. I hate the nurses' lousy charts. I hate the lack of privacy. I hate the crummy "community room" (the only place to go except your bedroom) where everyone lays around like zombies.

When Nancy first arrived at the Gaffneys to stay as a foster daughter, her mother brought her. Nancy knew her mother would soon leave her. She wrote of this moment:

Strange. I didn't remember the house being this dark before. I was going to live here? I stared at mom. She looked pale and I could see that she was fighting the tears. This was for real. My new foster mother kept talking, I guess to help fill the painful silence that came when she stopped. She showed me my bedroom. The bed just about took up the whole room. The heavy, dark headboard reached all the way to the ceiling. I could tell that you didn't slip into that bed. You climbed into it. I felt even smaller.

I'd been in this house before. I had visited my new foster parents about a year ago, in an effort to control my bleeding ulcers. They were hypnotherapists. My high school counselor had sent me to them. They had said if I ever needed a place to stay, I was welcome there. They had a license for that kind of thing.

Here I was. The doctor at the hospital had told mom I had to have twenty-four-hour supervision. Mom said she would see to it. I was so groggy from the thorazine they had given me, and so anxious to get out of there, I just kept nodding and agreeing to anything. But mom understood them. And she knew the next day what had been said the night before. That was when she called the Gaffneys. I had told her about them. They wanted me to come right away. Mom helped me pack, because I was still groggy and my arm had swollen up like a balloon from the shot. We didn't pack much. It was sort of like a hospital stay. Temporary. I was to stay for a week or two. Maybe three.

I think it was one of the hardest moments in my mom's life to turn around and leave me there. Especially after the night before. I was lucky . . . I still had enough thorazine in me to dull my senses. Good thing, too. Things were happening so fast around me, changing my life in such a big way, things I didn't understand . . . that I could not have let go of her at that point if I could have thought clearly.

I understood more of the terror in Nancy's life up to the day she entered the Gaffneys' home by what I learned from her mother. Nancy and her mother were unusually close. Since the age of five, when her father left the house, Nancy had been taken care of by her mother. Nancy's mother, undoubtedly the most important person in Nancy's life, played the roles of both mother and father as Nancy grew up.

In still another sense Nancy's closeness to her mother was revealed. She bore her mother's name. She was called Nancy, Junior. Nancy's father had suggested to his wife just after their fifth child was born, "This will be our last so let's name her after you."

Her mother called her "Junior" or at times "June." Nancy had the same color hair and eyes as her mother. One of Nancy's sisters was a redhead, both grandmothers had red hair.

Nancy's father referred to her as "my little princess" or "pumpkin" or "J.R.," the letters standing for Junior. Nancy's two older sisters called her Nancy. Her oldest brother, Steve, of whom she was afraid because he had a temper and sometimes struck her, called her "J.R." She adored Tommy, the next older brother, he brought her Easter baskets with money earned on his paper route, treated her gently, called her "June."

Nancy Phipps, her mother's name today, is an attractive woman, looking somewhat like Judy Garland. She is youthful, often taken for Nancy's sister. A realtor in Upland, she lives in a rented house with her youngest son, Timmy, seventeen, a senior in high school. She is married to a man suffering from Alzheimer's disease, cared for in a nursing home.

She says of her daughter that since Nancy was a toddler she "won the hearts of everyone who knew her." She was the most well-behaved of the six children, always "the perfect little lady, cheerful, loving, lovable and always striving to please. She was just too good to be true." Nancy told me, "I love my mother and would never do anything to hurt her."

Nancy's mother gave me a few details about the rape no one else disclosed. She recalled March 25, 1973 as "much the same as any other quiet Sunday, a bright, sunny afternoon, a relaxing kind of day. Nothing to hint we would see the depths of hell before our lives would ever be normal again." Nancy told her she was going to the nearby park to write poetry, would be home in a short while and "walked out the door with writing pad in hand."

This was 2:30 P. M. Shortly after five, Nancy's mother began to worry. Two hours later she felt deeply concerned and "a little angry that Nancy had not at least called to say she would be late—this was just not like Nancy."

In her mother's words: "Finally the door opened. Nancy almost fell in, staggering toward me. Her face was horribly beaten, her eyes almost swollen shut, her clothes torn, dirty and bloody. I was hysterical, crying, demanding to know who did this to her." At first Nancy would not say a word, finally she told her mother about the rapist. She begged her mother not to call the police, believing the man would then follow through on his threat to kill her. Instead, Nancy's mother called her ex-husband who went gun in hand to find the rapist based on a description of his car.

Nancy's mother said, "Thank God my former husband didn't find the rapist or my husband would be in prison. He would have killed the man for doing such a thing to his baby."

Nancy's mother also informed me it was soon after the rape she began to notice changes in Nancy's behavior, "changes that were not at all like her." Her mother also remembered an earlier time when Nancy was eleven and asked one night as they both stood by the sink washing dishes, "Mom, have you ever lost time?" Nancy's mother commented, "This was to be the most important question Nancy would ever ask me, and I, in total ignorance, had shrugged it off as nothing. I didn't realize how extreme was her plight. I should have talked to her about it, questioned her reason for asking, tried to understand what she was saying to me."

The school authorities started to notice that Nancy behaved strangely at times, sat at her desk as though in a coma. They suggested her mother find professional help for Nancy, mentioned the Fuller Institute in Pasadena. Her mother made an appointment for Nancy to see a doctor at the institute, believing her daughter was suffering the aftershock of the rape. But following a few visits to a young intern psychologist, Nancy refused to return. She threatened to run away from home if forced to visit the institute.

"This was so out of character for Nancy to throw tantrums, she was so threatening to me and her behavior so shocking, that I gave in and cancelled the appointment," her mother recalled. The psychologist then phoned to find out why Nancy had not appeared. When her mother told him Nancy refused to see him, he pleaded with her to get other help for her daughter, sounded almost frantic about Nancy's need for aid.

Nancy's mother then made an agreement with Nancy. She said she would not insist on Nancy returning to the Fuller Institute if she would see the family doctor, Dr. Wallace, in Alhambra. He examined her, then told her mother, "Go home, pack your daughter's clothes and take her at once to the Queen of Angels Hospital in Los Angeles. A doctor will be waiting for her in the emergency room at 4 P.M. Get her there!"

Tests had shown heroin in Nancy's urine. Nancy later told me, "What the doctor suspected was true. I had heroin in my body when I went in. But I did not know about the heroin. Only that I often felt sick." Nancy/John had been taking it in large doses, leaving Nancy, the core personality, to suffer.

The doctor at the Queen of Angels Hospital, informed by Dr. Wallace of his findings, ordered a nurse to put Nancy to bed. Her mother waited down the hall while the doctor examined Nancy. When he came out of her room he told her mother Nancy was "a very sick young lady." He asked her mother to go home, search Nancy's room, read her letters and diaries for clues about her drug addiction.

Her mother did this reluctantly, she had always respected her children's privacy, never opened their mail or listened in on their phone calls. "Never have I felt so guilty, so sneaky," she said, as she read Nancy's three diaries. They were difficult to understand, nothing in sequence, "so complicated it seemed almost in code. What I could make out was shocking. Yes, drugs were mentioned, but who were all these strange people she had written about? What was the meaning of all this mumbo-jumbo?"

She called the doctor's office in the morning, left a message saying he was right about the drugs. During her next visit to Nancy, the doctor asked to speak privately to her. In the hall outside Nancy's room, he told her he was transferring Nancy to Gateways, a mental hospital that would get her off the heroin. Nancy's mother said she would agree to anything that would help her daughter. The doctor asked her to return the next day and drive Nancy to Gateways.

When mother and daughter walked into the mental hospital they both were upset at seeing patients so disturbed. "Neither Nancy nor I had ever seen anything like it except in the movies," Nancy's mother recalled. "Patients mumbling to themselves, staring into space, bouncing up and down and singing to their own music. We heard screams from down the hall. Nancy was terrified. I did not want to leave her in such a chaotic place."

A doctor introduced himself, asked Nancy several questions, then assured her mother Nancy would be well in a short time. Against her better judgment, Nancy's mother agreed to let Nancy stay. A nurse led them to Nancy's room, assuring her mother Nancy would be comfortable. Her mother kissed Nancy goodbye, said she would return in one week, the time the doctor had set. She walked to her car praying this was the right thing to do, "even as the very thought of Nancy in such a place sent chills through me."

When she visited Nancy the following Sunday Nancy told her she "hated" the hospital, feared the patients. She cried, begged her mother to take her home. It was difficult for her mother to walk away but she felt Nancy had to stay for her own sake. She drove home, tears in her eyes.

The next Sunday Nancy again begged to be taken away from the hospital, clung to her mother. Her mother promised she would bring her home in one week, no matter what. The doctor told her mother Nancy was making progress though her mother could see no progress, only her scared, desperate daughter pleading to be rescued from an intolerable place. Nancy told of patients screaming through the night, living in fear of personal attack, said she did not know how much longer she could bear it.

As her mother walked to her car she looked back, saw Nancy standing by the large double-glass windows, watching her leave, tears streaming down her pale face. Her mother vowed she would not put her daughter through such torture longer than one more week.

That night she was cooking dinner for Timmy and herself when the phone rang. A male voice identified himself as a sergeant with the police department. He told her Nancy had just broken out of the hospital without anyone seeing her and had attempted suicide by slashing her wrists in Echo Park. She had been taken back to Gateways Hospital.

Nancy's mother turned off the stove, grabbed little Timmy and her purse, ran to her car. Reaching the hospital she parked in a spot that said "Emergency Vehicle Parking Only," holding Timmy's hand raced into the hospital. She was instructed to go to a certain room, see her daughter, then talk to police and paramedics who needed more information for their reports.

She told me how she "walked into a room where my daughter lay on a table. Her arms were outstretched with both wrists slashed lengthwise to the bone. The doctor was preparing to sew them. Nancy looked up at me with tears running down into her hair and asked, 'Are you mad at me, Mommy? Are you mad?' I put my hand on her forehead and then brushed the tears away. I said softly, holding back my own tears, 'I'm not angry, dear.' "

The doctor then asked her, "Will you step outside for a while, so I can repair this broken doll?"

While she waited the police explained a black family had been fishing at the lake in Echo Park, near downtown Los Angeles. They had forgotten something in the car and the wife returned for it, leaving their three children with her husband. On her way she came across Nancy/Jennifer "lying under a tree, barely conscious, blood pumping out of her wrists with every heartbeat."

The wife ran back to her husband, he dashed to Nancy's side, quickly loosened the laces from her tennis shoes, tied them tightly around her arms. Meanwhile his wife raced to a liquor store across the street from the park to call an ambulance.

Nancy's mother, while she waited for the doctor to sew up the "broken doll's" arms, called her ex-husband and he drove at once to the hospital. After the doctor finished his surgery, he told Nancy's mother she could take her daughter home. He prescribed exercises with tennis balls for Nancy's wrists, warned she might not regain full use of her hands if she did not perform the exercises faithfully.

The doctor also told Nancy's parents she had to return for a seventy-two-hour observation. According to Nancy's mother, "A look of anger flashed across her father's face and he lashed out at the doctor, saying, 'Like hell! She's not going back to that place, ever!' "

There echoed in her mother's ears the voice of a policeman at the hospital who said of Nancy within her hearing, "Jesus Christ, how do I get all the weird ones?"

Shortly after this near-tragedy, one afternoon when Nancy was at school the doorbell rang. Nancy's mother let in a plainclothes detective who asked, "May I talk to you?" He appeared "uneasy and hesitant, refused my offer of coffee, just sat on the couch looking around the room and watching me."

Then he cleared his throat several times, informed her, "Your daughter is in serious trouble and I need your full cooperation." He knew Nancy's mother was a policewoman and wanted to help her. He warned that Nancy was suspected of being a member of a gang that sold drugs and the police were watching her, "hoping under surveillance Nancy would lead them to the kingpins of the criminal gang. He warned me against telling her she was being watched, for that would place her in far more danger. She might tell the leader of the gang and they would kill her."

After the detective left, she said, "I felt a wild urgency to pack up and move my family far away from this dreadful city. Fear and anger raged through me. And I was supposed to act as if not a thing was different than before that detective's visit."

When Nancy walked in from school, "one arm around a stack of books, she was cheerful and bubbly and full of good news about winning a hockey game in physical education class. As I watched her standing before the open refrigerator door deciding what she wanted for a snack, I knew that detective had made a horrible mistake. Surely he was talking about some other girl. Nancy was so sweet, so innocent, how could that man think this petite, honor roll student could be mixed up with criminals, and even the Mafia. He had to be crazy."

Nancy's mother continued going to her job each morning at 7:30 in downtown Los Angeles, believed Nancy and Timmy were sound asleep by 9 P.M. when she went to bed. She told me, "I had no idea that after 10 P.M. each night my sweet and innocent daughter would dress in gang-type garb and head for the streets and the people she knew there. I later learned she would return about 3 A.M. yet manage to get up in time for school, keep up her excellent grades and appear to be living a very normal, quiet life."

She went on, "It seems impossible that there was not the slightest hint of her 'other' life. I had the best of police training, every day I saw the good and the bad of society and I felt confident in my ability to see people for what they were. Yet here, living in our own home was a suspect in the worst type of criminal activities known to the police and I never had a clue to the truth until the day that detective told me. To me, it was completely unbelievable. How could such a thing possibly be true?"

She lived through the gang "bust," saw Nancy brought home by the police and decided to move from the city at once when the police told her the Mafia had put a price of $10,000 on Nancy/Jennifer as informant, since she was the only one the police had allowed to go free.

Before Nancy's mother could make the move, on April 4, 1975 she received an emergency call while at work. She was told by her supervisor, "This time it is really bad. Go, just go to your daughter's school." When she arrived, Nancy's mother saw the same scene I did at Ontario High School when Nancy/Jennifer fled my class. Four police officers were closing in on Nancy and "the wild look on Nancy's face was that of a madman," said her mother. "The officers moved in slowly, then wrestled her to the floor. Once she was pinned down, the ambulance attendants literally straddled her, one sitting across her chest, the other across her knees. My little girl!"

After Nancy was subdued she was given "a shot to relax her, laced into the straitjacket without further resistance. As a stretcher was wheeled in and she was lifted up, I went to her to again assure her of my love for her. She only looked at me with sleepy eyes and said nothing."

Nancy's mother heard an elderly man, a bystander, say in disgust, as Nancy was taken away by the police, "These kids and their drugs, they all belong in jail." Nancy's mother told me, "I wanted to shout at him, 'She is sick! She is just sick!' "

The police allowed Nancy's mother to accompany her daughter to Los Angeles County General Hospital. By the time they arrived, according to Nancy's mother, "Nancy was her usual self. She asked me what happened. She remembered nothing. The officers could see Nancy was totally in control and they removed the straitjacket, walked us to the elevator, told us which floor to go to, said goodbye and left." Nancy's mother still wore her policewoman's uniform "of badge, insignia and belt with a holster hanging at my side."

Nancy turned to her mother, whispered, "I know these people think you just arrested me."

When they sat with the doctor, Nancy's mother told him how Nancy did not even recognize her, that Nancy had been like a "caged animal." Nancy's mother asked if her daughter could be admitted to the hospital, pleading, "Something is dreadfully wrong with her." Nancy now appeared normal, however, and the doctor dismissed them saying, "Hospitals are for sick people and your daughter is not sick."

Her mother asked, "Do you think hypnosis might help her?"

"It might," he said. "Why don't you try it?"

Nancy, Senior's concern probably saved her daughter's life. She was determined to find a way of lessening Nancy's suffering. I thought her a sensitive, articulate woman, willing to answer questions as frankly as she could. She had worked hard to support her large family after divorcing Nancy's father when she was thirty-four. Originally she wanted to be a lawyer, she told me, and "went into police work with the idea I could cure the ills of the world. There was satisfaction in responding to a 415 call [domestic disturbance], calming down a family that was fighting." She also worked in the assessor's office of the county of Los Angeles for a brief time.

I knew that to understand the daughter, you have to understand the mother and father for it is parents who shape the emotional destiny of a child. I asked Nancy's mother to tell me about her background, her childhood, her dreams and ambitions. She described how her ancestors came to this country in the early 1660s from Belfast, Ireland, bearing a coat of arms.

She was born in Berea, Ohio, grew up there. Her parents moved to San Diego, to be near her brother in the Navy, stationed at Long Beach. She was nineteen when she met Linley Cicero Gooch in San Diego. He had just returned to the United States after serving with the Marines in Okinawa during World War II. She called him "Lindy," explained, "That's what I thought he said when he introduced himself."

He stood six feet, two inches, was dark haired, slim and handsome, with an Alan Ladd face. Born in Danville, Illinois, he grew up on a farm with a father who drank heavily, laced his breakfast coffee with whiskey. His son refused to touch even beer. After he met Nancy, Senior they discovered they enjoyed figure skating, spent many a night whirling around the rink. She described him as "a very intense man, masculine, not deep, not the emotional type but often mellow."

They married, bought a small two-bedroom house in Covina, thirty-five miles east of Los Angeles. They wanted children but Nancy, Senior had been severely hurt in an automobile accident when she was seventeen and the doctor told her she would never have a baby. They adopted a boy just after his birth on July 8, 1950, named him Steve. He was one of twins, the other died in the hospital.

"I wanted that baby so badly," Nancy, Senior said. "We chose him special. But once Steve reached his teens, home was just a place to change his clothes. He wasn't close to anyone in the family." He is now married, lives in Oregon, works for the roads department of the city of Medford.

To her surprise, Nancy, Senior became pregnant three years later. Tommy was born September 15, 1953. He is married, works for the post office in Ontario. A year later, Nancy, Senior gave birth to Barbara on December 1, 1954. After another year, on March 12, 1956, Susan was born. Both daughters married early, left the house. Susan runs a day-care center in San Juan Capistrano. A year and a half after Susan's birth, Nancy was born on November 11, 1957. The last child, Timmy, was born on July 31, 1969 during Nancy, Senior's brief second marriage.

After fifteen years of marriage Nancy's mother asked for a divorce. She told me she found herself practically living without a husband. Linley worked nights, she worked part-time during the day in a lawyer's office to help support the family. Her evenings consisted of bathing the five children, then, after they fell asleep, sitting by herself until she felt tired enough to fall into bed. She grew more and more lonely. Linley wanted her to work the swing shift in the factory along with him, principally, she said, because he was jealous of the men in the lawyer's office who flirted with her during the hours she worked there.

"He was an extremely jealous husband," she said, "but then I was a jealous wife. He was friendly and outgoing, he'd walk into a restaurant and kid with the waitresses. He was faithful but that didn't stop my jealousy."

When she first asked him to leave he said, "I'm not going any place." Then he agreed to take a room in the home across the street which took in boarders, so he could see the children regularly and be there if she needed him. But after he moved, she said, "he sowed his wild oats, like a little boy in a toy shop," and she sued for divorce.

After the divorce, "because I was never one to warm bar stools or drink heavily, I wanted only to go to school and study," she consulted a counseling service. When asked, "What do you want to do?" she said, "I want to help people, maybe take up nursing." The service sent her to a hospital to train, there she was told she had "no call for nursing." They suggested police work as a way of taking care of people. This did not appeal to her at the time and for two and a half years she did paralegal work in the county assessor's office.

There she met her second husband. When Nancy was eleven, her mother married again, became pregnant with Timmy. Nancy, Senior told me this husband "oozed charm, made you feel you were the only woman in the world but half an hour later he'd be trying to make another woman feel the same way. He was a playboy." He had been a well-known trombone player, a member of Glenn Miller's air-force band and later joined the orchestras of Tommy Dorsey, Les Brown and Henry Mancini. While with Mancini, he played for several Academy Award evenings in Hollywood. But he became an alcoholic, lost his standing with bands.

When he learned Nancy, Senior was pregnant, he threatened to leave if she would not get an abortion. She refused, he left, after four months of marriage. She told me, "I chose the baby over him. I helped him pack. I had three girls at home who each wanted their own baby and were delighted with the idea of my having one. Timmy came home from the hospital to four mothers. But when the thrill wore off, it was always, 'Junior, take care of the baby.'"

Nancy, Junior said of her stepfather, "I liked him, he was good to us, though he did make an occasional pass at my two sisters and me."

Because Nancy, Senior worked so hard, Nancy, Junior became

Timmy's chief caretaker. She enjoyed it, said, "I was the one who wanted a little brother most. I fantasized I was his mother."

Shortly after her second divorce, Nancy, Senior started to go with the man she described as "very highly respected by all who knew him." He was a professor at California State University in Fullerton, with a Ph.D. in speech pathology. A highly intelligent man, he enjoyed museums, the world of art, classical music and exotic foods. Their romance was rocky and they never married. During a particularly stormy period, when Nancy was twelve and a half, her mother asked her to take year-old Timmy by bus to El Paso and stay with her brother Tommy. He was in the army, living in Texas with his family. Though frightened at leaving home to become Timmy's full-time caretaker, Nancy, who never opposed her mother, embarked on the journey. She and Timmy stayed several months and during this period Nancy told me later, she lost time as Nancy/Sarah once again came to the rescue.

Though Nancy's mother always had suitors because of her lovely face, slim shape and friendly manner, she admitted, "Men, really deep down, scare me."

There was reason enough for this fear. Nancy's mother recalled, "I had problems with one of my stepfathers—sexual problems—when I was twelve. He never actually did anything but he insinuated he would like to have sex. When I was a teenager he would stroll into the bathroom while I sat in the tub and talk to me. My mother suspected how he felt and one day confronted him with it. He admitted his feelings for me. Even though my mother was pregnant with my younger sister, Florence, she divorced him when she discovered he ran around with other women."

She said of her childhood, "I was never loved or wanted. I was tolerated." She called her mother, "a very difficult woman," added, "She never loved me, she looked down on me. She instilled a deep inferiority complex in me. I felt as I grew up that the house was my address, not my home."

Nancy's mother told me how hurt she felt the day her sister Jo-Anne was severely injured in an accident and her mother turned to her, sneered, "Why couldn't it have been you instead of my darling?" Nancy, Senior said, "I felt wounded. I vowed I would never be like that with my children. But I guess even out of the worst comes some good. I became independent. I told myself I didn't care that she was so mean to me."

Her mother married five times. She described her mother's second husband as "a real cad" and learned he was still married when a former wife showed up one day at the door. It was her mother's third husband that Nancy, Senior remembered as "father."

"He's the one I recall most vividly," she said. "He did have some good qualities, like playing Scrabble with us kids. But he could also whip off a belt faster than anyone could see and hit us when he got angry. Like if we spoke at dinner, which we were not allowed to do. The beatings started when I was ten. One day my grandmother took me home with her and was shocked to find stripes on my back from his leather belt." She added, "He could be the meanest man God ever let live. He sometimes even beat my mother."

He stood only five feet, three inches, weighed 115 pounds, but liked fat women, according to Nancy, Senior: "My mother weighed 190 pounds. And my father left my mother, after three years of marriage, for a big, fat nurse when my brother Harry was eighteen months old."

This stepfather also frightened Nancy's mother in another way. He was a flier for the air force, had started as a trainer of fighter pilots during World War II, made a good living. Sometimes he took Nancy's mother, then a child, up in his plane and in spite of knowing she was scared to death would "zoom the plane in loop-the-loops, turning it upside down," as she would plead, "Please, daddy, stop." She still hates flying with a "passion." Her stepfather "lived by flying and he died by flying. After he married the fat nurse he was killed one day in a two-plane crash in the sky, flying solo. No one could find out if it was his fault or the pilot of the other plane."

Her mother married twice after this though her daughter described her as "a real man-hater. She hated taking care of, cooking for, a man. She lives alone today and loves it. She doesn't have to slave preparing a meal for a husband and children."

I thought, This is the tragic and chaotic background of Nancy, Junior's mother, now doing all she can to help save her youngest daughter from a hopeless future. Perhaps a life that would soon end by her own hand if she did not receive the right kind of help.

Nancy told me her father was not there for her very much as she grew up and at times there were conflicts between her mother and father. She said, "Even so, I was unhappy when my parents divorced. I didn't understand why. I'm not sure they understood."

Against this background I wondered how I could reach Nancy's feelings about the trauma in her early life.

I felt like the blind leading the blind but not able to give up leadership because there was no one else Nancy would allow to take over. Of all those who offered help—psychiatrists, psychologists, hypnotherapists, counselors—she clung to me. If I thought she might do better in someone else's hands, I would willingly have relinquished my role.

It was to become a voyage of passion, of learning, of growing, of prevailing, often on an incredibly tense level. I was leader of the journey inward of a talented, tormented, emotionally crippled young woman as she slowly made her fragmented way from complete chaos and a wish to die into a wholeness and a world she could better order.

The story of Nancy Lynn Gooch, I realized as I stepped deeper and deeper into Nancy's life, is to some degree the story of us all. Each of us creates within himself both defenses against and outlets for our tortured feelings.

I consistently conveyed to Nancy the feeling I was in her corner all the way. She knew I cared about her from the first day I held her in my arms in the nurse's office, tried to comfort her. I am able to show affection easily, I am not afraid of touch. If a person feels terror or pain I want to hold them close, reassure them—what the hurt child needs. The warmth of someone's arms helps more than words.

Even as she desperately wanted my help, Nancy fought any sign of closeness. She admitted, "I want to be close to you but I am afraid of being close." Some psychologist once said any time we are asked to change our behavior we at once raise defenses against doing so. For the average person such defenses are like iron. For Nancy, they were a thousandfold stronger.

In her exaggerated wish to please, I sensed Nancy's plea not to abandon her. She feared abandonment more than anything except annihilation—she wanted to stay alive. I would discover all Nancy's personalities had a certain toughness that kept them survivors. This spirit made it possible for me to endure the difficult times, buoyed my hope that one day Nancy would become whole, no longer split into enemy camps.

As I worked to help the personalities stop their destructive behavior, I was at first the enemy. Then a tentative testing ground. Then anchor in a safe port where the storms of the terrifying past could be examined in new light. The light of reason.

Nancy's nineteenth birthday was November 11, 1976. As she described herself to me she was still, to all intents and purposes, "the good little girl who never harms anyone." Diane asked Nancy/Sarah, "Why is it so hard for Nancy to tell us how she feels?" Nancy/Sarah replied, "She is fairly honest but has to keep up a smile or the world will fall apart. She can open up some to Emily."

Notes in Nancy's diary revealed the suffering beneath her outwardly compliant behavior. One year after moving to the mahogany bedroom at the Gaffneys', in her first year at Chaffey Community College, she wrote:

> November 23, 1976: Today I had a fugue at college in the locker room. The L. R. [locker room] lady found me and was frightened cause I was shaking so bad. She thought it was a seizure. She told me this. I never knew what happened during a fugue.
>
> November 29, 1976: Another fugue at college. "No! No!" But the police and counselors and attendants grabbed me and carried me to the stretcher and strapped me down. Mrs. Campbell, whom they called, drove over, took my face between her hands and said "Honey, honey." They took me to the ambulance. I screamed, "No!" many times. Mrs. Campbell was *mad*. She hated them. She had asked me if I wanted her to go home with me. She held me. So here I am after once again being released when they find nothing wrong. I was in that fuckin' ambulance for 1 1/2 hours.
>
> December 3, 1976: I went to her school to see Mrs. Campbell. She walked in and put her hand on my face and said, "Hello." We went over to a bean bag couch and I took her hand. Tears started running down my face and she pulled me up against her. She put her hand on my face and we just sat there, with me silently crying. I tried to stop and she said, "Why don't you just let it go, Nancy?" She said I have shown stronger emotion now than anytime since she has known me. I said, "Do you still like me?" She said, "I love you."

One day Nancy showed me an undated letter she said Nancy/Jennifer had written to Zurdo, the gang leader. The letter, never mailed, was written after the police raid on the gang's headquarters. It read:

Dear Zurdo:
Where the hell are you. They said you got busted. I told
them you are too smart for that. You can come get me now.
Nancy is staying at 5052 Moreno, the Lady's name is
Nancy's mother. I haven't had nothing [drugs] for long
time. I couldnt get nothing. I miss the gang. What is it
where you are? I know you can get out. Don't get busted no
more. Keep the pigs away.

Jennifer (puppet)

The gang had called her "puppet" but the fact Nancy/Jennifer still
referred to herself as "puppet" told how a part of Nancy felt about
herself—deadened, a wooden figure, the strings pulled by other people
or her inner multiples.

Nancy also revealed more about her inner life when she gave me a
sheet of paper on which she had written dialogue for a brief show she
planned to stage in her communications class at Chaffey Community
College.

She played all the parts in the skit, as in real life.

Hi, everybody, I'm Nancy. I'm the main character in this
show. The others are just bit players, but nevertheless, their
parts are very important and do have an effect on my life.
There are four other puppets—Sarah, Lisa, Jennifer and
John. I say they are puppets but just the same they are real
people with their own personalities. If you pay close attention, you will have a little more information about them if
and when you meet them. Which you just might do! It's not
always easy to tell when you *are* meeting them—because
they look very much like me.

You see, they live inside me. Sometimes they come out
to be in the world instead of me. I must admit these other
people sometimes act very different from the way I chose to
act, but please understand that they are the result of many
different experiences, and they cannot help themselves.
Please don't be afraid of them. They can't hurt anyone.
More important than anything, please don't be afraid to
relate to me. I like people and I'm pretty normal with the
exception of my sidekicks. Besides, I'm a pretty nice person
once you get to know me. Of course, you may not be too
sure about the others, so I'll just let you meet them yourself
and be the judge. Okay?

Sarah . . . Sarah, where are you?

Sarah: Here I am, darling. Goodness, my hair must look atrocious! My name is Sarah and I do suppose it would be for the best if perhaps I shared with you some of the important factors pertaining to my existence. I'm nineteen, which is consistent with Nancy's age, although I am much more mature and intelligent than she is. Please don't get me wrong, it's not the poor dear's fault. It is just that our psychological makeup varies and I happen to hold some of the finer qualities. I prefer classical music to that infernal noise that is fondly termed rock-and-roll, for instance.

I wondered at first what purpose the multiples served. Because of my reading of the works of psychologists Carl Rogers and Abraham Maslow at college, as well as my current research, I was somewhat open to the idea that some troubled souls might resort to creating people within to lessen their panic, in spite of my original skepticism.

The only other personality of Nancy's I had met besides the well-informed Nancy/Sarah was Nancy/Jennifer, though I did not know it at the time. Not Nancy but the Jennifer part of her had fled my class, huddled outside, allowed me to comfort her in the nurse's office. Then returned three weeks later to thank me.

After our first meeting with Nancy/Sarah, Harold summoned her to appear at a session I did not attend. She revealed Nancy/Jennifer was a "time traveler," had the capacity to "travel in time." She might appear one day as five years old, the next, fifteen, her maximum age. No personality, Nancy/Sarah informed us, could be older than Nancy, the core personality.

Nancy/Sarah also reported, "Jennifer was first created when Nancy was five, maybe even at two. Some crisis occurred that produced Jennifer. Then she went underground for years. She was reborn at fifteen, at the hour of the rape by the Mexican."

Harold taught me how to summon, or try to summon, for sometimes they would not appear, a personality. The magic command consisted of two words: "Zenith, Zero." They signaled Nancy to go into a hypnotic state so we could try to persuade a multiple to come out, talk to us.

Thus far only Nancy/Sarah would appear. But one evening I tried to reach Nancy/Jennifer in our darkened hypnotherapy room. I said to Nancy as she sat in her special chair, the one that reclined, "I'd like to try to reach Jennifer."

Nancy nodded assent, I uttered the two magical words, her eyes closed.

"Jennifer, are you there?" I asked. "Jennifer, are you there? We want to meet you. Please come out, Jennifer. Jennifer, come out."

No response. Nancy's body did not move an inch.

I repeated the request several times. Suddenly Nancy's body slumped slightly in the chair, her shoulders fell forward, the expression on her face changed from its usually serious one to a softer, more youthful one.

The voice that spoke was almost apologetic, a whisper, "I'm Jennifer."

"We're so glad to meet you at last, Jennifer," I said.

"We're delighted." Harold's deep voice.

I asked, "Were you a member of Zurdo's group?"

"Yes." Almost inaudible.

"And you visited me at school to thank me for trying to help you that day you suddenly left my class?"

"Yes. That was me."

"Thank you, Jennifer." Then I asked, "How do you feel now?"

"I like my new home." She looked around the darkened room. "I feel safe here." Then, "The only time Nancy lets me out is when there's trouble."

"You don't often feel safe, do you?" I thought of the suicide attempts Nancy/Sarah and Nancy's mother had described.

"Some places are very dangerous." A little girl's voice.

"Which ones in particular?"

"That last mental hospital. I had to get out of it. And after escaping, I felt like dying. I had withdrawal symptoms because of drugs. So I drank a glass of Lysol."

"Lysol?" I was appalled.

"Yes, *Lysol.*" Emphatically, as though it held special meaning.

I would later remember this as another clue to what I thought of as the soul murder of Nancy. And each personality would reveal his own special clue.

Nancy/Jennifer went on, "I drank the Lysol because I wanted to die. I'm sorry if it caused Nancy bleeding ulcers."

Thus the bleeding was not from "psychosomatic" causes, as Harold had thought, but from Nancy/Jennifer's deliberate destruction of parts of the lining of Nancy's stomach.

"Were there other times you wanted to die, Jennifer?"

"Every time they put me in a hospital. I thought they might keep me there forever. I was scared to death of the crazy people. And of the police who came after me every time I ran away."

Police and ambulance attendants were Enemy, each time they caught up with Nancy she fought them off like a wildcat. Now I understood her reaction at my school, as though her life were at stake. I thought of the words of Dr. Walter B. Cannon, famed scientist. He theorized when danger confronts us we either resort to "fight or flight." Nancy/Jennifer perceived the police as danger, her one thought to escape, she knew she had broken laws as a member of a drug-dealing gang.

"Tell us of other times you fled mental hospitals," I said.

"One night at the San Bernardino Hospital a woman patient came over to my bed when I was trying to sleep and urinated on me. I panicked. I smashed a window, crept out of it. I ran down a dark road toward the mountains, hoping to hide in them. The hospital called the police and they came after me in two cars. I trapped myself by running into a dead-end road. I tried to fight them off but they were too strong. They took me back to the hospital."

"Were there other hospitals you fled?" I asked.

"There was Gateways. I broke a window there one night and ran to town. About a mile away I found a drug store, stole a package of razor blades. Then I walked to a nearby park. I took out one of the blades. I slowly cut both wrists. I watched the blood spurt almost to the bushes. Then I lost consciousness."

Nancy's mother had described this suicide attempt and how Nancy/Jennifer would have died had not the black couple come to her rescue.

I asked, "What do you look like? How do you see yourself?"

"I have black hair and dark eyes," she said.

Harold asked, "Like the man who raped you?"

"I don't know," she said. Then, "I can speak Spanish."

I thought of what Anna Freud called "identification with the aggressor." Nancy/Jennifer saw herself in the image of the rapist. We tend unconsciously to identify with those who are more powerful than we are in an effort to become, at least in fantasy, the victor in a terrorizing situation.

Nancy/Jennifer said, "The man who raped me smelled of sweat. I've never been able to stand the odor of sweat since. It makes me nauseous."

"Do you remember anything else about the night of the rape?" Harold asked.

She thought a moment, said, "Only that he put his foot on my chest as I lay on the ground while he unzipped his pants. The cowboy boots hurt. Then I felt suffocated, it was hard to breathe with him on top. And he beat me hard. Afterwards, my face bled a lot."

A raging stranger had raped Nancy, there was no show of tenderness or love. Only brutality and power—cowboy boots stomped on her frail breast. Nancy/Jennifer carried the terror of the rape victim but also, buried psychic fathoms deep, the burning wish for vengeance turned on herself—the emotion suicide hides. Nancy wore the disguise of Little Miss Sunshine who would never hurt a fly so no one could guess the depths of *her* need for revenge.

Nancy/Jennifer appeared to be tiring, we let her go inside. I was delighted to meet her at last, the one who had prompted Nancy to return to school to thank me.

The following week when we called for Nancy/Jennifer to come out she had regressed to a five-year-old, asked to be held and cuddled. She played with her favorite toys, bought by Harold and Diane—the monkey Bobby Joe and the rubber snake Rattles. I wondered if these were the names of Nancy's early toys.

Nancy/Jennifer loved animals, seemed to have special communication with them. This was true not only of squirrels and birds but lizards and snakes. She would sit quietly in the middle of the mountain woods as animals edged out, drew close to be fed from her hand. She marked what she called her "circle," a section of shrubbery near the upper parking lot of Chaffey Community College at the foothills of our mountain range. Warning signs for visitors instructed them to walk only on paved areas because of the danger of rattlesnakes. Nancy/Jennifer could read only Spanish, would have ignored the warning if she could have read it. In her outdoor circle she found complete acceptance and safety. She knew no fear of rattlesnakes, by some miracle was never bitten— Nancy could not tolerate the tiniest insect, much less the sight of a snake. Nancy/Jennifer defended her friendship with the rattlesnakes, saying, "Snakes don't hurt me, only people do. I like snakes better."

When she was afraid of a human being she would run as though from a steel trap—from the mental hospitals, from the police, from school authorities, sometimes from her mother's home and now at times from the Gaffneys. If she felt depressed she refused to eat, would starve herself. Or burn herself with cigarettes, drink rust remover or Lysol.

It was apparent Harold and Diane became very fond of the appealing Nancy/Jennifer. She sometimes came out at night as a frightened child, would head for the Gaffneys' room, snuggle between them in their large double bed. She called Harold "Papasan" and Diane, "Mamacita." To

Harold, she was the daughter he never had (Diane's son, suffering from cerebral palsy, was blind, cared for in a special home). On Nancy's birthday, the Gaffneys bought her an Opel car and paid the insurance.

Nancy/Jennifer spoke lovingly of her twin, John. John was described both by Nancy/Sarah and Nancy/Jennifer as a survivor of the dark streets. He had been a member of Zurdo's gang, both consuming and dealing in drugs. He would creep out of the house at night when everyone else slept, join the gang.

Evidently both Nancy/Jennifer and Nancy/John were accepted as twins by the gang—twins who never appeared together. Nancy/John wore a baseball cap turned backward, hair pinned up under it, spoke in a low, clipped voice, according to Nancy/Sarah. Nancy/Jennifer wore her hair long, almost to her hips, her clothes were feminine, her voice soft, she wore no makeup. She told us that the night of the bust she saw police with binoculars hide in nearby doorways, stand on rooftops with spotting scopes, sit in cars pretending to be lovers (men and women officers) just before they raided the gang's "pad."

After she split from Zurdo's gang, Nancy/Jennifer was like a child. She avoided looking into mirrors because she envisioned herself as a Mexican, with long, black hair. But she felt traumatized when Nancy cut "their" hip-length hair.

Diane and Harold had to bear the day-to-day crises in Nancy's life caused by Nancy/Jennifer. I was present only for the weekly session and other times if needed. Such as the afternoon I received a call at school just before my third-period class. Nancy/Sarah was on the line. I recognized her voice.

"Someone at the Gaffneys has just taken an overdose of pills," she announced, hung up.

I called the Montclair police, reported, "I've been told someone overdosed on pills at 5052 Moreno Drive, the Gaffney home. Will you check and let me know?" I gave them the school telephone number.

The police called back in half an hour. They reported they had searched the house, breaking a window to get in, but found no one there.

I became alarmed. At the end of class I raced to the car, then to the Gaffney home. I went in through the broken window. All was quiet, eerily quiet, the feel of death. I searched the house room by room. No body.

But I am a persistent person, as I have said. I opened every closet door. In the last one, a closet in the Gaffneys' bedroom, I found Nancy/Jennifer slumped on the floor. She looked more dead than alive. I picked her up, carried her to the car, drove her to Doctor's Hospital, within five minutes of the house.

The nurses wheeled her to the emergency room where they pumped out her stomach, sent her back to the Gaffneys that night. If I had not found her, Nancy/Jennifer might have died. The Gaffneys did not return until hours later.

Still another time Nancy/Jennifer took an overdose and Diane was on the front line. She gave mouth-to-mouth resuscitation, then rushed her to the hospital. When I next spoke to Nancy/Jennifer in a session I told her over and over in emphatic tone, "You will *not* kill yourself. There are people who care enough to stop you. You must learn to care for yourself."

Through Nancy/Jennifer I started to learn what the personalities needed—someone who would set limits so they would not continue to destroy themselves. I announced five limits for them all: 1. No drugs. 2. No alcohol. 3. No sexual acting-out. 4. No harming of the self. 5. No harming anyone else. These rules were essential if destructive acts were to cease. The good parent would set such rules.

It was not enough just to set limits, I had to repeat them over and over to get across the importance of survival. Nancy/Jennifer had made five suicide attempts, the sixth might be fatal. There were times I spent hours with her—once, seven hours straight—talking her out of her wish to die, trying to convince her life was worth exploring.

"Why did you never give up?" people ask, knowing the amount of time I gave Nancy/Jennifer and the others.

"I couldn't give up," I answered. If I let the desire to die rule the personalities Nancy lost and I lost. It was strength against strength—a war between the inner Nancy, the one who wished to self-destruct, and myself.

Nancy/Jennifer was one of the few personalities to show instant trust in me. Which I felt I earned that first day we met in the nurse's office. She called me "the lady with the ring," fascinated by my wedding ring, with its six half-inch-high sections of alternating gold and silver.

Nancy/Jennifer feared and mistrusted men—the police, the rapist, psychiatrists. If a man walked into the room, except for Harold or Clint, she tried to escape. As she did when she bolted out of my arms that day at school with the arrival of the men who wanted to take her to the mental hospital, as though this meant her execution.

At first as we worked together, Nancy/Jennifer was too frightened to show much loyalty to Nancy or anyone except her twin, John. Slowly she became more thoughtful about herself and the others.

We still did not know what caused Nancy's fugues at the sound of sirens. One Thursday evening Nancy/Jennifer told us that Andrew, the boy she loved, thought truly a friend, had decided to leave the gang. He was ashamed of what they were doing and told Zurdo, the leader, he wanted out. Zurdo decided to give Andrew a "hot shot," the pure drug, an overdose. Zurdo would not hear of anyone leaving his gang, that was treason. He knew there was no way the police could trace the murder to him.

Nancy/Jennifer told us she watched one of the gang inject the "hot shot" into Andrew's left arm. She saw him slump to the floor, fall on a mattress in the pad. She thought he was dead but Hal, one of his friends, whispered to her, "Go across the street to the phone booth as soon as we split with the body and ask the operator to call an ambulance. Give her the address. We'll put the body near the phone booth."

At this point in her tale Nancy/Jennifer's eyes filled with tears and she slipped to the floor, as though she were Andrew's body, then talked on.

She said, "I dialed the operator. She promised to call the ambulance at once. Hal and another member of the gang carried Andrew's body out of the pad, dumped him beside the booth. It was dark. No one saw them."

Tears streamed down her face as she lived out the scene. "I sat down beside Andrew. I held him in my arms. I begged, 'Please, please stay alive. I love you.' I rocked him in my arms. I touched his blond hair, his blue eyes, his wide forehead, even though I knew he had stopped breathing. I felt if I had been able to convince him not to get Zurdo mad he would still be alive."

She paused, sniffed away tears. "Then I heard the sound of a siren. The ambulance was racing down the street. I knew I couldn't be found with Andrew. They would arrest me. I lowered his body to the sidewalk. I ran across the street. I saw the ambulance draw up. Its sirens were still screaming. Two men in white stepped out of the ambulance. They went over to Andrew's body. They picked it up. Put it in the ambulance, took it away."

We now understood why Nancy/Jennifer went into shock at the sound of a siren. It stood for death. It stirred to memory the murder of the first boy she loved, perhaps the only one. She was also afraid she might be given a "hot shot" next for leaving the gang, something her mother, then a policewoman, made her do when she learned from a detective her daughter was a member.

Nancy/Jennifer was asked to bear not only the terror of the rape in Echo Park but the murder of a friend and lover. I wondered what earlier horrors in Nancy's life Nancy/Jennifer might also have been summoned to shoulder.

Nancy/Sarah had told us Nancy created her first personality when Nancy was two. What could have happened to her then that so terrified her she had to split off a part of herself?

Nancy/Jennifer had finally, after a year and a half at the Gaffneys, allowed herself to speak. She had lost some of her cowering, terrified state. She was able to say to Harold one day, "I hate you. I hate all men. You want to put me away."

Her growing trust in me was allowing her to talk more freely, to admit she even existed. Through her I realized that the strongest mandate of the personalities was never, *never* to let an outsider know they were present.

To reveal themselves was to die. This, though I was not aware of it then, was an important clue to the early terror in Nancy's life.

Shortly after Nancy/Jennifer first spoke to us, Harold and Diane conducted a session I missed on July 4, 1977. It was taped, then made into a transcript Harold showed me. The session concentrated on the appearance of our co-therapist Nancy/Sarah.

Harold called for her after his "Zenith, Zero" summons. He told me he recognized her at once as Nancy's posture changed. She sat straighter, looked regal.

Harold asked, "How does it feel to be out, Sarah?"

"It always feels good," she said.

"Do you think you'll be here tomorrow? I'd like you to meet Dr. Robert Postman." Dr. Postman, of the Voorman Clinic, was taking over the hypnotherapy on the advice of Ted Baldick, who advised Harold not to play the role of both parent and therapist to Nancy. Diane drove Nancy for her first visit to Dr. Postman's office. Nancy/Jennifer came out, smashed through his window, tried to jump off the balcony, so deep her anger at being forced to give up Harold, whom she loved. But gradually she adjusted to Dr. Postman, who joined the team for a while.

Nancy/Sarah said, with a toss of her sophisticated head, "I would like very much to meet him but I'd like not to be in therapy with him."

"I'll tell him there will be no therapy," Harold agreed. "This is a social meeting. I hope we are invited to sit in because I want to see how he handles you."

"*I* am not handled." Pride in her voice.

"Huh?" Harold, for once, was caught off base.

She repeated, "I am *not* handled."

"I have already told Dr. Postman that under no circumstances will you go into therapy."

"I will not be subjected to a hypnosis situation."

"There's no necessity for hypnosis. The only reason we use hypnosis is to bring the other personalities *out*. And you're *out*. I do want you to tell us what you feel is happening with Jennifer."

"I am *utterly* amazed." Surprise in her low voice. "I really am."

"Pleasantly or unpleasantly?"

"Pleasantly. I honestly didn't think Jennifer was capable of the potential she's showing."

"She accuses me of being a cheapskate."

"I heard her call you that. She has a wry sense of humor." Nancy/Sarah had told us she could observe and hear all the personalities.

Harold said, "The last time you were here, Sarah, you told us not to trust Jennifer too much, right?"

"I still go with that."

"You think she's playing a game?"

"I think she's trying not to play a game. She doesn't want to. If she is playing a game, it's certainly not very beneficial."

"Beneficial to whom?"

"To all concerned." Alluding to her suicide attempts.

Harold asked, "Do you realize the second year of college starts this fall for Nancy?"

"Right." Then she said, "Nancy's in a fugue. I waited for Jennifer to come out and when she didn't emerge I took over. Normally when Nancy reaches a certain point I will automatically take over before I even have a chance to emerge."

"Jennifer often beats you to the punch, doesn't she?" Harold asked.

"She is stronger than I am. And she's getting stronger all the time. But this trust she has, the basis of her strength, can be easily destroyed. She is supersensitive."

"That's why Diane and I are careful to keep *every* promise we make," Harold said.

"I think that's a wise decision."

Harold continued, "Jennifer doesn't hate Nancy so much any more. Though she leaves tape messages telling Nancy to drop dead."

Then he changed the subject, said, "I'm glad you're here. This is your fifth emergence, is it not? The first time was two years ago in November. Remember that Sunday afternoon when we all sat in the parlor?"

"I remember." The assured voice.

"Do you have any idea how long you stay when you come out?"

"I observe that if I come during the day, I often leave during the day. Often my departure is similar to my arrival. If I come in Nancy's sleep, I'm almost positive to return in her sleep."

Then she added, "This is my fifth emergence with *you* but this is more than my fifth by myself."

"You have been emerging since Nancy was eleven, right?"

"Right."

"And you have taken over for as much as eleven months, as I understand?"

"Right."

Harold smiled. "Well, all I can say is that I told Diane when I married her that life would never be dull." Then, "I will be bitterly disappointed if you are not here tomorrow because I want you to meet Dr. Postman. He's a heck of a nice guy."

"As I've already stated, I have no control." That low, even, sure voice.

He asked, "Are you going to take a shower or wash your hair tonight before you see Dr. Postman tomorrow?"

"I want to set Nancy's hair."

Harold sounded surprised as he said, "You're going to set *her* hair? It also happens to be—"

"*My* hair."

"*Your* hair. True, you both wear the same hair."

Diane commented, "Nancy washed your hair this morning."

"I noticed," Nancy/Sarah said. "I combed it but I want it prettier."

"And you're going to sleep in her bed tonight?" Harold asked.

Nancy/Sarah laughed. "I would assume so."

"In the nude, as usual?"

Nancy/Sarah giggled. "As usual."

"You don't like to sleep in any kind of nightclothes that Nancy likes to sleep in—Dr. Denton 'jamies and panties and bra. Nancy would never let Diane see her undressed. But you don't seem to have any false modesty."

There was silence, then Harold continued, "Why have you all come out over the years?"

"Well, we're a result of many different experiences."

She thought a moment, went on, "At the moment we were *created* Nancy's psychological state called for some type of protection, some kind of defense. We are defenses of Nancy's. In each instance where we were born, so to speak, there were sensitive areas. Nancy could not handle something, though there are parts of her that can. She had to call upon us, a way of breaking off, of preventing the total breaking of herself. She never realized she had this type of control—the creating of all of us."

Harold said, "I spoke to Bob Postman and I asked, 'Look, are these all parts of the same personality?' He said, 'They're *all* Nancy.' And do you recall, Sarah, saying you were not at all happy with the idea of integrating, disappearing? That you did not want to lose your individuality?"

"That's correct."

"In other words, you want to remain the way you are. You don't want to become part of Nancy? Even though Dr. Postman says you *are* part of Nancy?"

"I don't want to lose my individuality but I *am* part of Nancy. Nancy is, in a way, my mother. She has created me. And therefore I cannot be apart from her. None of us can. Although I think many of us would like to fight it out against that mother. I cannot deny I'm part of Nancy. We're *all* part of Nancy. But we all express ourselves, go through different experiences, sometimes in joy. I know Nancy most intricately. Not many people can know her as I do."

"You also told me three weeks ago when I drove you to school that you are essentially a virgin, that you have never had a sexual experience. Is that true?" Harold asked. "When you are in being, insofar as Nancy's body is concerned, her body is not a virgin's. But you said that you as a personality never had a sexual experience."

Nancy/Sarah shrugged her shoulders. "I wouldn't want you to confuse Nancy's moral standards with mine though they are very much the same. I have high moral standards and so does Nancy. When she does indulge in sexual relationships, she turns aside her moral standards though the guilt she goes through afterwards is proof of her moral standards. She is not herself, she plays a role when she's in sexual relationships. I think the rape had a lot to do with this. If Nancy had not been raped at *some* time, at one point, she would still be a virgin today. What she's trying to do every time she has sex is to cover the rape. In this way she can believe that it doesn't really matter because she wouldn't have had her virginity anyway."

"But do you feel that you are an individual yourself, Sarah?"

"Yes." With conviction.

"You are *not* Nancy?"

"It's like saying your right arm and your left arm are attached to your body but they can do very different things. You'd be amazed how much you can view each arm separately. Most people can't write with their left hand. Think how limited you'd be if you lost the use of your right arm, then you'd have to rely on your left arm. That's in essence what happened with us."

Harold changed the subject. "Are you aware that every time I tell Jennifer, 'All I want you to do is to like me,' she replies, 'That'll be fifteen dollars.' What she charged for a trick when she was with the gang. She tells us she thinks she's homely. We asked her to look into a mirror once."

Nancy/Sarah commented, "I was there."

"Remember how she studied herself for about fifteen minutes? Stared at herself from all directions. Like a monkey looking in a mirror for the first time, feeling curiosity. Then Jennifer said, 'I'm still ugly! And that's why I only get fifteen dollars and the other girls get twenty.'"

Harold commented, "It's hard to tell what she thinks of herself. We can't run an I.Q. test on a seven-year old, which is her age these days."

"I took an I.Q. test in the sixth grade," Nancy/Sarah said proudly. "I had a 166 I.Q."

Harold whistled in surprise. "That's genius." Then asked, "Do you happen to know Nancy's I.Q.?"

Diane put in, "The clinic said 128."

Nancy/Sarah repeated incredulously, "The clinic said 128?"

"Don't get us wrong, Sarah," Harold said. "Nancy is not stupid. Only confused." Then asked, "Do you think we should take Jennifer to Disneyland?"

"I would say she would be all right at first but if you get her into a crowd she would begin to panic," said Nancy/Sarah.

"She told us she didn't like crowds, she doesn't want anybody to touch her. I said nobody's going to touch her down in Disneyland. They may bump into you but nobody's going to reach out and touch you."

Then Harold added earnestly, "We're trying to get Jennifer to trust us. We're also trying to get her to realize that there are other things than drugs. All she talks about is drugs, drugs, drugs, drugs, drugs. I ask her to come outside and see the beautiful trees, the lovely flowers, the impressive mountains and the awesome sunsets. And she says, 'I can always see beautiful things when I get high.' I say to her, 'After the high, there's always the terrible depression.' She says, 'No, you can keep taking pills.' I say, 'If you keep taking pills you'll destroy Nancy's body.' And do you know what she says? 'In that case I'll give it back to her.' In other words, she will ruin Nancy's body and then Nancy can have it back."

"Jennifer's—"

Harold broke in, "A little bitch. A little snip. But she has told me I could touch her provided I don't get too close. She asks Diane to rock her to sleep. You know," in surprise, "as she falls asleep there is an inexorable, irresistible drowsiness. She gets sleepier and sleepier and all of a sudden she falls asleep. Her expression changes and Nancy is back."

Then he asked, "How did you get your name, Sarah? We know Jennifer was named after the opium poppy, she explained that to us. Do you recall the name of that poppy?"

"Yes. Papaver somniferum." This is the poppy from which opium is obtained.

"Thank you, as always, Sarah, for your inestimable help," Harold concluded the session.

Reading the transcript, I felt reassured. I was on the right track in my treatment. Nancy/Sarah had said she was "utterly amazed" at the way Nancy/Jennifer was changing, that Nancy/Sarah did not "honestly" believe Nancy/Jennifer had been "capable of the potential" she now showed. This warmed my uncertain heart. Come what may I was ready to tackle the explosions of the other personalities.

The regular sessions at the Gaffneys soon turned into a psychic Star Wars as two more of Nancy's subterranean personalities descended on us like rockets. Angry rebels, full of self-hate, wishing to destroy themselves and others. I would marvel at the vast difference between Nancy's outer persona, the one she displayed to the world, and the hidden people who took over for her in moments of stress.

Nancy/Jennifer turned her rage inward, punished herself for her vengeful wishes and her guilt. Whereas the two new people spit out their fury at the world.

The one personality I longed to meet was Nancy/John, Nancy/Jennifer's twin. I regretted being on vacation in August when the Gaffneys received a surprise visit from him.

Harold decided that day to call for Nancy/Jennifer. He and Diane knew "Jenny" would be furious because they had neglected her. They had promised to ask her to come out every seventh day but busy with other commitments they had delayed her visit for sixteen days, now wanted to apologize.

In his commanding, musical tone Harold started off, "Jennifer, you will write your name. Jennifer, you will write your name." This was to assure them it was Jennifer who came. Each personality wrote his name in uniquely different script, the younger ones in printed letters.

Expecting Nancy/Jennifer, Harold continued, "You will emerge, Jennifer. Nancy has given written permission for you to come out. Today will be devoted to you, so emerge very quietly, very peacefully and let's have a pleasant visit."

He gave the hypnotic order: "Number 1, Getting ready to emerge. Number 2, Feeling marvelous. Number 3, Safe, because you know we love you and we know you love us. Number 4, Ready to open your eyes for a very delightful visit. Number 5, Open your eyes wide, Jennifer."

Harold paused, then asked, "Hi, Jenny. Still mad at us?"

Silence.

"I'm sorry what happened to delay our seeing you. It wasn't our fault. I do not blame you for being angry. Now the question is, Jennifer, will you forgive us?"

Nancy's body, as he told me later, seemed to shift to a boyish shape, the head lifted to an arrogant pose. Harold waited, not knowing whom to expect.

There was more silence, then a low, clipped, tough boyish voice, slightly defiant. "I ain't Jennifer. I'm John."

Nancy/John had never come out before, we had heard of him only through Nancy/Sarah and Nancy/Jennifer. As I read the transcript I imagined the shock on the faces of Diane and Harold.

Always on top of any situation, no matter how unpredictable, Harold responded, excitement in his voice, "Are you really John?" Then, "We are Nancy's friends."

The defiant voice. "That doesn't mean anything to me." Accusingly. "You don't pay attention to me when all the others come out."

"I pay attention to anyone who comes out," Harold assured him.

"Depends who we are."

Harold changed the subject. "This is the first time you've ever seen this house, isn't it, John?"

"Yeah, but I know about you."

"We're Nancy's foster parents. We've heard about you for almost two years. You know Jennifer, do you not?"

"Yeah."

"I suppose you know Sarah?"

"Uh-huh."

"What's your impression of Sarah?"

Silence, then, "What is this? Some kind of survey or something? You writing a book?"

"Maybe. Would you like us to write a book?"

"I don't give a shit. What's with all the questions? How do I know you're not narcs or something."

Harold said slowly, "I'm not a narc. Did you ever see a narc with both legs off?"

"I seen a lot of things."

"You've never seen a narc with both legs off, though, have you?"

"No."

"Well, I have both legs off. I'm also sixty-eight years old. That's kind of old for a narc. True?"

No answer.

"I can assure you, John, we're not narcs."

"What's with the tape recorder?" Suspiciously.

"I want to keep a record of what you say because we're very much interested in—"

Nancy/John broke in angrily, "I don't need a record. It's just something you don't want. Zurdo told us 'No records.' "

Diane asked, "Do you know where Zurdo is?"

"Shit, no. It's been a long time."

Harold asked, "Do you know what year this is, John?"

"No." Then, "You guys are really off the wall."

Harold repeated, "Do you know what year this is?"

"It's seventy-three."

"It's nineteen seventy-seven, John."

"Bullshit. What are you guys trickin' me for?"

"We're not tricking you. Would you like to get a newspaper and see the date?"

No reply. Then, "Someone got a cigarette?"

"What kind of cigarette do you smoke?" Harold asked.

Contemptuously, as though no others were worth smoking. "Marlboros."

"Same as Jennifer."

"Yeah."

"You know you and Jennifer are twins, don't you?"

"Yeah, I know." Disdainfully.

"We've been getting along very, very well with Jennifer. And we've been waiting very anxiously to meet you."

"She didn't want to come today."

Harold asked, "Why didn't she want to come?"

"How would I know?"

"Just because she's a typical female?"

No answer.

Harold went on, silence did not daunt him, "I understand you and Jennifer are twins. Born during Nancy's rape. How do you feel about being here?"

"I only did it for Jennifer."

"Why did you do it for Jennifer?"

" 'Cause I hadn't been coming when she needed me."

"John, let's start from the beginning," Harold suggested. "Do you know Nancy?"

"Yeah."

"Do you know that Nancy has lived with us for two years?"

"I don't keep track." Contemptuously.

"We love Nancy very, very much. We've met Sarah about six times. We have met Jennifer many, many times. But the fact remains, John, we have been waiting for you because Jennifer has told us about you and Sarah has told us about you. I know this sounds like a stupid question, but you are male, right?"

With a slight laugh, "Yeah."

"You're the final piece of the puzzle. And the first thing is this. Do you think, John, you could learn to trust Diane and me?"

Without a pause Nancy/John said, "Hey, man, I ain't got no room for that kind of bullshit."

Harold said patiently, "Please, could you answer a question, John? Could you learn to trust *somebody?*"

Suspiciously, "I don't know. Zurdo taught us you don't trust nobody."

Diane said, "Zurdo didn't trust anybody and Zurdo's long gone."

"I don't care." Defiantly.

Diane requested, "We haven't told Jennifer he's in prison and we prefer you don't tell her."

"I don't tell her shit, man." Then he warned, "Better watch it, man She's listening."

Harold said, "We know she's listening and that Sarah's listening and ' we know, to some degree, Nancy is listening. Now, do you realize, John, that you are part of Nancy?"

"Yeah. I know it all."

"You share Nancy's body. And do you realize Nancy is one of five different people and you're one of those people? Do you realize this, John?"

"Uh-huh."

"How do you feel about it?"

"Don't make no difference."

"Now that you're here, could you answer some questions?"

"I don't answer shit to nobody." Slight anger.

"Not under any circumstances?"

"Hell, I don't know the first thing about you guys."

"I've already told you, John. We're Nancy's foster parents."

Diane explained, "Nancy came to us straight out of the psych ward."

Harold asked, "John, are you a drug addict?"

Without hesitation. "Yeah."

"What are you on?"

"Everything."

"What do you prefer most of?"

"Junk."

"In other words, heroin, horse?"

"Yeah."

"Or, in the vernacular of the street, they call it 'shit,' sometimes, do they not?"

"Uh-huh."

Harold asked, "How much a day is your habit?"

No answer.

"We're not narcs, John. We're here to help Nancy and you're part of Nancy."

"About a forty-dollar-a-day habit."

"How did you support it?"

"Zurdo."

"What do you mean, Zurdo?"

"When Jennifer works for it."

"In other words, Jennifer was supporting both of your habits, right?"

"I'd rip off things. And she'd turn tricks. We were a team."

"What did you rip off?"

"Tape recorders. Hubcaps. Anything."

Harold said slowly, "I can only say one thing, John. I'm very, very surprised that you're here. And so very, very pleased that you're here. Because we've known you were inside of Nancy. And we've asked Sarah and we've asked Jennifer very, very often why you haven't made an appearance. And now you're out."

"I'm not coming out for Sarah." Hostilely.

"Who are you coming out for?"

"Jennifer. I only care about Jennifer."

Diane asked, "Last time, when I worked with Jennifer and tried to get through to you, were you there for just a fraction of the time?"

"I don't know time. That little shithead. She goes back into time. She gets time mixed up sometimes. She calmed down when she thought I'd come but I wasn't going to come."

Harold asked, "Why are you so reluctant to come, John?"

"Jennifer's got to learn how to handle situations."

"We love Jennifer very, very much. We've been bringing her out almost every week, trying to help her. Are you aware of that?"

"I don't pay much attention. I only know when she's in trouble. Seems she's always in trouble."

Harold asked, "How well do you know Nancy?"

"I know her all right."

"Are you aware of everything that happens with her?"

"Sometimes I pay attention. I mostly pay attention when Jennifer is out. 'Cause if she needs me then, sometimes I come." He added wryly, "One of these days that chick's going to write a check her ass can't pay for."

Harold exclaimed admiringly, "I've never heard it said so beautifully! You have a nice way with words, John."

"It's an old saying from the gang, man." Contemptuously.

"You and Jennifer are twins, John. But you're much more mature. Jennifer is about eight or nine years old mentally and emotionally."

"She just don't want to take care of herself."

"You're about sixteen or eighteen?"

"Fifteen." Defiantly.

"How well do you know Nancy?"

"I know her all right."

"She has two kinds of ages, John. There's her chronological age and there's her emotional age."

Then Harold added, "I'm pleased because we've got all the pieces of the puzzle on the table."

"Hey, man, I ain't part of any puzzle." Angrily.

Again changing the subject quickly, Harold asked, "How does it feel to be out?"

"Okay. Jennifer's scared to death of everything. She's got to learn, man, you gotta make it in this world somehow." Reflectively. "She ain't going to make it."

Harold asked, "What do you mean she's not going to make it? What's going to happen to her in your opinion?"

"Shit, I don't know. She's just weak."

"She's told us that. And she's told us she depends on you and she's unhappy you haven't come when she's needed you." Harold added thoughtfully, "You came and took over when Nancy was being raped, didn't you?"

"Only cause she wasn't strong enough."

"I understand you beat hell out of the guy who raped her. Is that true?"

"Yeah."

"What did you do to him?"

"Not an awful lot. Shit, by the time I got there, I could hardly move."

"Because Nancy was so beaten?"

"Yeah."

"But the fact remains you came out to try to help Nancy. Right?"

"No. To help Jennifer."

"You love Jennifer?"

Defiantly. "I don't love *nobody.*"

"Then why do you come out to help Jennifer?"

" 'Cause she's my twin. We're a team."

"In other words, obligation a brother and sister have."

"If she don't make it, man, I ain't goin' to make it." Plaintively. "If she kills Nancy, or something like that, it's the end of me too. She doesn't seem to realize that. Dipshit."

Harold assured him, "We've told her countless times if she kills herself she kills Nancy. Or if you kill Nancy you'll kill yourself. And you know what she's always answered?"

"No." Interested tone.

"She's always answered, 'I don't care. I don't want to live anyhow.' "
Pause, then, "Do *you* want to live?"

"Shit, yeah."

"Well, how do you live if you never get to come out, John?"

"I live when I'm high. And that's about it. Nothing else seems worth coming out for."

"In other words any time we'd want you to come out, all we have to do is hold out bait—drugs?"

"I'd come." Then, ruefully, "Jennifer, she's had lots of chances, man. She just doesn't do shit. She just prowls into some little corner and folds. She could go anywhere she wants and get anything. She knows how."

Harold asked, "How does she get anything she wants?"

"Aw you can spot a contact a mile off. Zurdo taught her everything she needed to know. Shit, she's probably forgotten all of it."

"I don't think she's forgotten anything. But John, you're fifteen and much older than fifteen as far as knowledge goes and experience. Jennifer is the same age yet she is about an eight-year-old child."

"Well, they tried to teach her. She was always fuckin' up the group."

"You mean she had two left feet?"

"Yeah. She was scared shitless to do anything. Turning a trick was like pulling teeth."

"Well, it hurt her."

Scornfully. "Jennifer didn't hurt."

Harold said with emphasis, "She told me that having sex with a john hurt. She reported many times guys said, 'God, you're tight.' "

"She's tight only because she's scared shitless."

"I think because of vaginismus. That's contraction of the vagina. Because she's frightened."

"Half the time she didn't get the money." Ruefully.

"You mean she got stiffed?"

"Yeah. Her own damn fault too."

"She didn't learn to collect in advance?"

"She didn't know shit. Finally she caught on. But still they ripped her off. Finally the only way to get money was for her to turn the trick and then for me to take over at the end. No fuck was going to take her money and walk out on me."

"Have you ever turned any tricks?"

"Shit, no! Who's going to pay for guys?"

"There's lots of men who'll pay for guys. Haven't you heard of male prostitutes?"

"Well, I don't turn tricks, man."

"There are as many male prostitutes around as there are female prostitutes, if I believe what I read in the paper."

"There's easier ways to get it for free."

Harold was quiet, then said, "We're very glad to see you, at long last, John. The question is, how long are you going to stay?"

"I don't know."

"How long would you like to stay? Sarah says when we ask how long she's going to stay that she has no control. Do you have any control over how long you will stay out?"

"I'll give it back to Jennifer any time you want. But I don't think that bitch'll come."

"I think she'll come if you'll let her."

"Can I have another cigarette?"

"Diane, will you hand John a second Marlboro?" Then Harold said slowly, in his reassuring voice, "I've never met anyone so blasé in my life and I like you, John. I like you because you do care about Jennifer. And if you care about one person, you can care about others." Then, "When you've finished your cigarette, can we get in touch with Jennifer?"

"Yeah."

"How do we handle Jennifer? Do we be firm with her or do we be gentle with her?"

"Shit, the only thing she responds to is having her ass kicked."

"You telling us we should beat on her?"

"No." Silence as he puffed away. "Just can't teach her nothin', that's all."

"I want to ask you something John. How does it feel to be born at fifteen years old? You didn't grow up, you just appeared, right?"

"Yeah."

"How does it feel to come into a world with no former knowledge of it?"

"I catch on quick."

"I'll say that. Amen." Harold's approval. "You may be twins but you've got about eighty percent of the brains. Jennifer's got about twenty percent."

Nancy/John said thoughtfully, "It's there if she just wouldn't be so fuckin' scared of everybody."

"You think she's scared of us?"

"She's scared of her own shadow."

"What do you think of Diane and me, John? You've only known us about twenty minutes. Do you think we're square?"

"I dunno. I haven't seen you in action yet."

Harold went on, "In Jennifer I detect an undisciplined girl. In you I detect a very cold self-discipline. Am I right?"

"You learn it on the streets."

"Jennifer's alarm says, 'I don't love anybody. I don't need anybody. I don't trust anybody. I don't make promises to anybody.' "

"She's right about that, man."

"Do you refuse to make promises to people?"

"I don't need to."

"Do you think you can make it all by yourself?"

"Shit, man, if you don't rely on yourself, you're gone."

Diane put in, "You have to rely on your contacts to get drugs, don't you?"

"There's always a contact, man."

Harold said, "Prices are going up at a high scale, I've heard. By the way, is there any difference between a bag and a balloon?"

"Shit, yes. In a bag you get pills. In a balloon you get heroin."

"John, if you think you're never going to get caught, you've got another think coming." Harold's voice was a warning.

Nancy/John said nothing for a moment, then, "You would never have made it in the game, man."

Diane asked, "What do you want to do, John?"

"I don't like sitting on my ass. I like being out and doing shit. Hanging out. Ripping off. Shit like that."

Harold said quietly, "John, we don't want to preach to you but things are different since you first came out. It's tougher on the street now."

"It was tough then, man."

"The narcs are all over the place. But more than that there's evidence the price of junk has gone up 200 to 400 percent. You can't afford it any more."

"That's why you belong to a gang, man. You can't make it on your own."

"You'll land in jail, John."

"I ain't never been in jail yet."

"There's a first time for everything. Remember the first time you took a fix?"

Then Harold said to Diane, "I'm picking up on John as a very capable and a very cynical personality. But I don't see any sign here of someone who's going to go cutting their wrists or jumping out windows." To John, "You're a coldly practical person, John."

"I'll make my way." With assurance.

Harold said admiringly, "I don't think you've got a mind. I think you've got a computer in your head, John. Am I right?"

"You gotta learn to think fast, man."

"One other thing. How can we reach you when we want you?"

"I've seen all I want to see now." Leaving the question unanswered.

Harold asked, "You want to leave?"

"Shit, yeah."

Harold said, "Zenith, Zero. Go back to sleep, John. I want you to close your eyes. Take a deep breath. Then I want you to exhale. Go deeper into sleep. Five, going deeper. Four, all the way down. Three, feeling fine and perfect. Two, you're deeper and deeper. One, you're asleep."

Here the Long transcript ended. My introduction to Nancy/John came a few weeks later via Nancy/Jennifer. She delivered me a sheet of white paper from Nancy/John. He had scrawled in printed letters an inch high, "Fuck the shrink!!" Meaning me. He had no doubt heard me treat Nancy/Jennifer and speak to Nancy/Sarah, since they all listened to each other.

Underneath the inch-high letters, he wrote: "tell 'em [the Gaffneys] to listen to the record 'My Life' by Billy Joel. tell the woman [me] thats why it wouldnt be nice to have an adult in my life like it is screwed up. tell the shrink to fuck off. John."

He was created, as Nancy/Sarah said, to fight the rapist. I thought of Nancy's possible wish at that time to be a man. A frail girl would have no chance of conquering a rapist who held a knife at her throat. She would need someone strong, with "guts." Nancy/John, I thought, would be a tough psychic nut to crack.

10. September, 1977

One night about eleven as I was ready to fall asleep after thinking of what I wanted to say the next day in each of my five classes, the phone rang. An unusual hour for any of my familiar callers.

I thought it might be Nancy. But the voice was huskier, bolder than Nancy's. It announced without preamble, "This is Sherry. Are you the crazy lady interfering with my life?"

I swallowed, said, "I am only trying to help Nancy."

The voice snapped, "Why don't you go fuck yourself? You're nutty as a fruitcake. Get the hell out of our lives, you bitch. Or I'll report you to the police for pretending to be a therapist."

I heard the click of the phone—message delivered. Thus did I meet Sherry, quickly learn she was not one to hide feelings or mince words. Another personality had appeared, one about whom I knew nothing. I fell asleep wondering what role Sherry played in Nancy's life.

The next session at the Gaffneys I summoned Nancy/Sarah, she knew every personality well. I told her of the late-night call, asked, "What does Sherry look like?"

Nancy/Sarah said, "She has blond, flowing hair, soft and shiny, with bangs. She wears very little makeup. Her look of innocence belies her foul mouth. She expresses her anger easily, as you have just seen, Mrs. Campbell. She's not close to anyone. She thinks only of herself."

She laughed, added, "Sherry bleached Nancy's hair blond, which means all of us are blond. Once she dyed Nancy's hair red so we were all temporary redheads."

I asked, "Is she knowledgeable about men?"

Nancy/Sarah said "Sherry openly admits she's promiscuous, Mrs. Campbell. It's common knowledge among her friends you can make money as a prostitute with truckers who stop at Route 66 on Interstate 10. That's the freeway between San Bernardino and Los Angeles. This truck stop is a combination gas station, coffee shop and small hotel. Truck drivers pick up prostitutes here and vice versa. Sherry is known to the truckers as 'Sunshine Sherry.' She boasts she turns four or five tricks a night, sometimes four or five nights a week, if she wants to."

This was quite a lot of knowledge to assimilate about a part of Nancy's life unknown to me. I had not thought of Nancy, from the impression of propriety she gave the world, of living like a prostitute. Nancy/Sarah added, "She feels like a woman when she goes to the truck stop and she likes making the extra money."

The Gaffneys had mentioned Nancy/Sherry but she had not yet appeared at a session. I gathered she took pride in her sexual expertise, showed no conscience about acting sexually whenever and with whomever she chose. I saw this as opposite to the conservative Nancy who told me she had indulged in sex only a few times and did not enjoy it.

Nancy/Sherry had a way of withdrawing from a dangerous situation, Nancy/Sarah told me, leaving the naive Nancy/Jennifer in her place, as Nancy did with her personalities when she felt panic-stricken. If a drunken truck driver, "mark," "score," "john" or "trick" (as the girls called him), could not make it sexually and started to beat up Nancy/Sherry, she would "go inside," leaving Nancy/Jennifer, a five-year-old girl in trauma, to fend for herself. She was now stabilized at age five.

We asked Nancy/Sherry to come out at a session, telling Nancy in advance of our plan. Nancy/Sherry appeared in three-inch heels, tight green silk pants, a matching silk blouse that clung to her breasts, a pearl necklace and droplet pearl earrings. She carried herself as though proud of her body, wanted to display it. I thought she might be voicing Nancy's rage at her many frustrations—this generation seemed to be going through a wholesale "fuck you" stage. Sherry was the opposite of Nancy, who was a quiet, shy, vulnerable, generous spirit, always thinking of the other person. Yet I knew that in Nancy, as in all of us, there were those "depths beyond depths," Emerson's evocative phrase. Depths we carefully hide, show to no one, sometimes not even to ourselves.

The first thing I said to Nancy/Sherry was, "It isn't fair for you to leave Jennifer when you get into trouble."

Her answer was simple: "Just fuck off."

"You have to think of the others," I insisted.

"Let 'em think for themselves," she retorted. "That's what I have to do."

I saw a difficult road ahead, said little this first hour of acquaintance, let the Gaffneys ask questions. I knew I would have to spend time with Nancy/Sherry to try to convince her to give up her destructive way of living—destructive to herself and the other personalities.

She was intelligent, though it took time for her to realize she had to think of Nancy and the other personalities when she plunged into trouble. Time and again I would say to her, "You have to stop your promiscuity. You only hurt yourself and Nancy." At first she could not, would not, listen. Then a near-tragedy occurred that helped change her destructive spirit.

Nancy/Sherry (in Nancy's internal image) looked like an angel, flowing straight blond hair, blue eyes, slender yet voluptuous. One night she came out, drove Nancy's Opel to the truck stop. She parked in the large lot, walked inside the coffee shop, where she usually picked up men. (She told me all this a few days after it occurred.)

The coffee shop as usual was crowded but a trucker stood up, gave her his seat at the counter. She ordered the waitress, "How about a cup o' coffee? Hold the cream." There was a toughness, as always, in her tone, a certain coarseness in her choice of words. She combined the face of a madonna with the ways of a woman of the world.

In her self-assured, slightly insolent manner, she looked around to find herself a man for the moment. Three or four seats away she saw a trucker staring at her. He looked in his late thirties, a pudgy face with a black mustache, about five-feet ten. She tuned in to his obvious plea. She tossed her head, smiled faintly, thrust her breasts out even further.

He stood up, walked over to her. "My truck is parked outside. Twenty-five bucks. How about it?" Simple and direct, the voice coarse.

"Okay with me. One more swallow." Daintily lifting the coffee cup.

He reached for his pocket, tossed a dollar on the counter for her coffee. She stood up, aware dozens of eyes watched her. She followed him to his truck, surrounded by other trucks in their special parking area.

He opened the back door of the truck, pulled down a ladder. She climbed up. She faced a dark interior, a small cabinlike space set off for sleeping, a mattress on the floor, no sheets, no blanket. A nook for a nap or an hour of relaxation for the tired trucker. A spot also for instant sex.

She entered, started to unbutton her white silk blouse. He walked over to her, she smelled alcohol.

He said, a command, "Don't bother with the blouse. Take off your pants. And lie down on your stomach."

She stood frozen. He pushed her down on the mattress. Then he ordered again, this time with anger, "Take off your pants, slut! And turn over."

Nancy/Sherry suddenly changed from a self-assured hooker into a frightened young girl. But still trying to be tough, she said decisively, "I draw the line at that. No way."

She pulled herself up and away from the mattress. Nancy/Sherry was a survivor, she now asked herself, How do I get out of this? She turned, looked toward the door which he had closed. He understood her intent.

His face took on added anger, he snarled, "I'm gonna get it my way."

He moved closer, the smell of alcohol overpowering, she felt the surge of deep fear. Suddenly he lifted his fist, smashed her in the face.

She made a dash for the door, in combined blind panic and survivor cool, as she tried to close her blouse. He seized a large kitchen knife lying on a grimy wooden table near the mattress, caught up with her. He lifted the knife high, plunged it into her chest, ripping the white silk blouse.

He then pulled the knife out of her flesh, stared at it as if deciding what to do next as it dripped blood. She ran to the door, flung it open. Dashed down the steps and to her car in the parking lot.

She quickly found the key in her purse, unlocked the door, managed to slip into the driver's seat, locked the door. He caught up with her, she saw his snarling, mustached face through the window as he tried to figure out how to reach her. He smashed his fist against the glass just as she turned on the motor. She stepped on the gas, fled.

At this moment Nancy came. She found herself sitting at the wheel of her car, trying to make sense of what was happening. She realized Nancy/Sherry was embroiled in some escapade, had gone inside, left her to cope. She felt exhausted, weary, as if she had run two miles against a fifty-mile-an-hour gale.

Nancy took up the story when I asked her to write about what happened. As I sometimes did, knowing she liked to write and would provide details she might omit if she talked about the experience. The following week she handed me what she had written:

> One night I came back to find myself alone in my car. The motor was running. It was dark. The place was vaguely familiar. Yes, it was the truck stop. I trembled, but I wasn't sure why. I had a kind of sick feeling in the pit of my stomach. Something was wrong.
>
> I put the car into drive and made my way out of the parking lot. I turned up the hill, heading for the San Bernadino Freeway which led home. My heart was pounding, my head spinning, I felt shaky. I told myself, "It's O.K., Gooch, calm down. It was just a fugue. It's over now."
>
> I felt something trickle down my chest under my white blouse. I thought I was perspiring. I reached up to wipe the sweat away. I felt a hard knot on my forehead. I put my fingers to my cheek, it was swollen, it hurt to touch it. I licked my lips. They felt swollen too. I thought, I've been beat up. How bad this time? I don't feel any pain. What will mom say? Oh, shit. I can't go home. Not like this. I will

scare Timmy. What should I do? I didn't cry, it seemed too deep for tears.

That trickle again. I touched my chest, it felt soaked. My fingers were wet. I passed under a light and looked at my fingers. Blood. Mine, I think. I hope.

Even in the darkness I couldn't mistake it. There's nothing else in this world that feels like blood.

I began to shake. I pulled off the freeway because I felt faint. I turned the car off. I just sat there, not knowing what to do. The minutes went by. I'm not sure how long I sat. It was dark. I pulled into a gas station, intending to go to the restroom to see how bad my face was. Maybe I could go home and not scare everyone. I wanted to. I wanted my mother to help me. The station was closed. The restrooms locked. I had to think. Maybe I could think better if I went to Padua Hills in nearby Claremont. Yes! It's a quiet, wooded area where I go when upset. I'd think of something there.

I turned back to the car. It must be late. I'm supposed to be to work at eleven. Was it that late yet? Mom would be at the restaurant, she was working there too. She would know if I called. I got scared. Would she scream when she saw my face? No, not that. I've got to think.

I saw a pay telephone at a closed gas station. Mrs. Campbell. I stopped trembling. She would know. She would tell me what to do so I wouldn't have to be scared anymore. But what would I say?

I dialed. A man walked by. I turned away. One ring. Two. Please be home, Mrs. Campbell. Please. Blood was dripping from my chest onto my shoes.

"Hello?"

"Mrs. Campbell?"

"Hi, sweetheart. What's happening?"

"Mrs. Campbell?"

"What's wrong?"

"I . . . I got beat up."

"Are you hurt badly?"

"I don't know."

"Maybe you had better go to the San Antonio Hospital and get checked."

"No!"

"Why not?"

"The police. They'll come. I can't do it. I'm scared."

"Do you think you're hurt bad?"

"Yes. No. I don't think so. I can't tell. It doesn't hurt. But my face is battered as though I were beaten."

"Nancy, I'll come and get you. You'll have to go to the hospital."

Panic. "No! Please don't come."

"Why not?"

"I . . . I don't want you to see me like this." I was ashamed.

I felt the swelling under my eyes. I glanced down at my blood-soaked shirt. I watched the blood drip, drip, onto my shoes. I felt a rush, like sickness.

"Do you want to go home, Nancy?"

I swayed. Not home but Padua Hills. The mountains. There I would feel safe.

"Mrs. Campbell? . . . I . . . I think I've been stabbed."

"*What?*" Then, you must go to the hospital, do you understand me?"

"O.K. O. K. . . . I'll go."

"I'll come and get you if you tell me where you are."

"No! Please, I'll go to the hospital. I promise."

"Will you call me in an hour and tell me if you're all right? Will you call me if you can't handle it?"

"Yes."

"Do you promise?"

"Yes."

"I'll be waiting."

I walked unsteadily to my car. Damn. I felt dizzy. I turned towards the freeway lights. I drove with the traffic. How do I find the hospital? I'd been there before. But from the other direction. I turned off the freeway. I felt sick. Yes, I think I need to go to the hospital. I think I'm hurt. Bad. I pulled off the road, stopped the car.

I felt so tired. Nobody has this much blood in them, I thought, I had lost so much. I had to clear my head. A bright light. I looked up. A police car. Oh, no. Not that. Please. An officer stepped out of the police car, walked over.

"Anything wrong, ma'am?"

"No, officer. Just thinking." He could not see the blood in my dark car and for that I was thankful.

"Boyfriend troubles?"

I nodded.

"Well, just checking. There's been some vandalism here. We gotta check everything out."

"Sure. I understand. It's O.K."

"Hope it works out for you and your boyfriend."

"Sure. It will."

He walked away. I closed my eyes. They flew open in panic, I did not want them to stay closed. I started the car, and headed back for the lights. A few minutes later I knew where I was. I headed directly for the hospital. I stopped the car in the parking lot, got out of the car. I reached in for the coat on the seat. I held it close to me, hiding the blood. Don't let them rush me, God, I've got to stay calm.

I walked through the double doors. The nurse at the desk asked if she could help me. No, I thought, no one can.

"I . . . had an accident. I got hurt. My face . . . Maybe a doctor should check it."

"What's your name?"

"Nancy Gooch."

"Just have a seat and the doctor will be with you in a few minutes." She gestured toward a bench.

I turned. Good idea. Sit down, before I fall down.

"Hey! Is that blood?" It was a nurse.

Where did all these nurses come from—two, three, four. All reaching to take the coat away, reaching to take me away. The room swayed. The nurse had blood on her hands, and . . . the coat. They were all around me now. I saw the blood that covered me. Their white uniforms . . . If they got too close they would get blood on them, too. They kept reaching for me. I kept moving away, trying to save their uniforms.

"A phone call . . . I . . . have . . . to . . . call . . . my . . . friend. Please . . . it . . . will . . . be . . . O.K. . . . ." My voice sounded far away.

They brought me a phone. I dialed a number, then said into the phone after she said hello, "Mrs. Campbell . . . I can't handle this scene at the hospital."

"I'll be right there. Don't let them do anything until I get there."

I felt weakness, relief. It was going to be O.K. But the bleeding wouldn't stop. Strange, all that blood . . . it should hurt.

I felt no pain. The nurses placed me on a white table, took

off my bloody blouse and bra, tried to stop the bleeding with gauze.

Within ten minutes Mrs. Campbell walked in and silently took my hand. I felt calm. The nurse kept lifting gauze off my bare chest. I didn't want to see the blood-soaked gauze.

A policeman suddenly stood by my side. He started to talk to Mrs. Campbell. I didn't listen. Then he asked me questions. By law the hospital has to call the police when a weapon is involved in an injury.

"Who did this?"

"I don't know." I didn't. Only Sherry knew.

"What does he look like?"

"I don't know." Only Sherry knew.

"Where did this happen?"

"I think maybe at the truck stop." Which was where, sitting in the car, I had "regained time," not knowing what had happened since I had "lost time" late that afternoon.

"What were you doing at the truckstop?"

Oh God. "I don't know."

"What time did this happen?"

"I don't know."

Only Sherry could answer his questions. All at once this seemed hysterically funny, would anyone believe it? I started to laugh. I could not stop. I thought, I can laugh but I cannot talk.

But I did talk when the doctor appeared. He seemed tall, at least from where I now lay. Brusque. I said, "I'm sorry. I made a mistake. I shouldn't be here." I felt very heavy, very tired. "I've got to get out of here. I'm fine now."

His face closed in on mine. He said, sounding angry, "I advise you not to leave. You could die. Someone has stabbed you in the chest. The knife just missed your heart. Your lung may be punctured. You could bleed to death. If you don't get help, no one could save you in time. You would be *dead.*"

I began to laugh again. I couldn't help it. I must not cry. But it hurt to laugh. So I *was* human after all. I kept laughing.

"You will not get hysterical, Nancy!" Mrs. Campbell.

Right. I took a deep breath. Was I hysterical?

Ambulance attendants. The nurses say I have to be transferred to San Bernardino County Hospital for surgery. Half an hour away. Mrs. Campbell says, "You must go, Nancy."

Everyone is waiting. I look at Mrs. Campbell. No, she will not help me with this one. Careful, Gooch, you're starting to feel helpless. You're all grownup now. Don't cry. You have to make a decision. Be strong, for once in your life.

"Let's go."

Last-minute instructions. "Call my mom. Gentle. Don't scare her. Tell her I'm O.K. if nothing else. I have to know she will be O.K." I trust Mrs. Campbell. She will know how to say it.

It was raining. The ambulance ride went on forever. The two men argued about directions. The blood ran down my neck, my sides. Shouldn't the men try to stop it? The man with me was telling the driver about that stuck-up bitch on the third floor who thought she was too good to date anyone but a *doctor*. The I.V. bottle swung violently back and forth above my face, where it hung from a hook. I watched it and wondered when it would crash down on me. I pressed my hands over my flowing wound as hard as I could. The bleeding seemed to slow a little. The ambulance lurched and skidded on the wet pavement. "Goddam!" It was the driver swearing. I closed my eyes.

I felt the sensation of being lifted. I opened my eyes. They were putting me on a table. More nurses. One came and started to clean the wound. It hurt. For the first time I felt excruciating pain. I guess the wound went deep. The nurse said she had to clean it out. I didn't want it to get infected, did I? I gripped the rails and blinked the sweat from my eyes. Of course not. They didn't operate. Just a few stitches to gather the torn flesh together. Tape would heal the outside. Only a little scar.

A few days in the hospital. No. I didn't want to stay. Please. I would be careful, yes. Take it easy, yes. My mother walked in. She didn't scream or look terrified. She put her arm around me. We walked out into the night air. I had survived.

Nancy had called me and for that I was grateful. I phoned her mother, as Nancy asked me to do, then stopped off for her mother as she had requested. We raced to the hospital to give what comfort we could.

This event, even though tragic, marked an important turning point in Nancy/Sherry's emotional development. It was the first time she had not left Nancy/Jennifer, the youngest personality, who could not have possibly coped with the situation, to suffer pain Nancy/Sherry brought on herself. She had made a conscious choice to protect the little one. This, I knew, took massive effort on Nancy/Sherry's hedonistic part. I was proud of her, she no longer wanted to destroy the smaller, weaker ones but help them.

Though she had no way of knowing this particular truck driver would try to kill her, that sixth warning sense should have told her there was something very dangerous about this man. Not long after, he murdered a madam who had four prostitutes in her stable at the truck stop. I thought perhaps he felt cheated by one of her girls and took his rage out on her, she, unlike Nancy/Sherry, had not managed to escape. A police hunt went out for him, he was seized, arrested, charged with this murder, sent to prison.

One day before he was caught, Nancy's mother stood waiting in line at the post office with Nancy. They stopped for the moment, halting beside a wall of photographs of wanted criminals. Nancy's mother related, "With no warning, Jennifer suddenly surfaced, so excited she struggled to keep her voice down. In a high pitch of excitement she pointed at one of the photos and said, 'There he is! There he is! That's the man who stabbed Sherry. Mommy, there he is.' I glanced at the picture of a fat, mustached face. I had no knowledge one personality could observe when another was out. Nor did I know it was possible for them to communicate."

From our first meeting on Nancy/Sherry was frank with me. She had admitted with a shrug of her slim shoulders, "I use men as much as they use me. I take their money. This gives me power. Power is what that scared Nancy needs."

I was to think of these words in the final stage of therapy. *Power is what that scared Nancy needs.*

In a strange way, I thought, Nancy/Sherry, more than the others, gives Nancy a certain sense of false esteem. As though, for the moment, somebody, even an unattractive, sadistic truck driver, wants her. Nancy felt worthless, was envious of Nancy/Sherry, yet terrified that some night she would enrage a truck driver, fail to escape and both their lives would end.

I respected Nancy/Sherry's wish to be her own person but knew her prostitution was dangerous to Nancy. It signified a self-destructive, hostile way of dealing with the intense sexual desire of an adolescent. When I tried at first to reason with Nancy/Sherry, she would retort in contempt, "Go fuck yourself." Or call me, as she did several times, a

"Goddamned, motherfucking, cocksucking bitch." In part, this was description of herself—projection if I ever heard it.

In our next few sessions I was taken aback by her, kept silent, my way of discretion. One day I had said in a low, authoritative voice, "Nobody has ever talked to me the way you do. I'm going to stop you from using such language and from your destructive behavior. It is not acceptable."

She could not listen at first. It was slow going to help her develop into a more caring, self-controlled young woman. And now I was heartened in one sense by the stabbing incident. She had listened to me, she finally thought of the younger, helpless Nancy/Jennifer she had been leaving in her place when in a panic. Instead, she left Nancy, more capable of rescuing her bloody self.

As I undertook the responsibility of mothering and nurturing the personalities, sometimes I brought wrath down on my head. Particularly when I asked Nancy/Sherry to come during one Thursday evening session.

I said to her, "You *must* stop your prostitute activities."

Her reply, a snarl, "Fuck off!"

I insisted quietly, "You are not allowed to speak to me this way. You wouldn't talk to a parent in such a manner."

"You're not my parent." A sneer. Then, "Thank God."

The fight always centered on "Who's in charge? You or me?" The impulse in each personality was to feel, "*I* am in charge, *I* am the only one I can trust. I cannot trust a grownup. I have never known love or protection from a grownup. I must do it my way to survive."

Nancy showed me what she wrote in her diary about Nancy/Sherry in this year of 1978:

> May 7, 1978: Sherry came out and was soliciting on the street.
>
> May 9, 1978: Mrs. Campbell was wonderful, we talked for a long time. She kept telling me that it was not a blank state from which I suffered. I love her. We talked about anger. She promised to let me know when she got mad at me. She said maybe Sherry was my refusal to deal with my own sexuality, or from memories of sexual acts. She called me "love" and told me I was special.
>
> October 24, 1978: Tonite Jennifer called Mrs. C. They talked for a long time. Mrs. C. asked Jennifer if she had taken drugs. She said no and Mrs. C. said she was very proud of her. Sherry came. Mrs. C. talked with her hours! It really got rough. Mrs. C. said at one point, "I'm going to kill you before you kill Nancy and Jenny and the rest of them."
>
> Sherry told Mrs. C. she was a fucking bitch and she *wasn't* going to teach Jenny *shit.* Mrs. C. said, "Oh yes I am." She called Sherry a vicious bitch. She said Sherry just lived to screw men and Sherry was probably the dumbest person she had ever known. She said that what Sherry did to Jennifer was rotten (left her in a situation with a truck driver). Mrs. C. said she would fight Sherry till Sherry stopped hurting others. Mrs. C. was really rough on Sherry, not giving an inch.

She kept calling Sherry a coward, insisting she was scared. Mrs. C. said she had to stop Sherry because she did not want us to die. When Sherry told her that she turned three or four tricks a night, Mrs. C. was shocked. She tried to tell Sherry why she liked, respected, admired and cared about me but Sherry didn't want to hear it. Mrs. C. kept telling Sherry she was a worthwhile person when she wasn't trying to hurt anybody.

Week after week, month after month, the personalities and I engaged in fierce battles—passionate sessions that held an underlying intensity of various emotions, hate, love, defiance—that exhausted both patient and therapist. I was sometimes confrontive, directive. I insisted, "You *will* do this," when a personality taunted, "I will do what *I* want, you have no power over me." I would say, "You will suffer the consequences if you do not give up trying to destroy yourself and others."

At times I gave firm slaps to persuade the personalities to give up self-destructive behavior. I treated them as I did my own children. I rarely slapped my daughters, then only lightly and never after they were four. I did not hit a personality for threatening, or thinking of or wishing to carry out something destructive. Only if he acted destructively. If the personality threw a temper tantrum I would gently take his hand, say, "Here is your hand. I want you to raise that hand slowly. You do not have to act in anger. You have the choice *not* to act on anger. To control the anger as you control your hand." These were angry children who had not learned to handle rage or primitive wishes or their infantile sense of omnipotence. Nancy's emotional development had been crippled in many ways by the early trauma.

I had to see that limits were kept so no personality would destroy himself, which meant Nancy would be destroyed. When I occasionally slapped a personality the pain lasted only seconds, and the slap was not out of hate but of caring. Wanting that personality to mature, showing respect for the self and others. Each personality except Nancy/Sarah had a reservoir of hate and fury, needed to acquire some measure of self-control and self-esteem so he would not die. After all, Nancy/Jennifer had made five suicide attempts.

Diane and Harold, who served as parents, never slapped any of the personalities but they did not shoulder the burden of setting limits. I was the therapist-parent who had to help Nancy uncover and face the horror of persisting, overwhelming fantasies that rose from a sinister soul murder. Out of necessity I played a dual role, mainly steering on intuition. Plus a love for this anguished girl and a need in myself to discover the roots of her torment and ease it.

I believed implicitly in honesty. I never lied to the personalities or Nancy. If I said something, they knew I thought it true. I held the conviction, as I said over and over, "How you feel is an explanation for what you do, not an excuse. You are expected to control your behavior. If you do not, I will control it for you until you learn."

As I built a relationship with each personality I helped him accept responsibility for his acts. My philosophy was: "We'll take care of the behavior, then we'll worry about what caused it." Slowly they started to learn control. At first they tried to defy me or subtly get around me. Then they realized to show self-control brought a feeling of pride, while lack of control demeaned the self. Nancy had grown up with little pride in herself.

She had to learn to feel she was consciously in control. Contrary to what she had felt earlier in life when something, or someone beyond her control had hurt her deeply. She existed as if controlled by others, *she* was really the puppet on strings. To keep the "others" from hurting her further or destroying her completely, she had to face the fiery feelings she had assigned to her personalities.

Time after time I felt frustrated, moment after moment, frightened. Was I playing God? I did not feel comfortable in that role but there seemed no other way to halt the impulse-ridden, self-destructive part of Nancy. Someone had to stop her wild acting-out of promiscuity and anger in drug-taking and picking up strange men for sex. I empathized with the desperate feelings that prompted the destructive behavior but not with the behavior. I knew her need for vengeance on real enemies was strong but unfortunately she was turning the hatred on herself, not the enemies.

From the intense feelings of each of the personalities as they emerged I knew they believed they would die if anyone learned of them. They were not allowed to speak to anyone except each other. Nancy/Sarah had chosen to go against this unassailable rule when she courageously revealed herself.

The personalities had to learn—we all have to learn as we grow up—the wish is not the deed. Nancy's deep fear of her own violence and wish for vengeance was based on her belief the wish *was* the deed. This is the way our unconscious thinks, a thinking all its own. The unconscious does not know the meaning of "no." It insists all its wishes be gratified and at once. Part of my task was to instil a sense of the conscious "no" as applied to destructive wishes. To slowly help Nancy make conscious the intense rage and fear she had repressed over the years.

Her blackouts, "lost time," were a breakdown in communication between the conscious and unconscious parts of the mind. Nancy could not consciously be aware of the suicidal attempts, the prostitution, the drug addiction, the wishes for revenge, because of overwhelming fear of her intense sexual and violent impulses and desires. She had relegated her feelings to the escape valve of her mind—the unconscious.

Before she could make conscious the unconscious, I had to help her lose her fear of the feelings expressed in the parts of her that had split off. Only then could the personalities "integrate"—become part of her. She would then accept whatever emotion or need had instigated the creation of that personality.

It was not all defiance or hate I received from the personalities. Some of the younger ones as they appeared sought to be embraced, held. I believe in touching those you love. Everyone needs to be held close at times, whether one month or eighty years old. We never lose the need for the tender touch, the warmth of arms that protect. If this touch is missing from a life, nothing else makes up for the loss. To be held in love and tenderness is the most poignant and needed gift one person can bestow on another. A baby, especially, needs this from a mother. Many children and adults get the satisfaction of the touch from their pets.

I fed by bottle the few baby personalities who would appear, held them in my arms as they fell asleep. Possibly Nancy was never held much as a baby, I thought, the youngest of five children, each about a year or a year and a half apart. How would her mother, who worked to help support a large family, have had much time for her?

No matter what their age, all the personalities except Nancy/Sarah were at first childlike in their abandon. I knew what was good for children—what I had wanted as a child and lacked. I tried to do for the personalities just the opposite of what my mother did for me, and possibly what Nancy's mother could not do for her. Our mothers loved us but did not know how to take care of us. I said to the personalities, "*I* am the adult. I will protect and love you. It is *my* job to take care of you. To enable you to be a strong, happy adult. And if you don't do what I ask, there will be consequences." Only as they became protective of themselves and others would Nancy accept the personalities and the parts she had unconsciously scripted for them—parts that expressed her erotic and aggressive fantasies and wishes.

Usually I only fought one personality at a time, thank heavens. There were moments every ounce of strength I possessed was involved with a battle of wills as a personality used his formidable courage to fight against maturing. I had to help the personality develop emotionally to the point where he could accept the early terror, however diabolical its cause. Such acceptance signalled danger for Nancy. She *wanted* to keep each personality as he was, *wished* the horrifying memories to remain forever sealed.

But for Nancy to survive, the personalities had to face reality. And before they could do this, they had to feel safe, loved. They were wanton children, except for Nancy/Sarah. They represented Nancy's "unreal" self, her uncivilized self, as well as her hurt self.

To my complete surprise Nancy/John was the first to change. He started to show feelings of tenderness, responsibility, courage. Even as he rebelled against the limits I set, for he would not give up drugs, disobeyed my curfew, took part in street fights, occasionally cursed me.

Though he avoided the tender touch, when a session ended he would now say offhandedly, "See you soon." Music to my ears after Nancy/Sherry's "Fuck offs."

One late afternoon Nancy/John walked into my empty classroom as I sat at my desk marking students' term papers. Baseball cap turned backward, hair tucked under, the tough manner and defiant stride, told me who it was. He stood silent before me.

I looked into the steady hazel eyes, said, "Hi."

"Hi." The low voice.

He turned, walked around the classroom, looked at quotations from Hemingway I had written on the blackboard to illustrate the new literary style of the century. Something was obviously upsetting Nancy/John.

"Is anything the matter?" I called out.

"No." He returned to face me.

His hands were jammed into his pockets, his head lowered so the cap almost hid his face. I looked at his set mouth, knew something was wrong and he did not know where to begin. It was always difficult for any of them to talk about feelings.

I asked gently, "What's bothering you, John?"

He shrugged his shoulders, said nothing.

I stood up, walked over to him. I held his hand in mine, raised his head, looked into the serious eyes. We stood in silence, his eyes searched and questioned mine.

Suddenly the rough, boyish voice: "Sherry says you're not my mother. You are, aren't you? Tell her to stop lying." Body and voice pleading, "You *are* my mother, aren't you?"

I was not prepared for this. I had never told him I was his real mother, nor even implied it. Then I realized I had assumed authority over him, set rules, punished him for breaking them. I told him I loved him when I felt he was suffering. He was learning to acquire a small sense of self-discipline, I knew it took courage for him to give up some of his strong will, start to consider others. Learn to feel proud of himself when he was thoughtful. Who else could I be but his mother? He achingly wanted it to be true.

I was tempted to tell him Nancy/Sherry was lying and yes, I was his mother. But no matter how strong the temptation to relieve his pain, I could not do this. The trust between us was built on the fact we always told each other the truth. I did not want to endanger that trust.

"Sherry's not lying," I said. "John, I'm not your mother."

He pulled his hand away from mine, dashed for the door. I thought, Let him go, he will come to terms with this new information and then we can talk more. But I realized he felt deeply hurt, would keep running, trying to escape whatever he did not want to face as truth. Just as all the others did.

I ran after him, caught him at a corner of the building. I held him close, said, "I'm your *adopted* mother."

He relaxed, snuggled into my arms for the first time. An adopted mother was better than no mother. Thus the ritual of adoption started among the personalities. Nancy/John's breakthrough meant the others would follow John—the tough guy, the drug addict who said he had no obligations to anyone. His changed attitude also showed a growing courage in Nancy to deal with reality, dangerous though it might be.

The last personality to appear at this time was seven-year-old Nancy/ Danny. He set fires though no one was ever hurt. I took him to a fire station, explained to the firemen he needed a warning, that while he had not injured anyone or destroyed valuable property, he had burned down an abandoned, rickety old house. One fireman cooperated, drove us to the site of the house, now in ashes, told Nancy/Danny "he" must not destroy anything by fire, would be punished if "he" did. I knew he felt frozen inside, an icy void associated with Nancy's earlier terror, and might be trying to feel warmth, as well as finding an outlet for a burning rage. I told him over and over he would not be allowed to destroy the property of others. He stopped the fire-setting but kept lighting matches, as though he needed to see something burning.

Had anyone told me I would eventually face fifty-six personalities, even though most of them came out briefly, I do not know if I could have coped. I took one personality at a time.

I accepted them as they appeared, the destroyers and the helpers. I knew Nancy needed both at the moment. I also hoped one of them might aid us in understanding more about why they were created.

During a Thursday night session I first heard of Nancy/Carmen, as Nancy/Sherry referred to "a spacey broad inside." She added this broad's name was Carmen.

I asked Nancy/Sarah about Nancy/Carmen. She said, "You won't get far with her. She is blind, mute and deaf."

"How old is she?" I asked.

"No one knows. She seems to have switched off all conduits to her brain, shows no reaction. It is as though Nancy has provided her body with the ultimate escape. Carmen has walled off the outside world. She sends nothing to it, allows nothing from it to enter her. She seems as though she wants to erase herself. She has lost all will to see, to move, to speak, to hear. She is catatonic and cataleptic, rigid. There is no sensory awareness. You could stick her with pins and she wouldn't feel anything."

I thought of a short story I read in a literature course at college, assigned as an example of fine writing. By Dr. Bruno Bettelheim, it was titled *Joey, The Mechanical Boy*. It described an autistic child who would not speak or relate to anyone. Bettelheim speculated the unreal expectation of his parents that he be "perfect" was too much for him. His way of reacting to their demands for perfection was to turn into a mechanical robot. This theory helped me understand Nancy/Carmen's fears. She was a survival mechanism for Nancy as the mechanical boy was for Bettelheim's troubled child.

I called for Nancy/Carmen and a scene ensued that was to be enacted over and over, perhaps twenty or thirty times in the next few months. I would know Nancy/Carmen arrived when I saw a completely inert figure now occupying the position of the departing personality. I learned to say to the person about to leave, "Please lie on the floor flat on your back" or "Please sit on the couch in a comfortable position," so that I could work more easily with Nancy/Carmen.

I would try to leave the departing personality in the Gaffneys' living room, which gave me space to move Nancy/Carmen around. I would lift her seemingly lifeless body from the floor or chair until she stood rigid, hold her around the waist, drag her the full length of the room. Then I would lift one of her feet up, slide it in front of the other, walking her as an invalid walks following a stroke. I wanted somehow to make her move, rather than lying inert for the whole session.

Nancy/Sarah was right, Nancy/Carmen seemed without feeling. One time I moved her clumsily, she hit her head hard against the table's marble top but her face showed no expression of pain. To try to get her to focus her eyes, I commanded, "Look at me, Carmen. Look at me." At first she kept her eyes almost completely closed, except for a slight slit through which she could see somewhat. I pushed her chin up, ordered, "You *will* see. I will not accept you the way you are. You *will* hear. You *will* talk." By constant stimulation of her senses with my voice and touch, I slowly brought her to life.

I persuaded her to hear, talk, see, walk, learn how to write her name, my name, walk to the store with me, and eat, the ultimate symbol of wishing to live. She blocked the emergence of the other personalities, now they were free to come out.

In creating Carmen, I thought Nancy showed a part of herself that felt life hopeless, the world too dangerous a place to explore. Nancy/Carmen portrayed in essence the spirit of the three monkeys: "See no evil, speak no evil, hear no evil."

Nancy/Sarah wrote me a letter chiefly about Nancy/Carmen, addressing it formally, "Mrs. Campbell":

> I have left a note for Nancy explaining that I have worked for her [Sarah occasionally appeared as Nancy when the latter was too tired to go to work as peer counselor at Chaffey Community College] and that you asked that she contact you. I also explained to Nancy a little about what occurs when Carmen comes.
>
> Although Carmen has regressed somewhat back into her shell she is still mentally alert in the sense that I have observed her attempting to focus her eyes and has even attempted to repeat a few of the words she has learned. Her frustration at this difficult task has been the primary reason she has withdrawn, but she has now experienced sensations of life and I can sense her wonder and curiosity.
>
> I don't believe that she will choose darkness and silence over this. Carmen *is* capable of thinking and feeling, I am

sure of this from observing her. I have emphasized to Nancy in my note to her that Carmen is nothing to be afraid of now.

As she becomes free to feel, express and develop as a human being, Carmen will know the world as a real place and so, of course, will Nancy. It has occurred to me that previously Carmen came in times when Nancy just could not cope with reality. Perhaps Carmen is the key. Carmen in the past has been Nancy's strongest refusal of the realities of life. Her withdrawal was so complete that even those of us inside who attempted to, could not penetrate it.

Nancy is very resentful of Carmen; she feels she is going to have to cope with another personality but I am hoping she will realize that Carmen is an important part of what we are all about. Carmen's recent development is one of the biggest steps Nancy has taken toward a normal and complete life.

Nancy will never face responsibility when she can shut the world out. As Carmen was forced to walk and see and touch, Nancy can no longer escape, she will face life. I now believe she has the strength to do this; if only she could also believe this. It is really fascinating for me to observe Carmen as she gropes for understanding, and to some degree finds it. I know Nancy desperately wants to be "whole," and I feel Carmen is going to help her be a complete human being as Nancy accepts her as a person and Carmen learns to be acceptable as John, Jennifer and Sherry are learning.

Sherry is still desperate, she does not know how to help herself. She is frightened but cannot admit this, although I thought at one point that she would call you. She doesn't know how to let go, or ask for help. I do not know how to help her now and I'm not sure anyone does. In the meantime, if you hear from Sherry, please try to help her relax and know that everything will be o.k.

I am saving my energy in case I need to work for Nancy again soon, so I doubt that I will be talking to you in the near future, but if you need me for anything you know how to get in touch with me.

As ever,
Sarah

The other younger personality to appear was Nancy/Regan, who ranged at times from four to seven years of age. She personified hatred in its rawest form. She was the first to scream at me in scorn, "I hate you! I hate you! I hate you!" With a feral expression on her face, she set out on wanton destruction. A distorted, primitive animallike look on her face, she appeared obsessed by the desire to rip and tear up everything in sight. She seized the black drapes, tried to tear them from the walls. She shredded Harold's magazines and books. She stood close to the wall, hands behind her back, clawing at the wallpaper. Several times I wrestled her prone to the floor and sat on her to stem her violence.

I kept telling her, "No! No, Regan! You're not allowed to destroy things. You will *not* do that." At first I could not stop her, she suffered an overwhelming rage whose cause she could not recall, like a tantrum-ridden cat. I never saw a child so furious, as if fighting for her very breath.

She gave me a sense of the titanic rage within Nancy that swept to the surface through Nancy/Regan. I had to ask, What demonic feelings were buried inside Nancy, the "good little girl," caused by what demonic acts against her mind and body?

When one personality expressed fury the others seemed to calm down, as though their anger too had outlet. The outbursts by Nancy/Regan probably saved Nancy's emotional life, I thought. Without such expression of her inner fury she would possibly long ago have killed herself.

Nancy found herself of international interest when a feature story appeared in the *Progress Bulletin*, the local newspaper, about her therapy, written by Bob Nagey, staff writer. It was later reprinted in national newspaper services and some foreign ones. Nagey mentioned Clint, saying a local psychiatrist had been following the case at the invitation of the foster parents, quoting Clint's words: "There is no established treatment of multiple personalities. Everything has to be done through trial. The ultimate goal in cases of multiple personality is to integrate them into one entity, hopefully combining the best qualities of each into one person."

This meant, I knew from my latest reading, the "integration" of each personality into the core personality. Before this could occur the personality had to *want* to be integrated, had to *want* to give up destructive wishes. Which meant, essentially, Nancy had to want this.

I sensed that to achieve integration, first the personalities had to care enough about themselves and each other to give up the wanton behavior. They could only do this if they felt loved and accepted. I had to play the role of the loving, caring mother, they had to accept me as their "mom" and obey me, love me, know I acted in their behalf.

I thought how different each of the main personalities were. Nancy/Sarah was a scholar, mature, protective of them all. Nancy/Jennifer was childlike, lovable but very depressed, actively suicidal at times. Nancy/John took pride in false bravado but was protective of his twin and showed an underlying vulnerability. Nancy/Sherry was headstrong, brash, acted out her sexual impulses. Nancy/Carmen was still an unknown, might always be. Nancy/Regan was a bundle of fury.

Nancy was still self-destructive, as I learned from a letter she wrote me (she and the others often wrote instead of speaking when they wanted to clarify a certain conflict—Nancy was at heart a writer: I thought at times that perhaps writers create their own kind of "multiple personalities" in the characters they dream up.) I had spoken to Nancy about not seeing certain members of the local street gang that sold brain-damaging drugs, some of them to Nancy/John. Chico was the leader and chief seller, and Jim and Jerry had been friends of Nancy. She wrote of mourning the death of Jerry from drugs:

> Dear Mom,
> It's one of those long nights when I can't sleep, and as usual, I can't turn my mind off. It's been a rough week; I think about Jerry constantly and everything reminds me of him.
> When Jim called, his grief just seemed to intensify my own, but I understood his need to talk. He was really shook—he said he just needed to be with someone who was close to Jerry, too. After all, Jerry was his best friend, mom; they grew up together.
> Mom, please tell me how I'm supposed to grieve at Jerry's death. I've got a lot of guilt, anger and sadness that I can't express. I haven't shed a tear. I don't think you understood what I felt for Jerry, or how important I thought it was that he survive. I guess I wanted to make up for Andrew somehow. They were alike in many ways. When I found out that Jerry was dead, I hurt a lot. I didn't know how to cope with all that pain. I needed you, but something inside me prevented me from showing you that hurt—after all, you didn't approve of my even seeing him. I was angry at you for forbidding me to go to him even when I felt that I needed to be there.
> I know I didn't cause Jerry's death but I also know that

I didn't do everything I could to prevent it, either. That is not a good feeling.

I feel sadness, too, that you are so suspicious of *me*. I understand that I have given you reason to be, but it scares me that I can't be a daughter you can trust. I'm trying, mom. Even when I blow it, I'm trying. I know that's not easy to understand. I have to remind myself often that I have a real mother now, and I can't do everything I want to. Old habits die hard.

Most of the time it's easy to do what you want me to because I know it is right. I know you are worried that if I see Jim, I will take dope. But the whole thing was a different story this time. It wasn't for fun, or kicks, or pleasure. It was important. Even though it's too late, I want you to understand that. Please don't see me as that shallow. Or Jim, either. He's a human being, too. Even I want a better way to cope with this than getting stoned. That's the easy way.

Please believe me, mom.

Love,
Nancy

This moving letter was a request to allow her to grieve the death of a friend, to help her understand and express her "guilt, anger and sadness." She had been unable to cry, though she felt deep sorrow and this suppression of tears, I knew, was a vital part of Nancy's torment. In her words, "I didn't know how to cope with all that pain." Pain at the thought of her friend's death. And buried pain for suffering whatever she hid so carefully and at such high emotional cost from herself and the world.

Nancy and Clint became good friends, she appreciated his intelligence and empathy. He did not look on her as different or a freak but as a deeply troubled young woman in need of help, beset by fears and conflicts she could not as yet face. He never for one moment gave up hope she would someday confront them.

Clint was an education to me—a teacher, an ally and a friend. He called me a "revelation," told me that sometimes after a session he thought more of what I endured and accomplished than of what Nancy achieved. He praised my capacity to give, described multiple personalities as "vexatious" in many ways and lauded my patience and basic level of trust in Nancy. He called the interaction between us "beyond words." He told me one evening, "Your endurance, Emily, the whole spectrum of the time you give, your energy and ability to accept frustration is unbelievable. I know what it is to work with multiple personalities. You think you've gained an inch or two and in most instances feel you've lost a yard."

Clint described the first time he met Nancy/Jennifer. Nancy sat in a chair opposite him and "Harold told her to count backwards and spoke the key words 'Zenith, Zero.' Nancy's lips relaxed, grew fuller, her eyes opened wider, wider, as she focussed on me. The face and voice of a confused, frightened child emerged as she quavered, 'Who are *you?*' and then cringed back in the big recliner."

He replied, "I'm Uncle Clint. We talked on the phone two days ago."

She relaxed somewhat, said, "Stand up."

He pushed his chair back so he would not scare her further by looming too near, slowly lifted his six-foot, three-inch frame until he stood erect.

She said in awe, "You're so b-bi-ig!" She looked up into his face, leaned forward. They were friends from then on.

I found a long note I wrote to myself in November, a little over five years after first seeing Nancy flee my classroom in the fall of 1973:

> Sherry came to see me today. She was smiling and more relaxed than I have ever seen her. She is telling me what is happening to Jennifer. Jennifer is enervated, her life force is ebbing, she cannot appear at will. She cannot embrace or grasp her favorite stuffed animal, Bobby Joe. She is not aware of any feelings or desires or fears. For Sherry, there is a big hole where Jennifer's substance used to be. For John, there is fear and apprehension that the same thing will happen to him. He is drawing many pictures of Jennifer. Jennifer is crying.
>
> Jennifer's life force seems to be entering Nancy. Nancy is now remembering Jennifer's experiences and experiencing all the emotions that went with incidents Jennifer experienced. According to Sherry, Nancy is handling these bursts of memory and the accompanying emotion fairly well. Sherry says that when she integrates with Nancy, it won't be as traumatic for Nancy.
>
> Sherry has brought up the possibility that if Jennifer disappears altogether, there is a possibility that Nancy may never be able to come back because Jennifer is the necessary stage between the others and Nancy. I had a chilling thought that if Carmen appeared just after Jennifer completely disappeared that she would be the permanently dom-

inant personality. Neither Sherry nor John can come from Carmen.

Sherry now seems to take for granted that she must help Nancy. I wanted very much to hug Sherry today. I didn't dare because of the way she feels about being touched by me. She has said that she knows a way to get money which does not involve doing anything Nancy would disapprove of.

This note described important changes. Sherry was starting to think of others, to understand integration. Nancy/Jennifer seemed almost integrated. Nancy/John was using his artistic talent, applying his energy to creative work. And Nancy was handling "fairly well" the first integration, as well as emotions Nancy/Jennifer was experiencing.

But it was painstaking process, slow breakthrough, one by by one with each personality and also with Nancy. At times Nancy/Regan felt tormented by what she called "the pictures in my mind." She banged her head in frustration against the wall. I trusted she would emerge from this hopelessness and helplessness. Memories were allowed to break through only in minute, safe amounts.

I never knew which personality suddenly might be adversary. Except for Nancy/Sarah, *always* co-therapist. She was not often present these days but occasionally I would receive a message from her as impersonal observer of the people within. She would announce, "This child has broken the rules." She was the conscience, the highest order of the self-helper, protector of all. I felt I always had at least one ally. A part of Nancy knew where her survival lay.

Nancy was my challenger among challengers. At times we had four- or five-hour sessions—once we worked through the night as she despaired of living. I would go to classes in the morning exhausted. Sometimes I felt amazed by my foolhardiness even as I ploughed ahead, trying to figure out what else I might do.

I kept assuring Nancy and the personalities that the revelation of repressed memories would not cause me to abandon them, no matter how horrifying. Since their acts hid a knowledge of a past that terrified and they believed disclosure of memories meant death, I had to convince them the opposite was true. Disclosure meant life.

Several burning questions haunted me and must have haunted Nancy far more. Why had her natural feelings and desires been so stifled? What had driven them underground? What had happened to her earlier in life about which she could not speak because, if she did, instant death would result? What had so shattered her psychic world that it forced her to deny her senses, her feelings, her reason?

One personality had existed within for years, never saying a word, merely observing. I did not know of her existence. But she had been listening, watching me work.

This personality, when she was ready, would be the one to free Nancy by revealing the source of her pain. The early horror that had devastated her, made her a zombie emotionally.

Section 3

THE
FAILED
JOURNEY

12.   January, February, 1979

While I believed I had helped Nancy overcome much of her fear, I wondered if she might not travel more swiftly with someone who had achieved international fame in treating multiple personalities—Dr. Cornelia B. Wilbur, Sybil's therapist. She had established the Wilbur Clinic in Lexington, Kentucky where she lived and worked.

The Gaffneys and I talked it over, then asked Nancy what she thought of the idea. She had read *Sybil*, written by Flora Rheta Schreiber, was impressed by Sybil's recovery. Nancy appeared to welcome the chance to go to Lexington, hoping to have Dr. Wilbur, or some psychiatrist she had trained, as therapist. I thought I might study there that summer, then apply what I learned to Nancy's treatment as we both returned to Ontario.

Harold had a close friend in Lexington, Dr. Lloyd Mayer, an allergist, who urged us to send Nancy to the Wilbur Clinic. He offered to find her lodging near the clinic and help in any way he could.

Nancy had left the Gaffneys several months before to try living on her own though we still held sessions in their hypnotherapy room. The Gaffneys planned to move to San Antonio del Mar in Mexico within a year. They were building their own home on a cliff overlooking the Pacific, often visited the site to supervise proceedings.

Nancy planned to fly to Kentucky sometime during the winter of 1979. I knew it would be difficult for her to leave. Our group continued working with the various personalities, preparing them for the change. We thought they might regress to their former self-destructive behavior in protest against what they would consider abandonment by the Gaffneys and myself.

We held a session on Washington's Birthday, February 22, which Clint attended, and we told him of the new plans. We first called for Nancy/Jennifer to come out, she was preparing to integrate we believed. But by the stiffening of Nancy's body I knew Nancy/John had emerged, the voice that said "Hi" was low, succinct, boyish.

"Hi, John," I greeted him. "I don't think you've ever met Dr. Clinton Johnson. Remember I told you I would introduce you to him?"

Harold said, "Dr. Johnson, this is John."

Clint, in his warm manner, said, "Glad to meet you, John. I've been looking forward to this for a long time."

I asked, "How's it going, John?"

"It's goin' alright." A half smile.

"Are you getting any more phone calls?" He had left the drug gang but they were still pursuing him.

"No."

"They just quit calling?"

"Sherry talked to 'em, man."

"Do you know what she said? Were you listening?"

"No. Sherry would know."

"Then maybe I will talk to her and find out what they said. It sounds like they aren't trying so hard any more."

"Yeah, I hope not."

"Remember I asked if I could help you do something about the drugs?"

"Yeah."

"Think you'd like to try that?"

"Man, I still am not gonna take nothin'."

"I *know* that. What I'm wondering is if they can get hold of you and *make* you take drugs if you don't want to. Do you know anything about that?"

"I mean, you got a bunch of guys and they could force somethin' but they can't make you pay if you haven't got the money."

I asked, "Is it hard to say no? It would be for me, I think. If there were a group of people and they were all taking drugs."

"I wouldn't take drugs if they said to take it."

I asked, "Did you ever see anyone force somebody to take drugs?"

He thought a moment, then said, "Well, in Los Angeles I did."

"So it does happen." I wondered if he were thinking, as I was, of the overdose Zurdo forced on Andrew to kill him. I explained, "Dr. Johnson works with people who take drugs."

I turned to Clint, asked, "Do you know if people force other people to take drugs?"

Clint said emphatically, "*Very* seldom. I just speak from general experience but I would think probably not."

Harold asked, "John, you fixed Nancy's car, right?"

"Yeah."

"Where did you learn to fix cars?"

"When we had a car in Los Angeles, I used to tinker around with it."

"You did a beautiful job."

"Didn't go to no school or nothin'. I just watched other kids who had cars and worked on 'em."

Harold asked, "Still like to draw?"

"Yeah. But I haven't drawn no pictures or nothin'."

I said, changing the subject to integration, to which I had introduced the personalities as a long-range goal, "Jennifer's pretty sure she's going to be inside Nancy and not able to come out anymore. Can you feel that happening?"

"Yeah."

"So it's for real?" I felt quietly excited. This was partial victory after all our blood, sweat, tears and exhortation.

"Yeah."

Harold asked, "What do you think is going to happen to you, John?"

"Well, Jennifer and I came at the same time. Maybe we'll leave at the same time."

I put in, "I never thought about that! You think that's a real possibility? That you would leave if Jennifer leaves?"

"That's the way it works. I mean, like we came at the same time." He sounded resigned.

I said unhappily, "I would not like to lose you. We just got to know each other." He had become special to me, he had fought me bitterly at first but then, out of love, had given up most of his self-destructive ways. That is the way children learn control of primitive impulses, I thought.

I then asked, "Jennifer can feel herself going, can you feel something like that?"

"I used to be pretty strong and stay out, you know, for a long time. But now everything's really different."

I said thoughtfully, "You know what's different? I don't think it's because you're not strong any more. It's because you changed your mind about what you want to do, isn't it?"

"I don't know. Drugs and everything, it's like they don't mean nothin' no more."

Harold asked, "Would you draw us a picture? I'd like Clint to see your talent. Boy, you've got talent, John. Just some little sketch, if you please."

"Later, man."

I knew he did not want to be forced to produce, the artistic urge had to stem from him.

Harold asked, "You remember Sarah, John?"

"Yeah." Noncommittally.

"What's happened to her?"

"She's still there."

"She hasn't been out in a long time."

I asked Nancy/John, "Does she seem far away to you?"

"Well, she ain't around that much but she's still there."

"Do you have any idea what's going on with her?"

"Naw."

"You can't feel her?"

"Well, I can feel her there, you know, but I can't tell what she's thinkin' 'less she comes out."

Harold asked, "When Nancy lived here, John, you came out a lot at night, didn't you?"

"Yeah, I came out a lot at night."

"What did you do? Go looking through the house for drugs? Sarah told me you know this house better than we do."

Nancy/John shrugged his shoulders, remained silent. I suggested, "John, why don't you talk to Dr. Johnson? He will be your friend if you need him."

Clint asked, "Are you under any pressure, any danger from anybody outside, John?"

"I don't think so." A shrug of the slim shoulders.

"You burn anybody?"

I interrupted, "I don't know what that means. Would someone please explain?"

Clint said, "One way of burning someone is to take the dope, the merchandise, without paying for it. It works the other way, too. You don't get what you pay for."

He turned to Nancy/John. "They ever burn you, John?"

"I just deal the stuff, that's all."

Harold asked, "John, what were you shooting a couple of weeks ago? Heroin?"

Nancy/John did not answer. I quickly put in, "If Dr. Johnson is going to help you, John, he ought to know what the situation is."

Clint assured him, "If you're in any kind of danger, under any pressure, any threat, let me know."

Harold commented, "John is very thoughtful and very mature tonight." Then to Nancy/John, "What's Sherry been up to, do you know?"

"I don't know. She talked to Jim. Told him to get off my back."

I knew Jim was trying to get Nancy/John to take drugs. I said, "I'd like to find out what Sherry said to Jim. Just remember, John, in case anything happens, Dr. Johnson is here and will help you."

Harold asked, "Do you want to go away and leave Sherry?"

Nancy/John replied, "Okay."

I asked, "Shall I call her?"

"I can leave her," Nancy/John said. Meaning they were close, she could come through him.

As she did when, at my words, "Zenith, Zero," his eyes closed and Nancy/Sherry's presence soon became evident. The eyes opened wide, she sat straight in the chair, tossed her head, licked her lips as though to see if she wore lipstick.

Harold said, "Hi, Sherry."

"Hi." Voice lower than Nancy's, tone far more aggressive.

Harold went on, "Sherry, may I introduce Dr. Johnson?"

Clint said, "Hello, Sherry."

I explained, "This is the man who will help out if John gets busted or in trouble, Sherry. John told us that Jim called."

"Yeah." A shrug of the shoulders.

"What did he say?"

"You know, that they were gonna fuck around with John and stuff like that."

"You have any idea what they meant?"

"I don't take it too serious or nothin'."

"They don't sound dangerous any more?"

"I think they're more talk than anything."

"Very possible." Then I asked, "What did you tell Jim?"

"I told him, you know, 'Keep away.' He said they wasn't gonna do nothin'. They've had enough time if they were gonna do somethin'."

"That's true," I said. "The longer it goes on, the less likely they'll act. Dr. Johnson deals with people like Jim."

I turned to Clint, "The gang's been after John for about two weeks. Because they don't like his leaving the scene. They've been calling, threatening him. Apparently they informed on him. A police car followed Nancy and Sherry for a while though they seem to have stopped."

Clint asked, "What do they want from John?"

"They want him back dealin' for 'em," Sherry said. "Usin' and buyin' from 'em. Stuff like that." Then, thoughtfully, "Maybe John knows somethin' they don't want him to know. Or he got in too far."

I asked, "This is something you know about?"

"Naw, I wasn't gonna watch him shootin' up or nothin'. I didn't want no part of it. The reason I talked to 'em is I kinda figured if they talked to John, he'd be the one that would have to go see 'em. I didn't think he could take no more."

"You feel he's not as strong about it as he used to be?"

"Yeah. Especially with what's going on with Jennifer."

"Is that worrying him?"

"Yeah."

"He said something I hadn't even thought of," I mused. "If Jennifer goes, he might go, too. How does that seem to you?"

"Seems about right, I mean, that's all he's really been thinkin' about is what's goin' on with Jennifer. I don't know why he figures that way. I ain't goin' when she goes."

I explained, "He thinks that because they came at the same time. They're twins. Jennifer seems to be showing that she's going. Do you see any sign John shows he is going?"

Nancy/Sherry thought for a moment, then said, "He doesn't seem as enthused. He withdraws more."

Harold asked, "Been working for Nancy at all lately?" He meant at Alfie's Restaurant where Nancy now worked nights.

Clint put in, "Seems that Nancy really needs you sometimes, Sherry."

"I don't do nothin' for her." Arrogantly.

Harold said, "Yes, you do. You protect her."

"Bullshit! That's your opinion."

I said to Sherry, "It means something nice about you."

She sighed. "I told ya, I take care 'a myself. I don't do nothin' for no one."

I thought how much that sounded like Nancy/John before we worked together and he became more thoughtful. It would take time for Nancy/Sherry to give up the childish quality in her that made her feel the world was created just for her pleasure.

Harold asked, "Still figure you can make a lot more money than Nancy's making? For her?"

"Yeah."

Harold went on, "Remember, you said you could make more in a night than Nancy could make in a week?"

She shrugged her slim shoulders. "If it's gonna fuck everybody up, forget it. I'm just trying to keep everybody together. I don't want nobody goin' around committin' suicide."

"It's called survival," I said.

She pointed out, "Nancy's cryin' all the time and stuff, like it's part of Jennifer."

"She's showing Jennifer's feelings," I explained. "Is Nancy taking them over?"

"Yeah. She's real vulnerable and stuff. And she didn't used to be that way. It's like she's feelin' a lot of pain. And a lot of insecurity, or whatever goes with it. She's like, well, tryin' to stay herself. She's got this little record she bought. It's called 'Don't Cry Out Loud.' She plays it over and over."

I thought, This could be the theme of Nancy's life, she is ruled by the command "Don't Cry Out Loud," she cries, in a sense, through her personalities.

Harold asked Nancy/Sherry, "How do you feel about going to Lexington with Nancy?"

"Doesn't bother me."

"I have a very dear friend, Lloyd Mayer, a medical doctor, an allergist, who lives there. We grew up together. I just got a letter from him. He insists when Nancy reaches Lexington she is to call him. He will do anything he can to help you and Nancy get settled."

I asked Harold, "Does he know about Sherry?"

"No, but he will," Harold said. "I didn't want to give him any details until I got Nancy's permission. Somebody there has to know the story in case Jennifer comes out and gets lost. Which she will do once in a while."

Harold asked Nancy/Sherry, "You think Jenny is fading out of the picture?"

"Yeah. And I wouldn't be surprised if John went with her. I mean, they used to be real close. Now he acts like he don't like her. You know, she ain't as *smart* as him. She *was* at one time."

"As smart as John?" I asked in surprise.

"Yeah. She used to be streetwise. She could handle things. And then she got into the drug scene, she was pushing one thing and another. She didn't know what to do, so she did the kind of things he did."

Harold asked, "She was turning tricks at one time, wasn't she?"

"Yeah. But she didn't know what it was all about."

He commented, "She's pretty young to be turning tricks. And every time we see Jenny, she seems to be getting younger."

"I don't know what that's all about," I said.

"Neither does anybody else," he said.

I asked, "I'd like to see if Nancy could come back straight from you, Sherry, would you like to try that?"

"Sure, why not?"

Harold said jokingly, "I'll have to come in the restaurant some night and watch you waiting on tables, Sherry. Can I count on your not dumping coffee in my lap?"

She did not answer, she concentrated on leaving. A few minutes passed as she closed her eyes, we waited for either Nancy or Nancy/Jennifer to appear. By Nancy/Sherry's change in posture and facial expression to that of a frightened child I knew Nancy/Jennifer was now on the scene.

I said, "Hi, babe." Then reassuringly, "It's okay. You know what we found out? Nancy left a note for you and we didn't know about it. We wanted to tell you. I think it's in her purse."

Nancy/Jennifer tried to speak but no words came out. I asked, "Want me to read it to you?"

Faintly, "Okay."

"It says, 'Jennifer, I know what happened the other night. I am sorry you hurt so bad. Please know that it will be okay. You can come inside of me and I will take care of you. I promise your mommy will still love you. Remember that you won't have to be hurt any more. You will *always* be inside of me. I will be aware of you and so will the others. You won't die. I promise. I know you are a good girl. And I will try to make you happy. Please trust me. It *will* be okay. Nancy.' "

I looked up from the letter, said, "That sounds pretty good. She's going to take care of you. She likes you and wants you. You won't hurt. And I will still love you."

"She's not mad at me?" That little-girl voice.

"She's not mad at you. If she were mad at you she wouldn't say you are a good girl and she will try to make you happy. And you will still have me."

"But you can't hold my hand no more."

"If Nancy were here and I said, 'I want to hold Jennifer's hand,' you don't think I could do that?"

"I don't know how you're 'sposed to do it."

"There is no way you're *supposed* to do it. It just kind of happens." Then I said reassuringly, "I don't think it will be scarey."

"I will miss you." A faint protest.

"I know. I will miss you too. I promise if I don't see you before you leave that it won't be scarey. I know you won't get hurt."

"It would be like getting lost and nobody can find you." Sadly.

"I don't think it will be like that, Jenny. To be lost means you're afraid of something and I don't think you're going to be afraid of anything any more. When I see Nancy, I will be seeing you and knowing that you're there."

"Are you sure?" Plaintively.

"Yes, I am, sweetheart. That's what I'm trying to say to you. I will know you're there and I will love you."

"I can't hardly hear you no more."

Harold asked, "Can you hear me, Jenny?"

"Uh-huh. But I can't hear inside Nancy even though I try real hard. I don't want you to think I'm a bad girl."

I said, "I know you're not. It's okay now. With you and me."

"But maybe Nancy wants to make people feel bad inside."

I asked, "Why does she want to make people feel bad inside?"

"She likes to have you for a mommy. And John likes to be boss."

"I don't think Nancy does it on purpose, honey," I said. "I don't think Nancy can tell what she's doing."

Nancy/Jennifer started to cry, then voiced her real fear. "I don't want to be sent away to a strange city. I will be good. I won't never hit nobody, okay?"

I assured her, "Honey, you aren't going to Lexington because you have done anything wrong. You haven't done anything to make this happen."

She started to sob. I said soothingly, "It's okay to cry."

Then added, "Do you know what John thinks? John thinks maybe he is going to go when you go. If John goes, maybe he will be with you."

"He won't even be nice to people. How come?" Through her sobs.

"I wish I could say, honey. I don't know."

"He likes you." The sobs lessened.

"He likes to have a mommy, too. I'm glad I can stay your mommy."

"Even if you weren't nice at times. Remember when I told you I could love you even if I didn't like what you were doing?" Then I asked, "Do you think Nancy will feel like you when you're living inside her?"

"I don't know." Pleadingly, "Will you take care of Bobby Joe?" Her pet doll. "And Rattles?" A pet toy snake.

Clint assured her, "I like Rattles. I used to carry snakes around in my pocket when I was a boy scout."

Nancy/Jennifer said proudly, through her tears, "I caught a rattle-snake once."

Harold asked, laughing, "Do you remember when you put the lizard in Nancy's purse? She hit the ceiling. Didn't know how it could get there."

Nancy/Jennifer, wiping away her tears with her hand, said to me, "You want to talk to Nancy?"

"Yes, I do."

"I can get Nancy here."

I asked, "You're going to be good for the doctor in Lexington, aren't you?"

"Yeah, 'cause you want me to."

I said slowly, thoughtfully, "I will be glad when everybody is not having the problems they do now. But I have a whole different thought about it, Jenny. I think that everyone's going to be there, inside. I don't think anyone's going to disappear. It will just be different because you won't be out separately. That's what I believe."

"But will we be what we are?" Mournfully.

"One of the things that might be happening is that Nancy wants to be what you are because she likes you so much," I said. "Maybe that's why you are going inside."

"Why would she like me?" Sadly.

"Because you are lovable," I assured her.

"But I was bad, 'cause I hurt her." Thinking, no doubt, of the time she cut her wrists, defied the police, turned tricks, took drugs.

"She was angry then. But she said in her note she wanted you inside. And she wanted to take care of you, didn't want you to be hurt any more. I think she loves you now, Jenny."

"But how come she cries too?"

"Maybe she feels sad that you're leaving. Maybe she feels almost as sad as you." Then I added, "Honey, I know this sounds strange but there are *good* kinds of sad, too. There are times something good happens but you feel sad, too. I can see why Nancy would feel sad you're not going to be you any more but feels good you're going to be part of her. Maybe going inside Nancy will be like going home. You know that you came from Nancy, don't you?"

"I'm not sure what you mean." Puzzled expression.

"You were inside Nancy once. That's where you lived for a long time. So maybe it will feel good to go back. Like going to a place you're supposed to be."

"You'll forget me." Sadly.

"I will remember you," I said. "I will have Bobby Joe. And I will still think about you the same way I do now."

"You won't 'member when I was bad?"

Harold said, "Nope. Only the good things."

I amended this. "I will remember, Jenny, when you were bad. Because when you were bad is when I became your mommy and your friend. A good thing happened from that. When I was being your mommy, I was nasty to you at times because I wanted to stop you from what you were doing that hurt you. Did you stop?"

"Uh-huh."

"And it made you feel much better. Because you didn't like what you were doing. So when I was mean to you it did not feel good but something very good happened. You felt better."

"Will I remember you?" Forlornly.

"I don't know." I felt a bit forlorn myself.

"Will Nancy remember the times I knew you and she didn't?"

"I think that's what will happen but again I don't know. There will be the part of her that is you. There will still be your time when you were you but now only Nancy will remember that."

"I remember when you and I talked for a long time and at first you would really hurt me," she said. "Then I could tell you were different from the other people. And then I wanted to talk to you because you said it would be very important. That different things would happen to me. I couldn't stand the bad places I was sent. I would try to escape, run away. But it didn't work."

"This time you're going to a place where it's safe. Nancy will feel your emotions and you will feel hers," I assured her.

"*Will* I feel all grownup?" Hope in her voice.

"I think so."

Then I asked, "Want to go to sleep now, Jenny?"

"I have to go to the bathroom."

She stood up, walked out the door to what had been Nancy's bathroom at the Gaffneys.

I said to our team with a sigh, "I've never been present at a death scene with a last will and testament before."

"There's no question but that she's regressing all the time," Harold commented.

"She thinks she's getting ready to go," I said. "She's becoming used to the idea, apparently."

Clint put in, "I hesitate almost to articulate it but the feeling I get is that when you break down the partitions that separate the personalities you mainly become an assurance but also a threat. There is fear and apprehension of an emergency, of what might happen—the same fear and apprehension that necessitated the different personalities emerging. I have a feeling Jenny is feeling that fear."

"I can see that would occur," I agreed.

"I think it is unconscious," Clint added. "She is not aware of it."

Harold turned to Clint. "Now you've met the whole gang. You met John. You met Sherry. Sherry, as you heard, has a very robust vocabulary. John wasn't talking because you were here and he doesn't like shrinks."

Clint laughed. "At least he was civil."

"He wasn't always," Harold said. "Emily has changed him almost completely."

Then Harold added, "Jennifer is just ripping the heart out of me because I love her."

Clint said, "She's such a dear. I feel that what you all are picking up is her fear of integrating. I think she will be accessible, though as discretely different from Nancy."

I agreed with Clint but said nothing.

Harold asked Clint, "Do you like the way Emily works?"

Clint thought for a moment, then, "I don't want to say a word because it's pure primary process. It loses something if one attempts to translate that into intellect."

A great compliment, I thought, this psychiatrist really understands the power of the unconscious when there has been deep hurt in childhood.

Harold went on, "The last time Jennifer was here, Emily walloped her good for her destructive behavior."

I laughed. "Which also was primary process."

Clint turned to me. "That's security. If the personalities comprehend they have punishment coming when they're destructive, that's love."

Jennifer returned from the bathroom. Harold said, "Jenny, I'll always love you. Remember you. So will Uncle Clint."

Clint spoke for himself. "Whether you can hear or not, we will know and we will be talking to you inside. We love you."

I said, "Okay, darling. I'll let you sleep. I'll say 'now' and then I'll say the words and then you can sleep."

"Okay."

"Hang on real tight. All right. Now. Relax. You're not going away forever, you know."

"Are you sorry you got mad at me?" Still wanting reassurance

"Honey, I was just being your mommy. I wanted you to do something different. Something that wouldn't hurt you. I'm sorry you were upset and unhappy. I still love you. Now, Zenith, Zero. Jenny's going to sleep. Jenny's going to feel good."

We decided to end the session, we were starting to see in action the process of "integration," necessary for Nancy to become whole. We realized this vital step was not easy for the personalities, who had to give up their power, or for Nancy, who then had to face the conflicts inherent in the creation of her people.

Two weeks later on March 5, 1979 the familiar hypnotherapy room darkened as we started another session. Diane, Harold, Clint, myself and a woman who at that time headed the counseling department at Chaffey Community College where Nancy worked part-time, were present. Our total concentration was focused on the personality occupying Nancy's chair.

First we talked to Nancy to find out how she was. She complained Nancy/Sherry was drinking, leaving Nancy to suffer the hangover, hindering her work at Alfie's Restaurant.

Nancy said, "I didn't feel well last night at work and then I couldn't sleep when I came home."

I pointed out, "Sherry's only way of dealing with other people is to go to a bar."

"I know she drinks to fall asleep," Nancy said. "I haven't felt for days like I've been on anything except booze."

Diane asked, "Have you lost time this afternoon?"

"Uh-huh." Then, "I get sick when she drinks."

I said, "I'm going to tell Sherry that you're going to Lexington and you do not want her to interfere in any way."

"I'm beginning to feel like *they* [meaning the personalities] are arranging how it's going to be."

"They are in a sense," I pointed out. "Because they now say they will go anywhere you take them. They are not refusing to go to Dr. Wilbur's clinic even though they fear it means integration—their disappearance forever. They're saying, 'Yes, it's okay to go to Lexington.' You have to make some concessions to that."

"I'm flying no matter what they say." Defiantly.

"I'm going to tell Sherry you have arranged to fly," I assured her. "So she doesn't have to worry about thumbing it in the middle of a snowstorm somewhere between here and Kentucky."

"TWA goes directly to Lexington," Nancy said.

Diane asked, "Did you tell Sherry about Harold's friend, who will be there to help?"

"I told Sherry," I said. "She asked, 'Is he a shrink? Don't we know anybody else but shrinks?' I said, 'He's not a shrink, he's a skin doctor, which is different.' I also told her that Dr. Wilbur's name, phone number and address would be in Nancy's purse. And also that of Mr. Gaffney's friend, the allergist, in case anything happens."

Then I said to Nancy, "We want to speak to Sherry."

"Okay." She looked composed.

I conducted the customary countdown from five to one, encouraging her to relax, to sleep. In about two minutes the hazel eyes opened wide, the lips curled in defiance, Nancy/Sherry was definitely out. She crossed her legs, assumed a seductive pose.

"Hi." Flippantly.

"Hi, Sherry," I said. "I think you've met everybody here except the woman from the counseling service at Chaffey College," and introduced her. Then I said, "The last arrangement is that Nancy will fly by herself to Kentucky. So there's no problem about driving."

"Okay." Composed tone from the prima donna.

"I'm going to talk to John later. I will try to set it up so that he won't take any junk. Then I will talk to Jennifer to keep her going, see how she's doing."

"Well, she's been out."

"Has she?" I was surprised. "By herself?"

"I mean she comes after we do. But she's losing her memory. She maybe finds herself in Nancy's room and just looks around, doesn't know where she is."

"She's kind of leaving gradually," I said. "If we can keep her around until Kentucky, we're in good shape. Can you tell me how she's feeling about integrating?"

"I don't think she's got a whole lot of feelings."

"Nancy wants you to know that when you drink in the afternoon, it's a problem for her when she works at night," I said.

"It's good for her!" Contemptuously.

"She says it's hard for her to concentrate and do her job well. Because alcohol hits her harder than it hits you. If you feel slightly high she's really out of it. She just wanted you to know that."

"Yeah, but she does a lot of things I don't like."

"She just wanted you to know that your drinking is a problem for her," I repeated. Then, "What do you drink when you go out? If you drink hard whiskey perhaps a beer would be better."

"I drink like wine, or a screwdriver. It ain't nothin' heavy. And I don't drink that much. Two or three."

I changed the subject. "The job you've been doing at the restaurant to help Nancy out has been an excellent one." Sometimes when Nancy was exhausted, Sherry would fill in for her, instead of going to a bar or picking up a truck driver.

She said with her familiar shrug of the shoulders, "Last night some guy was acting up all over the place and hassling three girls. They went into the restroom and he followed them. One girl came out and told me to call the police, said the man was hitting one of the girls. I went in after him. I told him he wasn't allowed in there and if he didn't leave I'd call the cops. The girl he hit said to get a cop anyway, her nose was bleeding. There was a cop sittin' in the dining room and I went and got him. He took the man away."

"Good for you, Sherry," I said.

Diane asked, "Before I forget, Sherry, because Nancy has been very upset about it, what was the needle mark on her arm? We're trying to figure it out. Do you know how the needle mark got there?"

"Yeah, I know."

Harold said, "Tell us."

Nancy/Sherry replied, "I don't take nothin'."

I said, "We thought you might have given blood. Okay, we'll leave it at that." I didn't think Nancy/Jennifer took drugs but it could have been Nancy/John.

Nancy/Sherry asked, "What's Nancy goin' to do when she gets to Kentucky?"

"She's going to find a job so she can earn money. Maybe the same kind of work at a restaurant. And then she'll have an appointment with Dr. Wilbur. Find out who will treat her."

Nancy/Sherry asked the woman from Chaffey College, "Nancy ain't workin' up there at the college no more with you?"

The woman replied, "She tried but she was too tired."

I explained to Nancy/Sherry, "Nancy kept the job that paid the most money."

"There was no complaints or nothin' from the college?" Nancy/Sherry sounded amazed.

"No," I said. "They told her she was doing a good job, not realizing they were also telling you that you were doing a good job."

Referring to the times she had taken over, Harold commented, "Sherry, we're all grateful for your helping out Nancy. Is there any kind of work in Lexington you would like?"

"Not that Nancy would like."

I said sharply, "We're talking about *liking*, really *liking*. Not worrying about whether you're going to get beat up. Perhaps killed. So get that smirk off your face, Sherry."

Defensively. "I *like* making lots of money. And I *like* being free and easy. Doing your own thing."

I said, "Okay." This was not the time to argue with her sense of morals. "You could probably ask anyone here and they would say the same thing—'I would *love* to make lots of money.' " Then, "If Nancy waitresses in Kentucky she might get a job in a dinner house. The kind where there are drinks. Which means tips go way up."

"I get to know the regulars at Alfie's you know, and they're rowdy and shit, but they're cool and good tippers. I make more money than Nancy does. During the bar crowd one guy left like eight dollars."

"Wow!" I said. "He must have had too much to drink."

"Yeah, he was really stoned." She laughed, one of the few times I heard her enjoy real laughter.

Harold asked, "Have you had any marriage proposals, Sherry?"

Diane put in, "Nancy says you have."

"I can tell you about one," she admitted. "George, the night chef at the restaurant, wants me to marry him."

"Does Nancy like him?" Diane asked.

"I think she does," Nancy/Sherry answered. "I don't think *she* has ideas about him as a boyfriend. Just a person she works with."

I asked, "Sherry, do you like him?"

She shrugged her shoulders. "He's okay."

Harold said, "You're a very capable young lady. I feel certain if Nancy gets in a jam in Lexington, you'll back her up. I like you very much. I think we all do. As soon as Nancy gets settled, you'll be getting a phone call from us to say hello. We can ask for you, can we not?"

"Sure."

"You'll answer?"

"I'll be there. Where else?"

Diane said to Nancy/Sherry, "I really wish I had been able to know you better before you left."

"Well, there ain't much more than you see." Flippantly.

I suggested, "If and when you have a chance to talk to Dr. Wilbur or whoever else you talk to, you might suggest, if John is still interested, he take drawing lessons. I don't think Nancy knows how to arrange this."

"Okay."

I asked, "Is Carmen still around?"

"Yeah, she still comes once in a while," Nancy/Sherry said.

Diane interjected, "And usually curled up in a fetal position. I'm sure that's why Nancy feels so exhausted sometimes."

Nancy/Sherry said, "She's like a rock, man, that Carmen. Ain't nothin' there. It's like stuffin' cotton in your ears or puttin' blinkers over your eyes."

"That's scarey," I said.

"Well, it ain't scarey if she don't do nothin'."

"If she was the personality out all the time then everybody else would be smothered in a way," I explained. "And *that's* scarey." Then I asked, "You don't have any idea how you would go about breaking through her?"

"There ain't no way. It's like with Jennifer. You can wait 'til she's at a weak place, when she's not thinkin' real hard or is real uptight, and then take over. But you can't do that with Carmen. From the time she comes 'til the time she leaves she's the same. You don't see her relaxin' or nothin'."

I asked, "Do you have any idea what makes her come and what makes her leave?"

"Well, it seems she came when something real bad happened to Nancy. Like Nancy wasn't coping with something that was real heavy. It wasn't something *I* would cope with, you know, or Jennifer. Now it's like Carmen seems to be takin' over for Jennifer."

"So if anything bad happened to Nancy, Jennifer used to take over but now Carmen takes over?"

"Jennifer still takes over. Ends up comin' from Carmen."

Diane commented, "Maybe the one thing Dr. Wilbur has to do is to get Nancy to a point where she's not scared that Dr. Wilbur will meet Carmen."

I was dubious. "Possibly. But I would think Carmen is not the person who should be there."

Nancy/Sherry said earnestly, "The thing about Carmen is, man, that without Jennifer, we're all up shit creek. There's no way that any of us can get through."

Nancy/Sherry was telling us Carmen represented the hurt child in Nancy, the early damaged soul. Nancy as an infant, wounded, unable to speak, unable even to cry.

Harold asked, "Are you saying, Sherry, if Jennifer disappeared and Carmen came out, Nancy would not be able to get back? In other words, Carmen would wind up the final personality? Deaf and dumb?"

Nancy/Sherry said, "That's right."

"That's frightening to me." I had not thought of this.

Nancy/Sherry continued. "There ain't no way that nobody can get through from the outside, either. 'Cause Carmen don't hear or see. You can't sweet-talk her, you can't yell at her, or nothin'."

"I hear what you're saying," I said. "We'll talk to Jennifer."

"Well, she don't got no choice about it really."

Harold said, "Sherry, I don't know if you are aware of it but we used to bring Jenny out every week. Thursday was her day out. I feel this is how we kept her strength up. When we gave her time out, she exercised and had a good time. But as soon as we stopped bringing her out, she started to get weaker, fade away."

I said, "I think it's more than that. I think the integration is taking place and I don't think either Nancy or Jennifer is controlling it. It's just been happening."

"Nancy's starting to remember," Nancy/Sherry said. "Now Jennifer is in bits and pieces."

"It's as if her memory has been taken away," I commented.

"Yeah." Then, "I'd like her to hang around 'til we got to this doctor. 'Cause you know, Carmen ain't goin' *nowhere.*"

"I know." I sighed. "And that kind of scares me."

"She can't get on the plane, she can't do nothin'."

Harold said, "From what I gather, she just *lays.*"

"She doesn't hear and she doesn't see," I explained.

Harold mused, "She's blind, deaf, dumb and paralyzed. Vegetable."

Clint asked, his first words that session, "Does she have feeling?"

Nancy/Sherry replied, "I have no way of knowing, man. You can't pick up no thinkin'. There ain't nothin'. I mean she's not unhappy, she's not happy, nothin'."

Diane said to Nancy/Sherry, "If I don't see you again, I want to tell you how much I appreciate all you've done."

"Well, like I said, I didn't do it for *her.*" Scorn in her voice, referring to Nancy. "But for survival."

Diane asked, "Can you tell me, Sherry, the incident from which you were born?"

"Well, I seem mostly to be linked with John. There was no big thing like, you know, John and Jennifer were from the rape. Maybe I picked up strength from Nancy's sister. She's really cool. She did a lot of things I liked but Nancy couldn't accept, like going out with guys. Nancy saw it all and just couldn't handle it. She'd leave and then I'd come out."

"Are you saying you learned a lot from Nancy's sister about men?" Harold asked.

"I didn't need to learn it. It's just there. You pick it up, you know."

"Do what comes naturally, right?" Harold said.

"But Sherry does things that are not Nancy's lifestyle," Diane pointed out.

I thought, Not Nancy's lifestyle but perhaps her hidden wishes, she sees an older sister she admires going out with men and she wants to do the same thing but does not dare.

Diane asked, "Was it the sister who told you where the truck stop was?"

"No. It was a classmate of Nancy's in school. A few of the girls went there regularly." Then, changing the subject, "I thought Nancy was going by bus to Lexington."

Diane said, "She's flying. She hates the bus. One of the most traumatic experiences in her life was on a bus."

Nancy/Sherry asked, "What happened on a bus?"

"Every time she had to go to college on the bus she fugued out," Diane said. "She connected it to when she was twelve and had to take Timmy, then only a year old, all the way from Los Angeles to San Antonio, Texas, on a bus."

Harold added, "Tommy, her older brother was in the army and stationed there with his wife and children. His mother was having trouble with the professor, a man she expected to marry but never did. Anyhow, Nancy couldn't handle the baby on the bus and we think that's when Sarah first appeared. If you even mention 'bus' to Nancy, she looks terrorized. Every time we sent her to Chaffey College on the bus, before she had a car, she would fugue out. Especially at the San Antonio Avenue bus stop. I've gone up many times to rescue Jennifer from that bus stop."

Nancy/Sherry put in, "Just thumb it, man. Like I do."

"Right now, you're going to fly," I said.

"I don't think John should be driving a car in Lexington," Nancy/Sherry warned. "He's only fifteen, he ain't got no license and it don't work giving Nancy's license."

I suggested, "Can we talk to John, Sherry?"

"Sure." She closed her eyes, prepared to leave.

We said goodbye, Nancy/John came out. I asked softly, "How are you?"

"All right." Then, "Are you mad at me because I played pool with the guys?" He alluded to Jim and other members of the gang.

"I'm not mad at you," I said. "Nancy's going to fly to Lexington in about ten days. I'll see you before then even though afterwards I won't be seeing you for a while. We can write letters. We can talk to each other on the phone. I have told Sherry and I will tell Nancy that if you still want to, we'll arrange for you to have drawing lessons in Kentucky, because there's not enough time left for you to start here."

"All right."

Then I asked the others, "Do you think I could be alone with John?"

They all left, bidding him goodbye. I asked, "John, remember when I said I would like to try to get to the point where you don't need drugs any more?"

"Don't you trust me?" The look of innocence the guilty do not wear well.

"It's not a question of trusting you because you've done a better job than I could have expected about keeping your word to stay away from drugs. But I understand you recently took drugs and they made you feel so good you wanted to go out and get more."

He said nothing. I went on. "Do you understand that one of the reasons I'm not getting really, *really* mad at you is because I understand what a problem it is to say no? I understand how strong you have to be to say no. You weren't strong enough this time."

"I could say no."

"But you didn't."

"I didn't think it was any big deal. I wasn't taking nothing real heavy."

"But you said you wanted more."

"I said I'd try to stay off the stuff."

"That was not a promise, though."

"No, but—"

"Wait a minute, John. If you are going to break the rules, then I can't expect any promises to be kept. You start the chain of distrust."

"I still don't think it was that big a deal."

"Well, I do, apparently. You take drugs when you want them and then I have to start worrying. I don't want you *hooked* on anything."

"Can't get hooked on pot."

"If that's all you take. But once you've taken pot, is that enough?"

"I can quit there."

"Sherry doesn't think so."

"Sherry don't know everything. You sound like if I was shootin' heroin or somethin'."

"I want your mind clear. I want you to be living every moment. I want *you* to be there. I don't want you half out of it all the time. I want you to be *fully* you."

"I'm not *out* of it. It just feels good, that's all."

"I wish I could have a picture of what people look like when they're stoned. Ever seen a drunk staggering on the street?"

"Yeah."

"That's what you'd look like. What do you think I would feel if I saw you staggering around?"

"There ain't nothin' else to do sometimes."

"Well, now there is. You're going to Kentucky. There will be drawing lessons if you want them. There are other things to do besides get high."

He was quiet. I went on, "I know what I'm asking you to do is very, *very* hard. Most people could not do it. I would like to give you a little help. Sherry's very proud of you, by the way. She knows how hard it is to give up the stuff."

"When I'm in Kentucky there'll be no stuff around."

"Anywhere you go there will be people who will supply you. I know that. It's going to be a very hard thing to say no."

Then I asked, "Do you *have* to get high? Do you *have* to be out of it?"

"Yeah, because when you get high is when you have the fun. Everything's a trip. You don't fit in otherwise."

"You don't really want me to talk like this, do you, John? You would like to reserve the right to get high, wouldn't you?"

"I just figure it ain't no big deal."

"I don't expect you to be perfect. I don't expect you to be as strong as you feel you have to be. I don't expect you to be able to refuse 100 percent of the time. But I would like you to develop the ability to say no."

Then I added, "I am proud of how strong you are most of the time for resisting. And I hope when you go to Kentucky you can resist."

"Because I'll be on my own, you mean?"

"Not quite on your own. Because I will be writing you and you will be writing me. And Sherry will be writing me and Nancy will too. And if Jennifer feels like writing, she'll write. It's just that I won't be very close where I can talk to you easily."

"You've gotta trust me." Earnestly.

"I would like to. But it's not a question of trust, John."

"You don't really think I can do it." He sounded defeated.

"One of the hardest jobs in the world is to say no to that stuff."

"I'm a strong person. I've been out on the streets. I know what it's like."

"But you also think that the only way to make friends is to get high. And you'll want to make friends because you'll be lonely. You'll want to be able to meet people."

"I know Sherry'll tell on me. She did before."

"I don't think that's what she wants now. I think she wants everybody to get it together in some way."

"She still does whatever *she* wants."

"Like what?"

"She still drinks. She doesn't care what anybody thinks."

I said, "As I understand it, she is very concerned now that everybody stay alive and stick together. And, John, drugs are not part of that survival."

"You're worried because I'll be on my own?"

"I know it's hard, John. Very hard."

"Everything's hard, man. Nothin's easy. But I can do it. No problem."

"What will happen if you can't say no? I'm going to be far away. Once drugs were the *only* thing you lived for, right? Nothing else meant anything."

"Yeah, it ain't that way no more."

"What if a cop picks you up in Lexington and you're loaded? You could wind up in jail. Once you backed into Nancy's mother's car and smashed it up. You weren't in control of yourself, you were loaded. That's why I am worried."

"I'm not gonna get high. I don't know what the big deal's about. It doesn't seem fair. You don't believe me."

"I believe you. I'm trying to explain two different things. I admire your strength in achieving what you have so far. But I'm also worried because one little mistake could kill you."

"Pot doesn't kill you." Aggrievedly.

"Pot *can* kill you. You know how it kills you? If you're driving a car and you're not aware of what you're doing, you can get killed in an automobile accident. Or you can walk out in the street in front of a car and be hit by it. People get killed all the time because they don't know what's happening around them and they do things they would not ordinarily do."

"I'm used to being high. I don't do dumb things."

"Except you backed into a car and you hit curbs."

"Okay. So you tell me I'm not supposed to take dope or drugs or anything and I'm not gonna do that. Why can't you believe me?"

"All right," I said. "I'll talk to you again before Lexington. But I want you to think about the fact that I worry about you."

"No need to. Unless the police hassle me again."

I asked, "What if they come after you when you're in Kentucky?"

"You mean if they lock me up for something I didn't do? Or things I did before?"

"If you get hassled in Kentucky, Nancy will have Dr. Wilbur's name in her purse. That's the therapist she's going to see. And she'll have the name of Mr. Gaffney's friend, Dr. Mayer. He knows about different people living in the same body." Then I suggested, "Why don't you call me for the next ten days, until you leave? After that you're on your own."

"But are you gonna let me go out if some friends want me to go somewhere?"

"Yes. I'm going to let you go. But you have to think about whether it's going to interfere with Nancy's job. She works from eleven to seven."

He said, puzzled, "I don't know when that is."

"You don't know when she works?" I was surprised.

"I mean, I don't know ahead of time." He was telling me he never knew the hour he would come out.

"She works at night."

"That's the time when all the kids like to do stuff together."

"Maybe you can figure out some way you can fit in seeing your friends so it doesn't interfere with her job," I suggested. "Because if she loses her job, she will suffer."

"What if the police hassle me again here? Like last night, when I didn't even do nothing."

"They probably thought you had some drugs in your car."

"But I didn't." Strong protest.

"I know you didn't. Thank God, you didn't. It's a good thing you got rid of it."

"They was gonna search me." There was a long silence, then he said, "I thought you was just mad 'cause I went to the Boys' Market. I didn't know where else to go."

"I was *scared* again, John," I said. "What if Jim and the others were there? I still don't know what they would do to you if they got hold of you. I wanted you out of there fast. They scare me. They could hurt you. They've made threats."

"Would you have been mad if the police put me in jail? Kept me there, trying to find out where I used to get my stuff?" Pleading.

"Yes, I would have," I said.

"At me?"

"No. At the police, John."

I said goodbye to Nancy/John, asked, "Can I speak to Nancy?"

She emerged at once, said, "You look totally exhausted."

"I could use some sleep," I admitted.

"I don't get much now that Sherry is going steady with George, our handsome chef at the restaurant," Nancy said.

"Sherry going steady with George?" I was surprised, that was quite a change from her johns at the truck stop.

I was truly so tired I could hardly think. We parted with a hug.

As I drove home I hoped the Lexington trip would prove valuable to Nancy. Some of the personalities seemed to doubt it. Others put on the front of good sports.

We would have to wait and see, I thought. If the Wilbur Clinic did not work out, they could all return and we would take up where we left off.

The visit to Lexington was postponed again and again by Nancy. I wondered if Nancy or Nancy/Sherry had told George, the good-looking chef, about the multiple personalities.

I asked Nancy when we all met April 3 at the Gaffneys, "Does George know about the personalities?"

"Sherry told him," she said. Then added, "I worked with George all last night at the restaurant. He seemed happy."

I thought Nancy might have kept postponing the Kentucky venture to allow Nancy/Sherry to enjoy her first months of a fairly normal relationship. I asked Nancy, "How did George take the idea of personalities?"

"He seemed to accept it. He said little."

Diane asked Nancy, "Has it been rough coming back to the memories?" She referred to the integration of Jennifer. This meant Nancy would now remember the terror Jennifer felt that ended in her suicide attempts and desperate flights from mental hospitals.

Nancy said, "It's sort of one step at a time. You don't think of two things at once. That's pretty hard."

Diane went on, "Jennifer says it was the feeling level more than anything else in her that would upset you. Especially the terrorized times being chased by the police."

"Do you remember that, Nancy?" I asked. "When Jennifer was trying to reach the safety of the mountains?"

"Yes. All those police cars chasing me. As I ran away from the hospital and was just kind of crossing Euclid. One police car spun rubber and pulled out suddenly. A policeman jumped at me just as a second police car came around the corner, also peeling rubber."

I commented, "Like they were after some major criminal. As if you had committed armed robbery." A mental patient was as scarey as a burglar to the police.

"There was nowhere to go," Nancy recalled, "I ran down a dead-end alley. I had made a mistake."

Harold remarked, "I tell you, the worst is over, Nancy. The process is on its way. It's just starting by itself and going to go right on by itself, according to Sarah. We have set an assembly line in motion."

Nancy laughed. "Last night at work it was really weird. It was like a flashback. All of a sudden I felt high and I hadn't lost any time. I was walking toward the coffee machine and then out of the corner of my eyes I saw this tarantula sitting on the side of it. I froze. I didn't dare look but I didn't want not to look. Then it moved. It crawled right up the side. When I looked again nothing was there. It seemed odd, I don't know whether there actually had been a tarantula."

I said, "LSD is supposed to do that."

"We don't know whether John got anything yesterday, do we?" asked Diane.

"I don't think he did," Nancy said.

"Maybe you were flashing back and forth with another personality and didn't realize it," I suggested. "Or it might be your own medication." Dr. W. E. Sigurdson, a psychiatrist, was prescribing drugs to make her feel less depressed and to give her more energy.

"Medication never makes me feel like that. And the tarantula incident was like quarter to five in the morning."

"That was fatigue," Diane said.

"But I didn't feel tired. Just dizzy."

"You don't feel tired with medication. That's what is so dangerous about it," Diane said. "But if you get tired enough, you hallucinate."

"Maybe I was hallucinating," Nancy agreed.

Then she added, "When I first started taking the medication I would feel wired. I could concentrate hard and classes just speeded by. Like a two-hour class—I was there and then it was over. I took *pages* of notes. I couldn't write fast enough. I couldn't listen hard enough. Now sometimes I take one page of notes and don't even remember if I took the one page."

"Your conscious mind needs sleep, Nancy," I put in.

"My body seems to need ice cream constantly," she said. "Where you all need coffee, I need ice cream. It's helped me to put on weight, too." She was so thin at times she seemed almost a skeleton.

Diane asked, "Do you want some coffee, Emily?"

"Yes, I think I would, thank you."

Diane and I took time out for coffee as Nancy commented, "Sarah wrote me a note and asked when we were going to Lexington. I'm still going, there's no question about it, it's just that I have to wait for John to integrate."

Then she said, "My mom bought the book *Sybil* and it said Dr. Wilbur's no longer in practice."

Harold commented, "She's seventy years old."

"She may be supervising," I said. "She may not have her own case load."

"Clint told us much of the time she isn't even there because she's away giving lectures," Diane said.

Nancy, who had spoken with Dr. Wilbur on the phone, now reported, "When I talked to her she said she would be a consultant on the case. And that she'd meet with me and then meet with the doctors and if there was anything the doctors couldn't handle, she would step in."

"She has 'hand-trained' a lot of doctors," I noted.

Nancy said wistfully, "I would love to study under her."

Harold said, "I told my friend Lloyd Mayer that your mother would be there to help you get settled and you wouldn't need him for that. But if you wanted him for anything else, he said to call him. He can pass you on to people who could help you."

At this time Nancy's mother had decided to drive Nancy to Lexington, stopping on the way to see her mother and other relatives in Cleveland, Ohio, where she grew up. Nancy was relieved, she feared flying, like her mother, who was willing however to fly home, leaving Nancy the rented car.

Nancy turned to me, "I told Dr. Wilbur all about you. That you were my therapist."

I said, "Timmy asked me today if I was your therapist."

"Timmy?" She looked surprised.

"I called your mother's house and asked, 'Is Nancy, Junior there?' Timmy answered, 'Is this her therapist?' I laughed and said, 'This is Emily Campbell.' He said, 'That's who I mean.' "

Diane asked, "Nancy, did you want to say something to us about leaving for Lexington?"

"I decided I wasn't really set on a deadline," she replied. "With a deadline we all started to feel pressure. My mother got panicky."

I said, "Tell her how much the Wilbur Clinic may help you. It offers a natural development, where treatment begins and then ends. You don't stop in the middle."

Nancy asked, "Is giving up drugs part of John's development?"

"It's one reason integration can take place," I said. "As John is able to give up drugs he becomes more attached to a real world. He's not just living for himself selfishly, as a spoiled child does."

Diane suggested, "Nancy—I'm thinking of when you are in Kentucky—if you catch yourself withdrawing from a situation or from a person, sit down and take stock. Try to keep in tune with your feelings and see them as warning signals. Give yourself suggestions. Write a journal. Dialogue it. Your only dialogue is feelings."

"I've been keeping a journal," Nancy said.

"How is it working?" I asked.

"It's *crazy*. I don't want anybody to see it. It's just kind of a *running* thing."

I commented, "On an overall basis however it will show a pattern. Some things will jump out loud and clear. Basic feelings."

"When I go back and read it, it seems out of touch. I mean with being rational." Apologetically.

"But that's good for you to see and realize," I said. "Keep writing."

Diane said to Nancy, "My main concern when you get to Kentucky is you. I'm not concerned about Sherry and Sarah. The worst is over for them. My concern is your *learning* to cope so you don't have to create more personalities. That's why it's very important for you to be in Kentucky. Away from *every* influence in the world."

"Including us," Harold put in.

Diane added, "I think the trip is really important. It will give you the chance to find out 'Who am I?' Devoid of all of us."

"That's a lifetime job," Nancy said thoughtfully. Then, "Maybe I'll learn to use my own head in Kentucky."

"What I'm saying is that you need to be free, Nancy," Diane explained.

"I feel like Kentucky *is* freedom," she replied.

"You'll get a lot of physical exercise there," Diane went on. "I cut out an article saying exercise is the best therapy for anxiety."

Nancy recalled, "All through junior high school I didn't think I could ever make varsity in hockey because I didn't know how to play the game. But I *was* on the girls' varsity. I don't think it was me, though."

"Who was it?" I asked.

"I assume it was probably John."

"John wouldn't play on a team with girls. Are you kidding?" I was amazed she even suggested it.

"It couldn't have been Jennifer." Nancy sounded bewildered.

Diane said, "It could have been John."

I insisted, "John would *not* play on a team with girls. You can just forget John."

"Well, that leaves Sarah or Carmen," Nancy said. "And I can't see either of them playing hockey."

We all laughed at the image of the sophisticated Sarah or two-year-old Carmen with hockey stick in hand. Nancy went on, "I can't picture Jennifer that coordinated. She doesn't seem like the type to get out there and swing a hockey stick. But they had me at center—whatever that is."

"It might have been you, who knows?" I said.

"I always liked sports. But hockey? To this day I don't know how to play."

"Yes, you do," I said. "Somewhere inside you. Like you can twirl a baton and you say you never learned how."

"I think hockey is a little harder." Nancy was skeptical.

Diane said reassuringly, "I feel you'll be in Kentucky without the fear of the drug situation, Nancy."

"Hmmm." Then, "I have a hard time plugging into that," she said, "because I don't feel it's me who has control over drugs."

"Famous last words," I said sarcastically.

Diane pointed out to Nancy, "You certainly suffered the repercussions from the drugs."

"Oh, yeah!" Emphatically.

Diane continued, "What with the loneliness John might feel there, he could make connections, just the same as here."

"Walk into the nearest bowling alley, I'm sure," I said. Then suggested, "Before anyone else comes, I would like automatic writing to find out how Nancy feels about the integrations at this moment."

"So what happens if subconsciously I say 'no' to drugs and John goes ahead anyway?" Nancy asked. "Shouldn't you bring John out?"

"Yes, we still need to talk to him," Diane agreed.

"We'll talk to him but I don't think anything will happen in connection with drugs if you say no," I assured Nancy. "That's what I'm trying to tell you."

"I don't know." Dubiously.

I suggested to Diane and Harold, "Shall we put Nancy under hypnosis so she can do the automatic writing? And have some idea as to what's going on inside of her? Sherry, Sarah or John will appear."

Harold asked Nancy, "You ready for hypnosis, Miss Gooch? We just say ol' Zenith, Zero."

Nancy looked at me pleadingly. I asked, "Not ready yet?"

"Not yet."

"You backing off at the last second, Nancy?" Harold asked.

"I'm scared." A nervous laugh.

"You're afraid to go under?" Diane asked.

Harold suggested, "Emily, you put her under."

I said to Nancy, "We'll wait a while. Get yourself a little calmed down. I'll lead up to it gradually. I'm going to say the word 'now' and after I say the word 'now' you'll know when it's going to happen. Wait for just a minute."

"Try some mental imagery, Nancy. A bubble of light," Diane suggested. "You're safe in this bubble of light. It's no longer dark."

Nancy asked, "Did anyone see the rainbows this morning? Two of 'em. Up by the mountains."

"See yourself surrounded by this beautiful rainbow. This rainbow is your protection," Diane went on. "The rainbow is beautiful. Just meditate, knowing you're safe."

"I will say the words now," I told Nancy. I waited a few seconds then uttered the departure words, "Zenith, Zero."

The induction process, with Harold helping out, took about ten minutes as the countdown went from 25 to 0, this day extra-high numbers because Nancy showed such reluctance. I thought it might be her resistance to depart for Kentucky.

When Harold was convinced Nancy was hypnotized, he said, "Now question number one, Nancy, is not really a question, but an answer. You said you were ready to give up Jennifer and you did give up Jennifer. And while it wasn't pleasant it wasn't the horrible thing you thought it would be. We are now going to ask if you are ready to give up John. You will write either yes or no. At the count of three, your subconscious mind will guide your hand, your hand will write the answer to this question: 'Are you ready to give up John?' One. Two. Three. Write."

She wrote the word "no." He said, "That's fine, Nancy." He turned to me, asked, "Do you want to take over, Emily?" Then to Nancy, "As we take the pencil out of your hand you fall more deeply asleep."

I said, "Nancy, I want you to relax. You're safe. I want you to relax. I would like to talk to Sherry. When I count to five, I want you to stay deeply asleep and I would like to talk to Sherry. One. Two. Three. Four. Five."

Then I said, "Hi."

Nancy/Sherry's husky voice replied, "Hi."

"How are you feeling?"

"All right."

Harold asked, "How's your love life?"

"You always ask the same thing."

"Well, I'm interested. You've only been in love a short while, you know."

Sherry shrugged her shoulders. "What can I say?"

"That speaks for itself."

I asked, "Sherry, what is your impression of how things are going on?"

"Like what?"

"Like what's happening with John. What's happening with Nancy. What's happening with you and George?"

She said peevishly, "Aren't you getting reports?"

"Yes, but each person has his own impression. And yours have always been very reliable and helpful. I thought I would like to have yours too."

"Where's Nancy's purse?" she asked.

Diane said, "Is it the black one over there?"

"Yeah." Sherry sounded relieved.

I asked, "Did George buy that for you?"

"Yeah."

"It's nice." As far as I knew, this was the first gift a man had bought her.

She seemed edgy. I said, "I'm sorry. I didn't realize you would feel so uncomfortable."

"I ain't uncomfortable." Again the peevish tone.

I asked, "How is John doing?"

"What can I say?"

"I'd like to hear. It's important to me."

"Well, he's on his way out. What more can I say than that, you know?"

"Have any idea when?"

"There ain't no way to tell when. But he ain't got that much time, man. Fuck, he ain't got nothin'. He's just like *she* was." Referring to Nancy/Jennifer. " 'Cept like, you know, he don't forget shit and stuff. But he ain't even half of what he was."

"Are you out most of the time? Or is he?"

"He's still out."

"Do you have about equal time?" I asked. "All three of you?"

"No, I'm out most of the time. More than the others."

"Are you seeing George?"

"I saw him the other night."

"Is it better? At all?"

"I don't know. What's 'better'?"

"He was giving you a hard time," I said. "You don't see him as much now that he's on the night shift. I thought maybe you had talked to him about leaving for Kentucky."

I imagined how difficult it was for him to understand, much less tolerate the idea of unknown, imagined people sharing one body. I admired Nancy/Sherry for giving up her life of prostitution to try to settle down with one man. Though I doubted her or Nancy's ability at this time to sustain a relationship, difficult even without multiple personalities.

Nancy/Sherry was saying, "George and I talked about my leaving for Kentucky and shit like that. He don't say very much."

George was a quiet person, I thought, both Nancy and now Nancy/Sherry commented on his use of few words.

"Nancy is not definite about which day she is leaving," I told Nancy/Sherry. "She's leaving it open to see what happens."

Diane asked Nancy/Sherry, "Are you aware Nancy's mother is going to work in Alfie's Restaurant?"

"Oh shit." Anger. Then, "What shift is she working?"

"The graveyard."

"Well, I ain't working with her. Fuck, man. There ain't *no way* I'm gonna work with *her.*"

I said, "I thought that might be how you'd feel," thinking, This is how part of Nancy feels about her mother. I added, "You could see George more, though, if you did work nights. Nancy's mother will have at least two nights off."

Diane said, "I think it's important that we arrange with Nancy and you arrange with George to have time with him."

"*I'll* work it out. I mean, you know, it ain't up to Nancy." A command to keep out of her life.

"She'd cooperate," I said.

"There ain't no way she's got any choice about it. If I want time I *take* it. I'll see him in the morning. We usually meet in the morning. When he gets off."

Harold asked, "Did you know that Nancy got the birth control pills for you? They're over there on the table."

Diane suggested, "And it might be wise for you, rather than Nancy, to take them."

"Okay," Nancy/Sherry said.

Diane handed her the pills. "Three months' supply. And you should start them immediately. Dr. Johnson got them for you."

Harold asked, "How are preparations coming along that you've observed as far as Nancy's leaving?"

"Well, she's all packed."

Then he asked, "How do you feel about Jennifer being gone? John's taking it pretty hard."

"I suppose he's the next to go and I suppose I'm the next on the target, right?" Again the peevish voice. "You guys are causing all this. It wouldn't be happening if you weren't. I told you when I first started talking, 'You leave Jennifer alone.' Now you're working with John. Man!" Pure disgust.

Diane said, "Won't it be better in a way? You will have more time."

"There ain't gonna be more time." Angrily.

I said, "Can I back up a little? If I stopped seeing Nancy altogether then the integration would stop. Is that what you're saying?"

"If you would only have left John and Jennifer alone. I think it's too late for John, now. But if you'd stopped before. Yeah."

"I thought integration would happen no matter what *I* did," I explained. "I think that's what you and Sarah have been telling us all along."

"It would have happened someday. But it wouldn't have been like that."

Harold said, "Sherry, John has been nothing but trouble. You have been nothing but a comfort to us."

"Speak for yourself, Harold," I said. "John's my pride and joy."

"If he'd just stay away from the drugs," Harold retorted.

Diane said to her husband, "He's doing that, honey. He's really trying. He's working on Mrs. Gooch's car to get it ready for Kentucky. I don't think you're being fair."

"Well, maybe it isn't fair but that's the way I feel about drugs."

"He's given us some anxiety but what children don't?" Diane's voice was gentle.

"That's true." I backed her up.

Harold apologized, "I withdraw the remark. It was not well thought out. We all put our foot in it once in a while."

Diane asked Sherry, "Are you looking forward to Lexington?"

"I used to think it would change things, man."

"In what way?"

"I dunno. All this shit wouldn't be happening."

I asked, "You mean the integration will stop once Nancy is in Lexington?"

"Yeah. I mean, you knew what you were doin'."

"I was getting all my information from you, Sarah and John."

"Well, it ain't a matter of information. It's what you did with Jennifer and John." Added, "And me."

"By loving you all, you mean?"

Diane said, "Sherry, you were the last to come on the scene. Before that, we worked hard with Jennifer and John. It took us a long time to win Jenny over."

Nancy/Sherry said sarcastically, "That's what it's all about. Win 'em over, then wipe 'em out."

Diane said quietly, "It's not a matter of winning over and wiping out. It's Nancy's readiness to accept her total being. I think she's ready for Jennifer and John because she's not in the same place emotionally any more. When I first met Nancy four years ago she was using drugs. It's taken her four years to get off them."

Nancy/Sherry, still hostile. "I ain't talkin' about time. I'm talking about what you *do* with it."

"What do you mean, 'what we *do* with it'? I don't understand," I said.

"Well, you know, man, you get Jennifer to do what you want and to trust and believe you, and the same thing with John."

"Was that a sham, do you think? Do you believe I'm being deceitful, dishonest?"

"Well, man, look what that got 'em! Where's Jennifer now?"

"I had no idea what would be happening."

Harold asked, "Where *is* Jennifer, Sherry?"

Sarcastically. "She *ain't.*"

Harold said, "She's inside of Nancy."

I asked Sherry, "You mean to say that just my loving those two has made them disappear?"

In mocking tone. "Well, it ain't what they do, it's how they feel about *you.* And how they feel about themselves."

"How do they feel about themselves that makes them disappear?"

"They just started believing in themselves and shit like that."

"But that's why they disappear. *Because* they believe in themselves. Are you saying the same thing is happening to you?"

"Not no more it ain't. But it's too late as far as John goes, man. Cut half of me off."

"Sherry, I want you to think about the first part of your life and what was happening. Like your beatings. And the *kind* of people and *kind* of treatment you were getting. Remember it, right now. And then I want you to think about your relationship to George. As painful as it might be sometimes, there he is, crazy about you, wanting to do everything he can for you, loving you enough to want to make you his wife. Can you tell me that your former life was better than your life today?"

She was silent.

I went on, "I know that what John was doing out on the streets was not good for him."

"Yeah, man, but that's what he was *about*. He ain't even that no more. He's nothing. Maybe it wasn't good for him but he was alive."

"Anything to be alive—is that the idea? He was alive but he was not going to be for very long. He was going to die from drugs. Or somebody killing him."

Surly voice. "He can handle himself on the street."

"Not with harmful drugs, Sherry. Drugs that kill your brain," Harold said.

"This was a little before your time, Sherry, but John saw Andrew and others die from drugs," Diane said.

I added, "And he has seen others O.D."

Diane went on, "Andrew died in Jenny's arms from just one hot shot."

I pointed out, "And John has known others who deliberately gave overdoses to those who got in their way or hated them for some reason. I can't see John as happier before."

"How the fuck do you think he feels now? How do you think Jennifer felt? What's good about that?" The fury again.

I realized how real these personalities seemed to each other. They put themselves above Nancy, she was the outsider, the cannibal preparing to swallow them. I said, "Sherry, I can understand why you're mad. And I probably would be too. The whole thing doesn't seem fair to you."

She sniffed. "If you'd kept away from 'em, it would be the same as it was before."

"I was trying to keep John and Jennifer alive. And Nancy."

With contempt. "I suppose you're going to try and keep *me* alive, too?"

"You and I have not established anything like that. You don't *need* to be protected the way these two do."

"Well, I just see, man, like you know, they got set up. They trusted you guys."

"That really *was* the purpose," I said. "I *did* set out to make them trust me. Because I wanted to protect them. I wanted to keep them alive. I *did.* But what made them trust me was to *be* trustworthy. I have done everything I have promised. But I have not masterminded it from beginning to end because I still do not understand the situation. And I am not going to talk you out of your anger because you have every right to your anger. It is a very normal thing for you to be feeling anger now."

Nancy/Sherry asked suspiciously, "By making them trust you, you got them to do everything you wanted them to do?"

"All I want is to make them believe in themselves, Sherry. That doesn't sound like a bad goal to me." The goal could be achieved by the process we were going through at the moment, I thought.

"They believe in you?" Suspiciously.

"Right. I worked very hard at that. People have to work hard to make others believe in them. They have to say what they're going to do and do what they say. As well as work hard for their trust. I don't understand how that makes them die."

"They die by believing in you. And believing everything you say and everything you do. They can't be themselves no more."

"Because they *believe* what I'm saying?"

"Yeah. Just like Nancy."

"Do you think I am telling them a lie?"

"I ain't saying you lie to them." Aggrievedly.

"Then if I'm not lying to them, I'm telling the truth."

"Yeah, but all this time, man, they're changing."

"True. If they believe me, and what I'm saying is the truth, and it *is* the truth, do you think they would want to return to what they were three years ago?"

"They ain't got no choice."

"What if they had a choice?"

"If they knew what was happening to 'em? Maybe, yeah. But they didn't know what was happenin' to 'em."

"John did."

"Sure, in the end."

"John told me how he feels. I think John has decided he likes the idea someone loves and cares about him. I don't think he would choose to go back on the streets. I don't know for sure. But I think so. I think you would like to stay with George, who loves you and cares for you. And not be the person you were before. His love could do the same thing, if you trust him."

"He don't work at it or nothin'. We don't spend time like you do with John and Jennifer."

"Not the same way. Because George doesn't know how. But he is making sure you trust him and that you know he loves you. I'll bet he works at that."

"Trust don't get it, man. Trust kills. If you trust, you die." Coldly. "Jennifer and John believe you, man. Believe anything you say. Believe you're gonna make everything okay."

"I never said I was going to make everything okay."

"No, but they believe that."

"What I *do* say is that I will love them."

"They sure fuckin' don't know it. I mean, a lot of good it does 'em. You're gonna tell me all those hours you spent with 'em, there wasn't somethin' in your head? A *reason* for it?"

"Yes, there was."

Suspiciously. "What was the reason?"

"The reason was to get them to trust me so I could get John off the streets and see Jennifer live without her consuming fear of everything."

"What was it to you, man?"

"I told you, Sherry. I care for them. That is the truth."

"But you set 'em up. They're at your mercy, man."

"That's the way you see it."

Harold asked, "Sherry, are you claiming we have powers we do not possess?"

"Ain't got nothin' to do with powers. It's got to do with John and Jennifer. How they feel and how they react to everything. They believe, they trust you."

"Do you believe and trust us?"

"Fuck, no!"

Harold shrugged his shoulders. "Honest answer."

I said, "I think maybe you do believe me, Sherry."

"You're gonna tell me you wasn't thinkin' the whole time that Nancy should be the only one?"

"I was thinking the whole time that it would be better if there were only one." This was what I felt in my heart had to happen for Nancy to feel a whole self.

"Well, if you didn't know nothin' about it, how the fuck did you do it so fast?"

"I have no idea. I still have no idea what's going on."

"It didn't just happen, man." The anger again. "They've been around a long time. And all the time you spend with 'em, and shit. I mean *hours*. I seen it."

"Even if I spent hours with them, if there had not been that long time before, when Nancy was seeing doctors, and Jennifer was seeing doctors, it would not have happened."

"It would have happened, man. I seen the doctors."

I reiterated, "I understand why you're angry. But when I first met John and Jennifer I had no idea there was a possible integration of the personalities. As far as I knew, this could have gone on for the rest of Nancy's life. An integration is not necessarily the thing that happens in all cases like this. If there were going to be a lot of different people in Nancy's life, what I really wanted was to have life be the best possible for each one of you. I was not kidding when I said I did not want *you* to be living a life where you were regarded with no value. I would like to see you valued by others. I think it's every person's right to have that."

She was silent, stared at me.

I went on, "You can feel the difference, Sherry, I am sure, between the men you used to know and George. He values you. As a person. And you have a right to that."

"Yeah, but he don't work on changing me so hard, like you do. He just accepts me as I am."

"Do you understand he accepts you *because* you have come a long way? Because you *have* changed? You have believed I was telling the truth when I said people did not regard you as valuable when you were selling your body to truckers and picking up men who were killers."

Defensively. "Maybe I wouldn't have met George, maybe I would have. I ain't that different."

"Come on, Sherry. You couldn't meet him as a prostitute and have him love you. You know better. You told me enough about him so I know him better than that."

"Well, what me and George got ain't nothin' like what you had with John and Jennifer." Implying she and George had a sexual relationship.

"Okay, you can choose to believe me or not but I thought that as long as there were this many people sharing the same body, each should have a decent existence."

"How come?"

"John was not having a decent existence, Jennifer was not having a decent existence and *you* were not having a decent existence. As soon as they saw someone valued them, they started changing."

"Yeah. Changing into nothing."

"I have no control over that. Do you think I should have just thrown them out again? Is that the idea? Send Jennifer off to be picked up by the police and anybody else who wanted to chase after her? And John out into the streets where he had to defend himself to keep alive?"

"You could have helped without so much hard work. All the hours you spent with them."

I said coldly, "I think you should apologize for that. I worked hard for what I thought good reason. I valued Jennifer and John enough to want to spend hours with them. I think you are seeing two happenings at the same time but I don't know if one is causing the other. You think the time I spent with them is causing them to be integrated. I believe the changes that occurred in them as a result of the time I spent with them has caused them to wish to be integrated. Or a wish in Nancy for their integration."

"Everybody disappearing forever." A mutter.

"You may be right. Nancy may be wanting this to happen."

"You been doin' stuff with her, too." Accusingly.

"I talk to Nancy. What do I *do* to her? What is it that you see happening with her?"

"You make her think a lot more about John and Jennifer and me, and *everything.*" As though this were a hideous deed.

"So she will know what's going on. I think that's only fair. All of you know what's going on with her. She should know what's going on with you."

"Yeah, but by her *knowing* and then changing, there ain't no more control. John and Jennifer, they lost control, man. They couldn't fight for survival any more. It wasn't the Number One thing."

"Something may have been more important than that kind of survival," I said. "I realize that you're inside and you have your feelings."

"I know John and Jennifer used to be real strong and could handle things. I mean it was rough. What isn't?"

"Jennifer could not handle it," I said. "You wouldn't condemn anybody to live the way she lived. Running away in terror from everything, forever. That would be very cruel. Nobody should be maimed by that kind of a life."

"Well, how do you think they felt, man? Like they didn't have the answers no more. Everything was what *you* said."

"Jennifer never had the answers. Just the fear. She was in sheer panic most of the time. Maybe that doesn't mean anything to you, but it upset me. It also upset me that John was a drug addict and had to have drugs to survive. Deal in them."

"I ain't sayin' that was good." Sullenly.

"I'm just telling you what my motives were. I'm seeing two people who look like they're in very deep trouble."

"Yeah, but from the beginning, man, they know you wasn't a doctor. Point in your favor. But you been doin' everything a doctor would do *and* more. More than any doctor I ever saw, I bet."

"Do you know what that 'more' is, though, Sherry? Do you have any idea what the 'more' is? That I personally care for each of the people. Not just Nancy but each one of you. You are all important to me."

"Yeah, but when we feel like we are important then we don't have to fight no more."

I thought about this—fighting was their existence, not to fight meant to die. I said, "You may be right. But I do different things than doctors because I really care."

"What's fucked about it is that John and Jennifer don't even know what's happening to 'em. I don't put myself in that situation, man."

"I don't ever try to put anyone into that situation, Sherry. You do not need to be protected."

"You keep sayin' 'protected', man."

"John and Jennifer were very young and did not know what they were doing to themselves."

"That's for sure!"

"They needed someone to protect them."

"And now they're gone. It's Number One to all of us to keep on going. Keep on *being*. The more you saw 'em, the more you did whatever you was doin' with 'em, then they didn't have to fight so much. It wasn't Number One no more to fight. They didn't have to care so much."

"I don't know if that's true." I was caught in trying to understand the role they all played in Nancy's life and their feelings about integration as "vanishing" forever, dying.

Nancy/Sherry accused me once again. "You got the whole system fucked up. Got Nancy all turned around."

"How can I turn her around? As I understand it, she's doing more now to help you lead your own life than she ever did in the past."

"She's doin' the same fuckin' thing you are."

"Which is what? Caring about you?"

Sullenly. "I don't know what it is. But I know you're makin' her do it, man."

"I'm just giving her information. I can't make her care about anybody."

"Yeah, but she can see what you do."

"Okay. I *know* you're mad but being mad is emotion, not rational thought. Emotions don't have brains. They just *are*. Should I pretend I don't care about everybody?"

"We know you care. That ain't no big problem. It's all the time you spent with 'em, man."

"But even when I did not see them, I was getting calls from them constantly. They called *me*. There would be days when I did not see them but talk to them when they called me."

"Well, you yourself said, man, they're young. They can't think nothin' like that out. That was new to them, man."

I asked, "Nobody had ever cared for them before?"

"I don't know. But they was changin' because of it."

I smiled. "Be my guest. You can be mad at me for that."

Harold asked, "Sherry, how many of you share Nancy's body? Or did, all told?"

Insolently. "You can count, cancha?"

Harold said, "There were seven important ones, right? Nancy—"

Sherry broke in, "I wouldn't count her."

"But there were seven main ones and many other minor ones. Are you aware this is very, very unusual? That most bodies are not shared at all? That there's only one person in one body?"

"Yeah, I know." A *so what?*

"And all of a sudden comes one body shared chiefly by seven different people. It's *extremely* rare. I don't think you are aware that several of the entities in Nancy have tried to kill her. Darn near succeeded a couple of times. Seven people can't live in one body, Sherry."

I put in, "If they were trying to kill her, then everybody would die. They obviously did not know that."

Harold went on, "Jenny was going to watch them all die, she said. Emily told her, 'You won't be around to watch them.' Jenny never thought of that. If Nancy had not come into our life four years ago, none of you would be alive today. Because of the suicide attempts and the drugs."

Diane said, "I saved her one night when she had a heart attack. If she had died, you would not be alive."

"Pain was a way of life for Jennifer and John," Nancy/Sherry said. "They understood it, they knew it."

I recalled, "One night Jennifer ran out into the street in front of a truck because she was in a blind panic. As she was most of the time."

"Well, I ain't sayin' it was good. I ain't sayin' what they was and the things they did was the best. I'm just sayin' you take away the pain and they ain't nothin'. That's all they know. All Jennifer knew was people treatin' her like shit. People hurting her."

I said quietly, "I know." Some of the psychic pieces were starting to fall together. The personalities reflected the pain inside Nancy, along with those wishes she dared not face consciously. As Nancy/Sherry had just said, the personalities existed for Nancy "to remain alive." They gave outlet to sensations and emotions that, if denied expression, would have driven her mad or long ago caused her to kill herself.

Nancy/Sherry had also said, "Trust kills." Someone Nancy had trusted long ago, perhaps even before she had learned to think in a mature way, had hurt her so acutely that never again could she trust a human being. To trust was to invite horror to return.

Nancy/Sherry was saying, "John was out there to be tough. And you changed that, man. Where does that leave him? Maybe it felt good to him to be tough."

"I want you to consider, Sherry, that maybe Jennifer and John have made the trade to integrate rather than live forever the way they have been living."

"But this is the pits, man," she protested. "One by one, we're all supposed to watch each other disappear?"

"It doesn't seem fair to you, no doubt about it," I said.

"Diane and I and Emily love Nancy dearly," Harold said. "We love Jennifer very much and we feel very bad that she's gone. I care a lot for John."

"I love John," I said.

Harold continued, "And Sherry, I wish we could get to love you. I wish you'd let us love you."

"You don't have to go to all that trouble, man. I'm half of John, that's where I came from. He goes and man, half of me goes."

Harold said to us all, "Jenny said that Nancy had taken a lot of her away. And now I hear Sherry saying that if John goes, half of her goes."

"Yeah, man. Like when Jennifer went, that was the end for John."

I asked, "Why do you feel you're half of John? Because you are not. Jennifer and John were born of the same trauma."

"I was there too because Jennifer was changin'. John needed me.

Jennifer wasn't there for him all the time. He couldn't depend on her to make money with tricks to keep him supplied with drugs."

Nancy/Sherry went on, "John needed a hooker. For his drugs. He couldn't go out and hook himself. He couldn't get the money and had to have drugs. So I came for him. I mean, he didn't make me come or nothin'."

But Nancy did, I thought, another piece of the puzzle falling into place. At a time Nancy/John needed money for drugs, Nancy/Sherry started working the truck stop.

Nancy/Sherry was saying, "I mean, everybody's connected. Jennifer and John are connected. John and me are connected. Sarah and Carmen are connected. Nancy and Carmen are connected. Nancy and Sarah are connected. Everybody's *part* of everybody else."

And in some way, I thought, each one is connected with a wish of Nancy's so intense and threatening she could not consciously face it, handle it in a mature way. The reasoning part of her mind, what psychoanalysts call her ego, which is largely conscious, was unable to cope with the wish.

"I came for John," Nancy/Sherry explained further. "I mean, it wasn't *directly* for him. But, man, I supported his habit for a long time."

Diane asked, "But who taught you how to support the habit?"

"What's to teach, man? I learned from one of Nancy's friends at school. I learned it better than she did."

Harold asked, "A friend of Nancy's taught you the ropes?"

"Anybody could walk down to the fuckin' truck stop and turn tricks. Just a matter of bein' a good hooker or the *best* hooker."

A thought occurred to me. I said to Nancy/Sherry, "You *stopped* being a hooker before John stopped needing drugs. How does that fit in?"

Nancy/Sherry said calmly, " 'Cause I listened to you."

I held back my surprise. "Does this also mean that—"

"I know what you're going to say," she said. "That fuckin' word 'integrate.' There's only one way I'm gonna go. That's the same way as the others. I wasn't goin' to go just 'cause I wasn't hookin' no more. Jennifer was there for John, helped him out. I was there for him, helped him out."

I asked, "If you stopped hooking, do you think someone else would have come to be the hooker for John's drug habit?"

"If he kept on, maybe. But he started changing."

"You know, Sherry, somebody has to pay the price. It was you for a while. To be used by other people. Then you decided you didn't want that. So another person would come to be used. Jennifer was *used* all the time. Somebody has to be *used* in Nancy's life."

Angrily. "I knew what I was doin'. I got something out of it."

"Jennifer didn't know what she was doing."

"She didn't. But I did."

"What did you get out of it?"

"Money."

"But apparently that was not enough to keep you hooking."

"I could go back to it tomorrow if I wanted."

"Even after an experience like George? Knowing the difference between one kind of man and another? One who loves you and one who just uses you?"

"Yeah. If I wanted to."

"Maybe you could do it but it wouldn't be exciting and fun any more."

Harold said, "Sherry, there's nobody in this room that's happy about what's happening. But we don't have much control over it."

"Man, I'm not saying it's hocus-pocus power. Just the little things that change things." She sighed. "Like their trust in you, man. That changed things for John and Jennifer. Then they were helpless."

He asked, "Helpless against what?"

"Not against anything. Just helpless."

"So what you're saying, in essence, is that we made them so weak they couldn't survive? Is that what I hear?"

"They didn't have no more guts."

"That's the same thing. They got so weak they couldn't hack it and faded away."

"Because of you takin' care of 'em, man. Like if you raise a kid, you make that kid what he is. That's what you did with John and Jennifer. And that's what they are. Nothin'."

I said, "I did with them what I would do with my own children. The ultimate goal is to make them strong, decent adults."

"John and Jennifer aren't your own kids, man."

"They're people we love, Sherry. Believe it or not." Harold's voice was strong with conviction.

I added, "John and Jennifer are, in a sense, my own children. I do the same things with them."

"Well, you got John helpless now, a little kid, man."

"Which is what he really is. Right? He's acting like a normal kid acts, rather than a street-wise drug addict." I added, "As I've said, Sherry, I understand your anger. I do not want to give up John but I don't know how to change what's happening."

Insolently. "Maybe if you give up now he'll make it."

"Back in the street? That's an awful choice to ask him to make. I'll have to give him up one way or the other. I can't have him if he's going to be the same person as before. So I have to give him up no matter which way is chosen. That's why I feel angry."

Harold said, "I feel very sad. Everybody is getting a raw deal. Nancy's getting a raw deal. Sherry's getting a raw deal. Jennifer's getting a raw deal. Sarah's getting a raw deal. But we didn't cause it. There's nothing we can do about it."

Nancy/Sherry asked earnestly, "Would you really want me to pull out on John?"

I said, "Pull out? And let him go back to the streets?"

"Well, it beats the way that Jennifer goes. The way we all seem to go."

"You think it would be better to die in panic in front of a truck?"

Sarcastically. "At least you see the truck comin'."

Harold said, "Sherry, have you noticed I have both legs off? Those legs were amputated to save my life. So the rest of me could keep going."

"I think what's fuckin' about it, man, is it had to happen. It's shitty."

She turned on me, snapped, "*I* started listening to you. *They* started listening to you."

"I was telling you about the real world," I said quietly. "What was really true."

"But we don't want to live in the *real* world!"

"You are living in it now. You have a man. You are a woman. You *are* in the real world."

A confession. "But I can't live with him."

"I know that," I said. It would have taken a miracle to transform that swiftly from a prostitute into a loving, nurturing wife.

"I can't have his children. I can't be his wife. I can't feel like a married person would."

This honesty on Nancy/Sherry's part showed, more than any ardent declaration, her trust in me. I felt elated.

She went on, "Because I *don't* live in the real world."

Harold asked, "Would you like to have children?"

"Not now. I don't know if I ever would. But I don't have no choice, anyway."

Harold persisted, "If you lived in the real world and were going to be here permanently, would you like to have children?"

"How would I know, man?"

"Well, if you don't, who does?"

Angrily. "I *don't* live in a real world, not a whole one! How am I supposed to know what it's like? With the few hours here and there I can grab with the man I love." Meaning when she could be the one outside and Nancy inside.

Harold said, "You live in segments. You get a little time out and Nancy gets some time out and Sarah gets time out. For two years we didn't see Sarah and now she's coming out quite frequently. She doesn't stay long but she comes out."

"You ask her, she's the expert, if this wouldn't be happening because you guys were doin' what you're doin'."

"I'll ask her," I said.

Harold reiterated, "Sherry, if we hadn't been doing what we were doing, you would *all* have been dead."

I added, "And Sherry is saying she would have preferred to die, from what I can hear."

"I think Jennifer and John would have, too," Nancy/Sherry said. "A kick in the teeth, man, is what's happening now."

Harold continued, "I'm not going to argue with you. Whether you know it or not, I respect and like you."

"I don't need it." Nastily.

"I know you don't need it. But I *feel* it. I'm *God damn* angry with the deal that's been handed out to you and all the rest of the personalities."

I interspersed, "Some of the things I told you, Sherry, about the real world is what makes George possible for you. And other things make the time with George better. Because I have given you some information about the real world you would not have found out by yourself as a hooker."

"Maybe so." Grudgingly. "But that's a pretty price to pay."

"It is," I agreed.

"I mean, I been watchin' John for a couple of months now. Like he goes from being strong when he's on drugs, livin' on the streets, to a helpless little boy. It's like growing senile."

"But Sherry, there's nothing we *did*, really, except trying to talk to him and love him and give him appreciation," Harold said.

I added, "He might have killed himself and everybody else. Or be thrown in jail for many years as a pusher."

Then I said, "If I had known ahead of time—" I did not finish the sentence.

Nancy/Sherry asked, "Would you have done what you did?"

I said truthfully, "I don't know. I can't answer that."

"You could have only talked to Nancy, got her trust and made her change. Nancy would be whole. And the integration would happen, right, man?"

"I don't think I could have done it that way. Maybe I could have tried but I don't think I would have been believable. I would have been playacting. One of the reasons for seeing Nancy every week now is because she is very disturbed at the idea of going to Lexington, as you well know. The whole idea is to try to settle *her* down. To do that, we are seeing everybody. Everybody talks to me of their own volition."

"I'm not saying that's wrong, man. I can see it's good for you to care about the kids and for them to trust you. I mean, those aren't *bad* things. I'm just sayin' it all leads to one thing."

"We don't have a quarrel. But I can't do anything about what is happening. I am not God, I do not have the power to change this."

"I ain't talkin' about *power*."

"But you keep speaking as if I could do something to change matters. The thing I can do is to send John back on the streets but I don't know if I could bring myself to do that. In effect I'd be saying, 'John, I don't want you any more, I don't care about you, go take care of yourself.' What would that do to him?"

"That would work. 'Cause John knows."

"What does he know?"

"That somethin's all over. You got him helpless, needing you."

"But I'm not willing to give him up. My problem is I have two choices and I don't want either of them. Either I keep loving John and he integrates or I stop loving John and he goes back to the street and drugs. What kind of choice is that?"

"I can see that it's really past the point of no return. Maybe he wouldn't go, if you didn't see him. Maybe he'd get strong again and fight for survival. Because he *knows* survival."

I said, "Sherry, just last week there was a girl on my campus who took angel dust in the morning before she came to school. She started hitting pupils and teachers, anyone in sight. She belted a person whether she knew him or not. It took five men to hold her down and she's not very tall. Because her mind was so screwed up by the angel dust, all she wanted to do was hurt people. The same thing could happen to John."

"Maybe he wouldn't go back to drugs."

"You really believe that?"

"I don't know!" Defensively. "I can't *predict* nothin'."

Harold said, "John was out looking for angel dust just yesterday, according to Sarah. He didn't get it but he was trying."

I pointed out to Nancy/Sherry, "You took care of Chico when he came to find John to sell him angel dust."

"I told him to fuck off."

"You were brave. John was afraid Chico would beat him up if he refused."

"I don't think Chico knew it wasn't John. I was wearin' the clothes John was wearin'."

I changed the subject. "Nancy thinks that if John integrates she'll be in good enough shape to go to Kentucky because the worry was that John would be out taking drugs in Kentucky. Sarah told me he did want to integrate but not in Kentucky. If it happens, it happens. John wanted it to happen here. And *then* Nancy would go to Kentucky."

"But if you can keep John alive then it ain't gonna happen no more. Just Jennifer is gone."

"John and Sarah are saying that it's going to happen anyway. Very soon. Even without me around."

"Well, it could happen, man. Like I said, he's more than half dead."

I was exhausted, I had made the point over and over. I said, "When you're ready, I would like to talk to Sarah and see whether she's saying the same thing."

"Maybe she can say it better, man. She's got to know it."

"She said John and Jennifer will go close together but the rest of you may take longer. I don't know if she's changed her mind. Nancy may still need you all."

"No, man. She just needed John and Jennifer. We came on our own because we wanted to do something different."

"Sarah, too?"

"I don't know. I wasn't around when she came."

"I think John and Jennifer were there because Nancy wanted certain things and she didn't want to realize she wanted them. And I think Sarah is the same."

"I don't understand what you're saying, man."

"Nancy *wanted* the escape of drugs."

"But John and Jennifer were born when Nancy was raped."

"I know that. But why the drugs, then?"

" 'Cause John and Jennifer couldn't cope with the rape. It happened to them. That was their welcome to the world."

"Nancy couldn't cope with it, either. She wanted the same escape into drugs as John and Jennifer did. Only she didn't want to admit it. That's why she needed them, so they would do the drug-taking for her."

Harold asked, "What was your welcome to the world, Sherry?"

"I wanted to be here."

I asked, "Do you remember your first time?"

"It was slow. It wasn't like bam-bam."

"You just kind of gradually grew?"

"Yeah. Then I just went out and found what I wanted."

"That must be strange, to begin like that."

"It ain't strange if you live that way."

Harold asked, "You're seventeen years old, Sherry, how does it feel to be born at seventeen?"

"I don't know! How does it feel to be born at zero?" Contemptuously.

Diane asked if we would like something to drink. Sherry took wine, I and the others, coffee. As we drank, we continued to talk. I opened the conversation, saying, "I would like to share an observation with you. I met Nancy when she was fifteen. She was in terrible shape. And when she was eighteen, nineteen and twenty, she was in better shape. I don't know if that was a result of seeing doctors or if she was just better able to handle things."

Nancy/Sherry said, almost enviously, "Look how she feels about you. Look at the relationship she's got with you. I mean you're super-duper important to her. Those doctors never were."

"But she was improving all those years. The doctors must have been doing something."

"Sure, man. They kept her goin' by stickin' her in hospitals, tyin' her up, keepin' her on drugs."

"That is not my idea of keeping her going. When I say she has improved, I really mean it. Not that she is just still alive. But that she is feeling better as a whole."

"She fought those doctors, man. She didn't listen. She didn't believe 'em. She believes you. She listens to you. So do John and Jennifer. They never listened to anyone else."

"I'm glad they're listening to me. They're learning that what they do affects each other's lives and they are responsible for each other. The reason John did not go out Saturday night to take angel dust is because I told him that when *he* gets high, either you or Nancy are going to suffer. He felt responsibility for both of you for the first time. That was one of the big reasons why he did not take any drugs."

Then I added, "Nancy is concerned now in helping you in your relationship with George."

Snippily. "I can handle that on my own. It's *my* relationship. *My* man." Then sarcastically, "How would you like to share your man with another woman?"

"I wouldn't," I said.

Diane commented, "But Sherry, I don't think you're really sharing George."

"Not in the sexual sense. It ain't like Nancy goes to bed with him or nothin'."

"She's not even involved with him," I said. "Except she thinks he's nice, a polite person."

"It ain't *involved*, it's how he feels toward her when he thinks she's me."

"But it's really you he's feeling it for," I said. "And Nancy knows that. You have your own clothes, your own gifts, your own love."

"George helps me to be a full person," she admitted. "Maybe not in the sense that I can cook for him. Or whatever. Like have his kids."

Then with a sigh, "We're all kick-offs from Nancy. You know, like she's whole. She knows love, she knows pain, she knows working, she knows education, she knows about relationships. She knows what it is to feel good, to feel bad, to feel all kinds of shit."

"You're feeling these things now, too, aren't you?"

"No." Silence. "And I never will. I could say goodbye to George tomorrow and I wouldn't feel the same about it as if Nancy said goodbye to you."

I felt surprised. "No?"

"Yeah. I mean, I can handle it. We're plannin' on goin' to Kentucky. So I say goodbye to my man. Maybe I don't ever see him again. What if something happens? Suppose we all integrate? I don't see him again."

"You won't suffer the same kind of pain you think Nancy would on separating?"

"No. I won't allow myself to get put in that position."

Diane asked, "What about the wonderment of experiencing life with George? Being out with him, going places, doing things?"

"It's okay. I'm a good-time gal. That's all I am. I seek pleasure. I don't seek it in the way Nancy seeks it. I don't seek it in the way you guys seek it. For *me*, it's minute to minute."

Sherry had stayed a long time, we said goodbye, called for Nancy/Sarah. We wanted her advice about the Kentucky venture and to find out if she intended to go. We could always depend on the competent, knowledgeable Sarah's words of wisdom.

"What does Nancy expect of me today?" I asked her.

"Perhaps I can explain it this way." Nancy/Sarah's brisk, assured voice. "There will be times when you're in contact with Nancy in the future and she is completely whole but still needs you to hold her. There will be times she will feel much freer to express her anger. And to be more frank and blunt about her feelings."

"Like Sherry?" I asked.

"Right. There will also be times Nancy will want drugs. That's a tough one with John because he's not exactly divided in half but he is torn between his need for drugs and his love for you."

"But he's willing to accept love, apparently."

"I think he is. I think *very* definitely that one of the reasons Jennifer was able to integrate was because of the love John received from you. Love she received prior to that, and understood and accepted. When John could accept that love, the twins were no longer separated."

Nancy/Sarah then announced, "I need to use the restroom," excused herself.

After she left, Harold said, "It's a mess."

"I don't think it's a mess at all. I feel very good about everything." Diane smiled at us.

"I understand Sherry's feelings." There was sadness on Harold's face.

"God, yes," I echoed.

Then added, "But she also explained it's not an intense relationship. She can give it up without too much pain."

"Emily, this is something not one psychiatrist in a hundred thousand ever sees," Harold marveled.

"Not one in a million, I would imagine."

When Nancy/Sarah returned I asked, "Is John going to integrate?"

"I don't think so, though it's a strong possibility."

Then I asked, "What can we do to help Nancy?"

Nancy/Sarah replied, "I don't think at this point positive suggestions are going to have a lot of effect on the devastating emotions Nancy feels because of Jennifer separating. With John, she has a little more warning. The feelings differ with each personality. When Sherry integrates, Nancy is going to feel intense anger. The anger that Sherry shows."

"Nancy can't get anger out," Diane observed. "She pushes it inside."

"That's why Sherry is here," Nancy/Sarah explained. "When Sherry integrates Nancy will need to be able to express that anger. And accept it."

"What will happen in Kentucky?" I asked.

Diane said, "Nancy might feel freer there to express her anger."

"But she might not have anyone she trusted to do it with," I said.

"I don't think she will feel freer in Kentucky to express her anger," Sarah said. "If Nancy goes to Kentucky I don't think John will integrate. At least, not immediately. And because of the separation from all of you, he might even possibly become stronger. Because Nancy would need to escape more, in the way John has, to overcome her pain at the separation."

"Nancy needs a sounding board for her anger," Diane said.

Nancy/Sarah went on, "Nancy is a very sensitive person. Not necessarily more than John but in a way a doctor will find difficult to help. He can give supportive therapy and help her understand her feelings, though at this point Nancy understands her feelings quite well."

Diane asked, "Is there anything else, looking long-range, Sarah, that you think we can get for Nancy, materially, that she needs before she goes to Kentucky?"

"I think she has everything, material-wise. Her mother is giving her necessities, like dishes for an apartment. Nancy isn't going to need a lot."

Sarah added, a warning, "When Nancy first made the decision to go to Lexington, it was extremely positive. Now she's not certain whether she wants to go. She's going to run and you don't run to find answers."

I asked, "What about Carmen? We don't ever see her."

"I would hate to see Nancy and Carmen alone," Nancy/Sarah said, "Carmen lives in the most unreality of them all."

"She has *no* awareness of reality," I said.

Nancy/Sarah mused, "If you picture someone in a mental hospital who cannot cope with reality, that's Carmen. I would assume the therapy process involved in bringing that person back to reality is to give them experiences. This is hard to do with Carmen second-hand because she doesn't observe. And touch is something she's not used to."

Diane asked, "What about the suggestion to Nancy that she can cope without the need of Carmen?"

"If it were that simple I'm afraid we wouldn't have gone through all this."

I marveled once again at the wisdom of Nancy/Sarah. Part of Nancy was well aware of her need for multiple personalities, as well as knowing their specific purposes.

Sarah went on to prove my point. "Nancy *will* grow stronger. But this is not going to happen any faster than she can accept it. Subconsciously, she will accept she does not need this particular personality any more. But when the personality integrates, she will experience explicit memories and acts that have frightened her. She will now have to cope alone with the trauma of her past."

Diane asked, "If we can strengthen Nancy will she inevitably be able to cope?"

"Oh, yes! Nancy has become stronger with her trust in the three of you. She is able to take the chance, the risk, the emotional trauma. For one thing, you are not doctors. She *has* been hurt by doctors for many years and resists them. The ones before you met her left a lot to be desired. Nancy was very desperate at that point. They told her many things she couldn't understand and didn't bother to explain them. All she knew was that she was beginning to hurt a lot more. She had no self-worth. But here, friends are giving her support. One of the reasons she is so casual at this point is because she's afraid she's going to change. And I have heard you say that will not affect—"

"How we feel about her," I put in.

"Right."

Diane said, "No matter what her memories are, we love *her* even more because of the courage she has shown to grow. We also love her because she's Nancy."

"Be careful with that one," warned Nancy/Sarah. "Because she's Nancy/Jennifer now."

I said, "I love Jennifer. So if Jennifer is part of Nancy, then in no way will that be more difficult. If I love Jennifer then I can love whatever Jennifer was that is part of Nancy. And the same with John."

Nancy/Sarah looked at me approvingly. "I would say that is one of the easiest ways for Nancy to accept herself. She is having trouble accepting this."

I admitted, "I guess if there's a pet, John's my pet. Because I knew him better than Jennifer. Very often when I was with her, she was in a blind panic. I saw her only in the most unusual circumstances. Diane and Harold have seen her in normal circumstances. With John, I have a normal kind of relationship."

"This is what Nancy has been struggling with," Sarah said. "These things are more important than being herself. Because to Nancy, more important than being acceptable to herself is being acceptable to other people. And she cannot understand why you would accept all her personalities."

Diane commented, "It has been difficult for her to understand how I could love her. Or for any of us to love her the way we do."

"I don't think she really does understand," Nancy/Sarah said. "Jennifer could see love for what it was. This person cares about me. This person will see I'm not hurt. And this person gives me love. For Jennifer, that's all it took."

"As simple as that," I said. They all laughed.

"Right." Sarah went on. "Jennifer felt this need in spurts, whenever she was out. She certainly grasped for love. Stronger love and to be held tighter than any one of the others. She was a very honest child in the sense she knew what she needed. Nancy finds it very difficult to ask for love."

Diane commented, "As difficult as it is for her to express anger."

"I would say it's about the same." Then I granted, "Well, maybe it's easier for Nancy to express a need for affection than to express anger."

"The only time I have ever seen anger in Nancy was when she felt her mother was trying to take advantage of her, giving her orders she didn't want to follow," Diane said.

I pointed out, "She is allowing some of her resentments and hostilities to show."

"But there's a lot there," Nancy/Sarah said. "I *do* like Nancy's mother and I *do* believe everything she does is with the best of intentions. But with her mother's divorces and so many other things, Nancy was more or less forgotten. Perhaps not forgotten, but certainly she didn't receive the care she needed."

I had to remind myself in amazement this was really Nancy speaking about Nancy, not another therapist speaking about Nancy. And I felt, once again, that all the agonized hours spent with the personalities, trying to help them mature, were not wasted.

Diane was saying, "I like Nancy's mother very much. And I've tried to help her. But right now I'm the whipping boy for momma."

"I don't understand." Nancy/Sarah looked puzzled.

"Nancy's mother needs support. And yet she won't allow you to support her. Or allow anyone else, outside of Nancy. Nancy's the only one she's ever *allowed* to support her. Because this is the problem she had with her own mother. Her mother was very destructive to Nancy, Senior. Nancy, Senior has had one hell of a hard life."

"Definitely," Nancy/Sarah agreed.

Changing the subject, Nancy/Sarah assured us, "The integration of Sherry is going to be positive. Sherry has developed an independent lifestyle with which she's happy, she expresses her feelings freely. It will help round off the picture. As for Carmen, it's a guess."

I observed, "Nancy has a very unrealistic anticipation of what can happen in Kentucky. Kentucky to her is green grass and horses. She expects to feel good the minute she sets foot on Kentucky soil."

Nancy/Sarah commented, "I don't think she's even concerned with the therapy in Kentucky. It's the *going.*" She added thoughtfully, "If anything breaks in Kentucky and she's not really forced to fix it, she won't have to face it. Here, with you, she knows she has to."

"You mean no one is going to confront her with her behavior?" I said.

"Nancy's world in the past has been to hide," Nancy/Sarah answered. "But I have seen her world change because of you. She *has* fought, though she has resisted at the same time. Fighting is all she's ever really thought about. It has occupied her entire life."

Fighting through personalities, I thought, who hid the sweet, gentle Nancy. Personalities who now threatened to integrate, which meant she would have to *feel* what they felt, deal with *their* conflicts.

I asked Nancy/Sarah, "Is there something I can do to help John?"

"I think what might be a comfort to John is the secure knowledge that *you're* in charge."

"Be real tough?" I asked.

"Be real tough."

Then, concern in her voice, "I hope Sherry's anger didn't upset you too much."

"I have a personal philosophy that says feelings are not something to be avoided. Even bad ones."

Sarah smiled in approval, suggested, "I can leave now and let John come. What time is it?"

"Quarter to nine." We had been in the darkened room almost two hours.

At this moment Clint entered, silently slipped into a chair as I called for Nancy/John. He emerged swiftly, said "Hi," his usual greeting.

I responded, "Hi, sweetheart." Then told him, "Nancy is going to stay around a little while longer."

"You mean we're not gonna go to Kentucky?" He sounded pleased.

"Maybe soon. She had planned to leave in four days but decided to delay a while longer."

"How long?"

"She didn't say. I don't know for sure. Diane thinks it's because maybe she didn't have quite enough money. It might be another week or two."

He leaned toward me, his face grew unexpectedly tender, and said, "I was gonna draw a picture of you. And one of Jennifer, Sherry, Sarah and me. So that after we was all gone, you could keep them as a reminder of us. But it didn't work out."

I assured him, "Whatever happens in Kentucky, John, I will still love you. And I'll be right here. I'm not leaving you."

He pleaded in a low voice, "Don't leave me. Don't leave me."

I took him in my arms, said reassuringly, "Even if you can't see me, you can hold on to me and know I am right beside you. As I've always been. You will be able to feel my love. There's nothing to be afraid of." I sensed he was feeling deep fear.

He called out, "Mom! Mom!"

"Yes, John. Yes, dear, I'm here."

"I don't wanna be scared, mom. But I *am* scared." He breathed deeply, then started to shake and shiver, as though in convulsions. I took him in my arms, held him close, tried to calm him down. I said softly, "Let it go, John. Let it go."

He broke down, cried, then whimpered, panting on and off for about fifteen minutes as I tried to console him. I heard Clint say to him, "Let it happen, just let it happen." And listened to Nancy/John's steady moans.

And then his words, "I hurt, Mom. Mom! Mom?"

"I'm here," I said. "I'm here, John."

I had never seen him so forlorn, I realized how frightened a part of Nancy felt at leaving us. The moaning and the whimpering went on as I tried to soothe him by holding him close. I kept silent, wanting him to express himself. Neither of us spoke for another ten minutes.

Then he pulled himself together, dried his tears with Kleenex I handed him. He said in his normal, clipped voice, "I wanna quit now. I wanna quit."

"Okay, John." I relinquished my hold on him.

He started to mumble, broken phrases I could not understand, in a self-comforting trance. He whispered as a frightened child whispers. I caught the words "the wall." He pointed to a distant spot in the room as though trying to reach it. Then looked horrified, as if he should not have made the gesture, it was betrayal of someone dear.

I called out, "Sarah. Or Sherry. Sarah or Sherry. This is too much for John or Nancy to handle. I would like you to come." I repeated the message. "Sarah or Sherry. This is too difficult for John or Nancy to handle. I would like you to come."

The whimpering stopped. Nancy/John's body straightened up. I heard Nancy/Sarah's calming voice, "I'm here, Mrs. Campbell."

I asked, "Was it too much for him?"

"It was too much for both John and Nancy."

"Do you know what the problem was?"

"He is afraid both of going to Kentucky and of being integrated. He feels he has no choice but to vanish. To die."

"I can see him panic-stricken because he will be alone with Nancy," I said. "Through his moaning I could hear the words 'the wall.' Jennifer once spoke of a wall she kept trying to break through. Do you know about this wall?"

"They've all erected a wall against the outside world. They are not allowed to destroy it. If they do, they will all die. The outside world must not know they exist or this wall exists."

"John seemed terrified of this wall."

"It's their protection against the cruelty of other people," Nancy/Sarah said.

We all build inner walls of protection against the hurts of life, keep part of us prisoner within, I thought. Nancy's wall was a psychic fortress. She saw her wall as solid concrete, not a fantasy wall.

Clint commented, one of his few but always pertinent perceptions, "Since Jennifer is gone and apparently the purpose she served was to protect Nancy from pain and trauma, John may be bearing the whole burden of that displacement. He may be protecting Nancy from memories Jennifer formerly served to protect."

"I thought of that, too," I said.

Clint said to Nancy/Sarah, "The question comes up repeatedly, and you're the one who phrased it, that Nancy wasn't ready to let go. You said it wasn't John hanging on but Nancy. Would it be feasible to reassure Nancy that if John is ready to go she need not hang on to him?"

"She's never experienced anything like John just went through," Nancy/Sarah replied. "What happened to John tonight is new to her."

That open exposure of the pain within, of suffering the agony of abandonment by someone loved, was new to me too. I knew it came out of Nancy's stark soul. A menaced baby screaming for its mother.

Clint asked, "Is Nancy holding the wall John talked about? Does he feel he can't climb over it? That this would be too dangerous for him?"

"That's one possibility," said Nancy/Sarah.

I pointed out, "He said the wall was right here. He was reaching for it as though it were in this room. And he felt he was doing something wrong."

Everyone retreated into silence. I finally asked, "Well, what shall we do? Shall we call for Jennifer?"

"She's going to be exhausted. She'll be wiped out," Sarah said.

"It's getting late. Maybe we've all had enough." Diane's voice.

I sighed. "I think I have."

Thus the session ended, one of revelations. John's breakdown stunned us all. He had never expressed himself so openly, with such raw emotion and acute need. This supposedly tough, street-wise urchin had allowed himself to regress to a helpless child pleading, "Don't leave me! Don't leave me!"

I felt apprehensive about the Kentucky venture. There was now no doubt a strong part of Nancy did not wish to embark on it. Yet I knew she thought it a challenge she must accept.

After a final postponement of the journey to Lexington, Nancy announced at the end of April she would definitely leave on May 7 with her mother. This time I felt she meant it, had set herself this inexorable deadline.

Four days before the exodus we held a last session on May 3. Nancy was the first to speak to us. She said, "I don't seem to feel very well."

"Is Sherry around?" I asked.

Usually Nancy did not feel well when Nancy/Sherry was active at night, which meant Nancy went without sleep. By now Nancy/Sherry had given up trying to hold together her rocky relationship, she separated from George. He had been unable to cope with part of a young woman "possessed" by inner voices.

"Is Sherry up to her old tricks?" Harold asked.

"Sarah reported Sherry came out and called George and they spoke on the phone for ten minutes," I said.

"What time was it?" Nancy asked.

"Two in the morning."

"Well, I lost time about one so she probably was calling George at that hour. Maybe even went to see him. How does she get back and forth?"

"She thumbs," I said.

"Blind?" Diane asked.

"Yes, she makes no bones about it. She gets out and thumbs and gets in and thumbs and says, 'I want to go to such and such a place, just let me off there.'"

Nancy asked, "How close is she to integration?"

"Sarah is no longer able to tell much about it," I said. "Things are too scrambled. But Sarah's been quite happy with the way things are going."

"She never is anything *but* calm," Nancy said.

Diane pointed out, "She was not calm the day she knew Sherry was hitching a ride to Yuma with those two truck drivers."

Earlier in the year Nancy/Sherry decided suddenly to take off for Arizona, wearing her tight jeans, furry jacket, high-heeled shoes. She fled because she was protesting integration. She hailed a truck, the drivers had been civil, no lewd remarks. But when they stopped for an overnight stay at Gila Bend, she became frightened, left Nancy in Nancy/Sherry's high-heeled shoes. Nancy walked to a phone booth, called me. I advised her to pay for her own room—she said Nancy/Sherry had taken money with her—stay overnight, then call her mother the next day to come and get her, all of which she did.

"Shall we go to work?" Harold asked.

"I'm not sure what we're working on," I said.

"I never have been," Harold retorted. We all laughed.

"What do you suggest, Clint?" Diane asked.

Before he could answer Nancy jested, "Shall we pull a name out of a hat?" We laughed again. There *were* moments of merriment in this most serious of psychic pursuits.

"Not deferring to Clint for the moment, I think we ought to get hold of Sarah," Harold said.

Clint agreed, "She's always briefed us well."

A new personality had come into the picture during April named Julie-Renee. I explained to Clint, who did not know her, "Whenever Nancy has trouble with vision, Julie-Renee seems blind."

Nancy asked, "How long has Julie-Renee been here?"

"She does not know, Sarah does not know, therefore we do not know," I said.

"Sounds like a lot of things we don't know," Nancy commented.

Then Harold asked, "Where the hell did Julie-Renee come from?"

"I don't even want to think about it," Nancy said emphatically.

Harold addressed Clint. "I'm looking forward to meeting Julie-Renee. She sounds like an interesting personality."

Nancy said, "I went to talk to George today. It was very frustrating, the relationship is really cold. George would hardly speak. He came out of the restaurant kitchen and said he didn't want to see me. I told him I would be leaving next week for Kentucky and might be gone some time. All he said was 'Okay, okay, whatever.' He didn't seem upset, he just didn't seem to care. I also talked to my boss at the restaurant, he said he was sorry to see me go and when I come back my job will be waiting."

"I imagine George was hurt," Diane said.

"I'm sure of that," Nancy said. "But he scares me. Sometimes he's a stranger. I don't seem able to communicate with him."

"We want to reach Sarah," I said. "Are you ready, Nancy?"

"I'm ready." She settled back in the comfortable chair.

We went through the "Zenith, Zero" procedure, Sarah emerged within two minutes. I asked, "So what is new?"

"There's a lot of inner turmoil," she reported. "I feel more and more that Nancy needs to leave for Kentucky as soon as possible. She's still battling her mother on how she's going to go. She wants, as she has from the first, to get on a plane by herself, which I think would be the wisest thing. But her mother insists on driving her there and Nancy has difficulty, as we know, asserting herself, especially with her mother."

Harold interrupted. "Excuse a slight digression. It has to do with Sherry's relationship. Sarah, you told me that Sherry was very, very good as a prostitute. That she'd never had a complaint from the customers. Is that correct?"

"She'd boast about that, yes."

"Never a complaint?"

"I don't know whether men file complaints." A smile. "But her customers, except for the one truck driver who tried to kill her, never said a word. She was building a clientele, regulars, and had her own way of pleasing them, make them satisfied."

"Thank you, Sarah. Glad you're back in the picture."

I asked, "Was Sherry out last night?"

"No, she was not. Jim called Nancy at about quarter to one in the morning. She told him she could not see him any more and was leaving Ontario. There was no way that she was going to have any more contact with him. At that point she was shaking but very serious about her decision."

Harold asked, "Sarah, is what we've been doing all in vain?"

Nancy/Sarah and I chorused, "No!"

I added, "It's all inside her now. This is Nancy against Nancy, I think."

Nancy/Sarah bore me out. "There's a tremendous struggle going on. Nancy's had to battle many things. Anything related to her as a human being, you might say."

I listened to what Nancy was telling me about herself. That she felt being alive was constant conflict, that nothing had ever felt pleasurable or acceptable.

I said, "Just think of the pressure we're putting on her. She will be leaving all of us to settle far from home. To try for the first time existing on her own. Living with strangers, getting therapy from a stranger. She must feel terrified."

Nancy/Sarah commented, "And she knew when talking to Jim last night that she would not and could not go back to her old life. She's got to find out what lies in Kentucky."

Amen, I thought. More of the battle won. Nancy was willing to risk parting from her mother, almost our whole country between them.

Nancy/Sarah reported, "John got high."

"What did he take?" I asked.

"I don't know, Mrs. Campbell. I am totally unfamiliar with drugs. Whatever it was, they took it together, he and Nancy. When he takes drugs, she takes drugs."

I said, "John takes anything he can get hold of. He takes uppers, he takes downers, he takes speed, he has been known to take heroin, angel dust. Anything he can buy."

Clint asked, "Do the drugs affect each personality differently, Sarah?"

"Yes. If Sherry drinks, I feel a little numb, Sherry will feel fantastic and Nancy will feel half-sick to death. I don't know how it affects Jennifer but we all feel it to different degrees. John feels pretty good on drugs, seems able to cope with the highs. Nancy gets paranoid. Sherry gets angry and I think this makes her a little clearer in the head."

Then Nancy/Sarah warned, "I think when Nancy goes to Kentucky there will be a drug problem as severe as here. Nancy is being pulled from both ways—toward and away from drugs."

Nancy is warning us what lies ahead, I thought. But we cannot stop her now, perhaps something beneficial will come out of the Kentucky experiment.

Diane asked a question we all wanted to ask, "Why is it, Sarah, that Nancy can't talk to Emily or us or anybody and tell how she feels? She always says everything's fine. When she says this I know it's absolutely at its worst."

"I think she's pretty honest with you all along," Nancy/Sarah said. "I think she's so used to putting on a smile because she's afraid if she doesn't the world will fall apart. I think she's learning that's not necessarily so but she's still working this through. She's not confident about her feelings. I don't mean that feelings have to be appropriate but Nancy seems to feel they do."

Bravo, Nancy/Sarah, I thought once again, you are right on the psychic beam.

Diane asked, "What has been her anxiety about leaving?"

Harold answered. "She talked about this last night with me. She's terribly afraid she will miss all of us and that Emily will be away a long time, so there will be nobody to comfort her."

I had planned to take a trip to Europe with my husband, our third visit abroad. For us it would be the last chance to decide whether to make our marriage work or divorce.

"Nancy's fears are very legitimate," I said.

"I told her I had to face the same thing when I left New York," Harold went on. "I was in a state of terror. I was leaving for a whole new life three thousand miles away. And that's what Nancy will be doing, the only difference, two thousand two hundred miles away."

Clint asked, "What does Nancy's mother really think about Nancy going to Kentucky?"

"She's being outwardly very supportive," Nancy/Sarah answered. "She has tried to make it as easy for Nancy as possible. Her mother has said, 'I will find a way to get you to Kentucky.' She has worked five days a week on the graveyard shift as a waitress, banking every dime so that Nancy can reach Lexington. She has contacted the doctor there, she has been very effective. All along she has done far better than I would have expected."

We remained silent, listening to Nancy/Sarah. "This has been difficult for her mother because she is very close to Nancy and in some ways dependent on her. Nancy feels she now needs to be independent, she is twenty-one years old and has never lived on her own. She has told her mother she needs to live alone. And her mother said, 'When I was your age that was how I felt and I can understand and while it's hard for me I will help you do it.' "

Harold commented, "But on the other hand, Sarah, her mother turns right around and insists on driving Nancy to Kentucky instead of letting her go alone as she wants to do."

"I think that's between Nancy and her mother," Nancy/Sarah said. "Allowing each other that much room. Nancy says, 'Okay, you can come with me and help me get set up and then you will be able to accept my leaving.' And her mother is saying, 'I know this is going to be hard on you and Kentucky is not going to be the paradise you think it will be so I will go with you and help all I can and then leave.' "

Nancy/Sarah added, "Once Nancy gets to Kentucky, this will be the first real and complete break from her mother. Nancy's mother is not particularly prone to a stable environment. I think she'll find a place for herself when she comes back. That will give Nancy and her mother room to grow. They have held each other back in different ways. With dependency on both parts. And possession on both parts. Nancy's mother comes from an extremely loyal family. I've seen several members of her family through Nancy and it's the same with every member."

I had to remind myself this was Nancy talking about her mother as she would never have dared before therapy, nor still dared except under the guise of one of her personalities.

Diane said, "They're a close-knit family and have no friends."

"Nancy's mother does have acquaintances and she's popular on the job," Nancy/Sarah said. "But her children are her life. Particularly now that there's just Timmy and Nancy. So with Nancy leaving this is difficult for her. Nancy's dreading the moment her mother has to say goodbye. Her mother has told her she *will* break down. But she'll get past it."

"That's a pretty common thing when mothers and daughters part," Harold said.

"Nancy will break down *after* her mother leaves," Nancy/Sarah predicted. "And then she'll be fine once she's familiar with her surroundings and confident about her environment."

Harold commented, "Nancy makes friends very easily. There's something about her that's warm. You have it, too, Sarah."

"Thank you." A faint smile.

I thought of Nancy's mother telling me that *her* mother hated her. If a child senses such hatred the child will have little self-esteem. A child's self-esteem flows from the esteem a parent feels for the child.

Diane asked Nancy/Sarah, "What is happening with Julie-Renee?"

"Remember that she first came out when Nancy bought drugs from Jim and couldn't handle it. But as much as Nancy has been under tension recently, she's only taken drugs once, about a week ago. She felt guilty and paranoid because she really does not want to be high. But she was feeling a lot of pressure and looking for an escape. This new personality, named Julie-Renee, was created when Jerry died and Nancy could not handle her feelings."

"What is Julie-Renee like?" Harold asked.

"I sense a lot of anger in her. Certainly confusion. At first she was blind, though she has been able to see at times. She is searching almost desperately for some clue to her identity."

I asked, "Sarah, what would you suggest we do to help Nancy feel more at ease, since she's leaving in a few days?"

"I think you should meet Julie-Renee and tell her what lies ahead. I believe she's going to be around a *lot.*"

"What about Sherry? And what about John?" I asked worriedly.

"I think Sherry is still upset over what happened between her and George but I don't feel she's a threat. She may decide to have an occasional fling but she's not going to be turning four or five tricks every night. I think she's content to work this out on her own. She never has been a dependent person."

"How about John?" I persisted.

"I don't see there's anything we can do with him."

I turned to Clint. "Dr. Johnson, do you have suggestions?"

In his measured, genial voice, Clint said, "First, review the facts and see how the plans of battle and strategy are shaping up, though in a sense we've been doing that. I would also like to be sure that Wednesday is the day of the planned departure."

"D-day," Harold said.

Clint repeated, "D-day. The day Nancy and her mother are set to leave."

Harold said, "I would like very much to meet Julie-Renee."

"She should know she's going to Kentucky," Sarah advised. "She is actually pretty stable. She's not a drug addict or unhappy or angry. She seems to have a normal range of emotions. I picked up that her anger was merely frustration at being temporarily blind. I suggest you tell her a few things that might keep her from getting into trouble. I don't think she would try to do anything that would get her arrested. Though John might."

"I think that's a good possibility," I sadly agreed.

"There are bad parts in every city, Mrs. Campbell," Nancy/Sarah said. "Maybe if John knows you're behind him that would stop him."

"I think we should meet Julie-Renee at this time," I suggested, thinking, Why run away from a possible enemy you might convert to a friend?

I started the "Zenith, Zero" induction with a countdown to ten, calling for Nancy/Julie-Renee. Nancy/Sarah's perfect posture suddenly changed to a slump, a blank look took over her face, her eyes glazed, unseeing.

I asked, "Julie-Renee? This is Emily Campbell."

The face remained expressionless. I said to the group, "I think she cannot see."

The mouth opened, a cold voice asked, "Where am I?"

"In our home," Harold said.

"Who's *that?*" Again the chilling voice, this time with cynicism.

"That's Harold Gaffney," I explained. "He's a friend of Nancy's."

"One of the spirits?"

"No. Not one of the spirits."

"Where *is* Nancy?"

"You and she seem to be trading off. About who's going to see and who's blind," I said.

"How did I get here?"

"Nancy was here first. Then I called for you. We wanted to talk to you."

"Some really weird stuff's been happening, man. Really crazy."

"Such as what?"

"Like sometimes I can see and sometimes I can't." Accusingly, "Do you know anything about that?"

"The same thing is happening to Nancy at times. I don't know why. I can't explain it."

"Could it be because you guys are giving me drugs to make me forget the bad vibes? You're making me have amnesia. You're making me not be able to see."

"We are not doing it, Julie-Renee," I assured her. "We do not have anything to do with drugs. If drugs are involved it's one of the other personalities in your body. Nancy is just as upset about the blindness as you are."

"You mean one of these spirits doesn't know anything, either?"

"Nobody really understands very well what's happening," I said. "There is a doctor in another part of the country who has had some experience with people in the same position as Nancy. She wants to see that doctor to find out what has been happening to her. She will travel there in a car with her mother."

"Am I gonna be drugged during this trip?"

"No," I assured her.

"Am I gonna remember everything?"

"You will remember *only* when you are out. That's apparently how it works for you. Only when you are able to see and hear."

Nancy/Julie-Renee said in exasperation, "I've been trying to understand this. And it still doesn't make sense. Except one time when somebody must have given me too much of something."

"There's a boy personality who takes drugs and the last time he took drugs you felt it," I explained.

Harold asked, "Julie-Renee, how old are you?"

"Twenty-one."

This was Nancy's age, I thought, so perhaps we had a fairly mature personality who would help out in Kentucky. Though she sounded at times like Sherry with a Pollyanna twist.

"Do you know how to drive a car, Julie-Renee?" Diane asked.

"I don't know. I don't remember ever having driven a car."

I said, "There is a possibility that while Nancy is in the car driving to Kentucky you may appear while her mother is with her. I want you to be prepared for that. Her mother will be somebody you don't know."

"Doesn't appear like I know anybody."

"That's true," I agreed.

Diane assured her, "There is a possibility that as you talk to us, your sight will return."

"Well, if you can control that, I would appreciate it." Sarcasm.

"It's not a matter of control, it seems the blindness comes in phases and goes in phases, both for you and Nancy," Diane explained. "Nancy is terrified. She doesn't know what to do. She just lies in her bed. She has missed work because of the blindness. It's very upsetting to her."

"When Nancy came tonight she drove her car and *she* saw," I said. "But she also has been blind in the last day or so."

I wondered whether it was the result of drugs, medication or a psychosomatic symptom—her wish *not* to see—to prevent her from embarking on her emotionally dangerous trip.

Nancy/Julie-Renee was indignant. "*She* saw? And then you guys bring me and I *can't* see. And you say you have nothing to do with that?"

"We cannot make Nancy see or not see," I said.

"Do people know you're doing this?"

"The doctor in Kentucky has been informed of the blindness," I said. "You will probably meet him."

Diane changed the subject. "Julie-Renee, there was an article in the newspaper recently about the work we are doing that went all over the world. We have a copy. You can read it and maybe it'll help you understand."

"When you get your sight back," I added.

"So the *world* knows that you're doing this to me." Still the fury. Then she asked, "How many people would believe a crazy story like this?"

"Not too many," I agreed. "It is a *very* difficult thing to believe."

"You *didn't* drug me?"

"No. One of the personalities who live inside Nancy's body took drugs."

She complained, "I don't know how I get places. All of a sudden I'm there. And I can't see and I don't have any memory."

"Sometimes you can see."

"Maybe if I was just blind I could understand. But where's my memory? Am I supposed to be kept in the dark about what's going on?"

"No, that's why we wanted to talk to you. To let you know what's happening," Diane said.

I explained, "Julie-Renee, just now when you are blind, Nancy can see. When you can see, Nancy seems blind. You two are switching back and forth."

Harold said, "Emily, may I suggest this might be a form of hysterical blindness that comes and goes."

Nancy/Julie-Renee repeated her charge. "You seem to have a lot of control, all of you."

Clint came to our rescue. "We have the possibility of some degree of control but we have not been controlling you in any way, Julie-Renee. All we have done is call you out tonight."

"I don't seem to know anything. Just blank memory. How can this Nancy do such a thing?"

"She doesn't know she's doing it," I said. "She wonders if you're doing it to her."

"How can I do it to her? I don't even know who she is."

"She doesn't know you either. She's quite upset."

Diane said, "We feel confident this doctor in Kentucky can help you."

"Help me how?"

"Help you understand what's happening and help you to see and possibly—"

"To remember," I put in.

"You seem to remember more about me than I do," Nancy/Julie-Renee snapped.

Harold explained, "We know more about Nancy than you do. I think you're a part of Nancy."

"So I'm not even really a person. Is that what you're saying?" Accusingly.

Harold turned to Clint, asked, "Would you care to take a whirl at that?"

Clint addressed Nancy/Julie-Renee. "Emily spoke of several spirits, to use your word. Several different personalities occupying the same body. All sharing the body that is yours. At this time. But later on, your body will be dominated by Nancy's spirit and you will not remember for a time what's happened to Nancy. We hope that when you go to

Kentucky, the doctor there will help put it all together so you can remember and be aware of Nancy and Sarah and John and Sherry."

"Which one takes the drugs?" Worriedly.

"Nancy takes a prescription drug to keep up her energy so she can work at night as a waitress," I explained. "It's a very strong drug and we're quite upset about it."

"What happens to her is very cruel," Diane commented. "The other personalities take up her sleeping time, wherever she happens to live. At first it was at her mother's home in Los Angeles. Then a number of mental hospitals. Then here with us. And now in her own apartment. She doesn't get her sleep and then she can't function. So the drug helps her to keep going. She has to work to eat. Most people don't eat if they don't work."

Nancy/Julie-Renee said, "I don't think it's normal for people to take pills in order to work."

"You're right, Julie-Renee," I agreed. "But you must remember Nancy gets no rest because of other people like John or Sherry."

"And the boy takes drugs?" Disapproval in the voice that was, however, warming up.

I explained, "He likes the feeling of getting high. Nancy takes the prescription drug to survive."

The combination of the two might be enough to kill her, I thought, if John resorted to drugs in Lexington, should living become too painful for Nancy.

"Nancy has a problem also in keeping her energy level up because of her stomach ulcer," Diane said. "She vomits a great deal."

"We have the same stomach?" Nancy/Julie-Renee asked in alarm.

"Some of you may. But apparently the others have no stomach problems. Only Nancy. She can't keep food down at times and doesn't get proper nourishment."

"How many other people are there?"

"There's Nancy and you and four others, now. Most of them are integrated—no longer in evidence," I explained. "Which means they won't come back."

I was to prove a poor prophet as far as the Kentucky trip was concerned.

Nancy/Julie-Renee asked, "How does Nancy feel about me being here?"

"Very upset," I said.

"She probably thinks I'm somebody else. Like I think she's somebody else."

"I think she is beginning to understand everybody is a part of the same person, though," I explained.

This was the heart of the therapy, I thought. Once Nancy accepted that all the personalities *were* her, the battle would be well on its way to victory. There had to be a fusion, the personalities would not disappear, they would always be part of Nancy but she would be in control of her impulses—as much as any of us are.

Diane asked, "Do you have any prior memory at all, Julie-Renee?"

"I just know I've been here for a long time and that I must have gone to school somewhere. I must have learned how to talk. I must know *somebody*. I must have parents and a home. But I don't remember people or places. I know what cigarettes are and what food is. Though I must seem retarded, that I don't know anything."

"You're sharp as a steel trap, sweetheart," Harold said. "You know anything about sex?" His way of trying to relieve her anxiety.

"I know what it is but I don't remember ever having it," Then she asked, "Do I turn into a boy, like this John?"

"With John, the body is still Nancy's body, that of a woman," I explained. "Only when John thinks of himself he experiences himself as a boy. He looks just like you but when he moves, he moves like a boy. He likes to throw footballs and fix cars. He does boy things."

"And you're his friend?"

"He is like my adopted son and I am like his adopted mother. Nancy is the only one who has a mother. Jennifer also adopted me."

Clint said to Nancy/Julie-Renee, "We first became aware of you through a dream Nancy had."

"So I'm a dream?" Again the sarcasm.

"No," I said. "She dreamed *about* you."

"I know that I'm a real person but I wouldn't know how to convince anybody about that."

"You don't have to," I said.

"How can you tell the spirits apart?" she asked. "We all look the same."

"You all act very differently," I pointed out.

Clint explained, "Even though you're in the same body, your appearance, your voice, your handwriting, your movements, are all very different. Different ways of holding your head. Of wearing your hair."

"If John walked into the room you would know it wasn't me?"

We all chorused, "Yes."

"There's six of us now that—what do you call it?"

"Come out and take time," I said. "Apparently no one of you can come and stay the whole time. It sounds like you get tired of controlling what goes on and that gives someone else a chance to come."

"How long have I been this way?" A hint of sadness in her voice.

"We don't know."

Diane said, "We believe Nancy has had separate personalities because of some terrible trauma in her early life. Sarah came when Nancy was eleven and flunking her classes. Jennifer and John were born when Nancy was raped at fifteen."

Nancy/Julie-Renee commented, "Sounds like Nancy's had a lot of bad experiences."

"You can say that again," boomed Harold's deep voice.

"And everyone wants to go to Kentucky? They believe this doctor will help us?"

I answered, "Sarah does. Sherry does. I think even John does. I know Nancy does."

Harold asked Nancy/Julie-Renee, "The question is, Do you want to go to Kentucky to get help?"

Without a moment's hesitation she replied, "If that doctor can help me to remember and know and understand, yes, I would go."

Clint explained, "He is supposed to have had much experience with multiple personalities. The intent of the people in Lexington is to help the multiples recall and understand."

"Is this a physical thing?"

"No. It's emotional and mental. The doctors there are psychiatrists and psychologists."

Harold pleaded, "Julie, please trust our judgment. And try to be patient. Will you do that?"

"I guess I have to."

Then she asked, "When will I see you again?"

"I am quite certain you will see us soon," Harold said. "I think you're very lonely and very frightened, young lady, and I don't blame you one bit."

"I'd just like to understand, that's all."

"So do we. We want answers and you want answers."

"I want to know why I'm here one minute and I'm not here the next."

"The others have gone through it enough so they are used to it," I explained. "They know they will come back even if they are gone for a while."

"Can they all talk to each other?"

"No. But they can observe what the person who is out is doing."

"I don't understand." Puzzled expression on her face as her lips twisted.

"For instance, as we talk, Sarah is close to the surface and knows what you and I are saying to each other."

"You mean she can hear when she's not present?" A startled expression now, the eyelids quivered over the blank eyes.

"Yes."

"But I cannot do that?"

"Apparently you can't. Maybe you haven't learned how yet. Nancy has never done it. You cannot hear or observe the others. You and Nancy are the only two who cannot. The others don't do it all the time though it's possible they could. If one of them gets into trouble, someone else will come out to help."

Nancy/Julie-Renee asked, "Will there be a person in Kentucky who will know me? A doctor who won't think I'm crazy?"

"He won't think you're crazy," I assured her. "He knows about the situation, knows it's real." Then I asked Clint and Harold, "I think the doctor's a 'he' though I'm not sure—do you know?"

Clint replied, "The first name is 'Kim' so we're really not sure either. Kim Larmore."

Harold asked, "Julie-Renee, you have seen before, have you not?"

"Yes."

"You will see again, then. You may count on that."

"Do the other people see now?"

"They see almost all the time. Carmen was blind for the first few times we met her. Until Emily broke through to her."

Harold turned to Clint, said, "Emily didn't know that you can't break through to a catatonic, cataleptic, deaf and blind person. And because Emily didn't know, she went ahead and broke through." He chuckled.

Clint commented, "Emily wasn't handicapped by knowing too much."

Harold explained to Nancy/Julie-Renee, "Emily did not know what she wanted to do was impossible so she just plunged in and did it."

I said to her, "Though Carmen seemed out of it and did not know anything that went on around her, the human mind is always working. Awake or asleep."

"Even when you are not consciously aware of what's happening?" she asked.

"Right." Then I said, "I would like to speak to Sarah for a moment. Would you help me do that?"

"Sure," she said.

"I'm going to see if I can call Sarah without hypnosis. One way you might help is to squeeze my hand. Concentrate on squeezing my hand and think *only* about that."

"All right." She took my hand.

"And while you're concentrating, I would like to talk to Sarah. I would like Sarah to come and talk to me. If you can, Sarah. If you can, I would like you to come and talk to me, Sarah."

Nancy/Sarah emerged swiftly, settled with her elegant posture in the chair. She answered, without needing to be asked, "I *was* observing. Seems as though Julie-Renee is settling down some."

"She believes, I think, what we're telling her," I said. "Things she never believed could happen."

Harold asked, "How do you feel right now, Sarah? Do you feel tired?"

"Not really. Julie-Renee was not very draining. Like Jennifer. Or John. Or as sometimes Nancy is. What was *your* impression of her?"

Harold said, "I like her. She's bright, she's logical. She's very patient. That's one thing blind people have to learn—patience."

Nancy/Sarah asked me, "Would you like to bring John now or later?"

"I don't know." I turned to the others. "What do you think?"

Harold said, "It's eleven P.M. I don't see anything would be gained by talking to him because his promises aren't worth a hoot in hell."

Diane addressed her husband. "That's not necessarily true, honey. And, let's face it, I think John really has something strong to fight against."

Harold answered, "I got news. He's a hype and I have no use for hypes. Sorry. Their promises are absolutely worthless."

Clint said, with humor, "Harold, you are maligning the meat of my profession." He treated drug addicts.

Harold changed the subject, indicating the night's work was over, by asking, "Are you all aware of the fact that once there was a $25,000 contract on my head?"

"What do you mean?" Clint asked.

"I was working part-time in a hospital in New York City and we were successfully breaking drug addictions of as much as $200 a day through hypnosis. Suddenly I get a couple of phone calls warning me to knock it off. Then I am informed it is all over the street that there is an open contract on my head for $25,000. Some of the peddlers didn't like losing their girls who were giving up their addictions because of my treatment. I also get news the peddlers play it rough. So I'm a little bit jaundiced in my attitude to hypes. I had to leave New York. That's when I came to Southern California."

Clint said, "In other words you were salvaging the street hypes and the *dealers* were being hurt."

"Well, when a guy gets a couple of girls prostituting for him and all of a sudden loses them, he can't support his habit. And the underworld plays rough."

Diane asked us, "What do you want to do now?"

I said, "I feel quite fatigued. I was fatigued when I arrived at seven."

"Is Nancy planning on working right up to the night she leaves?" Sarah asked.

"She told me she was leaving at five in the morning on Wednesday," Harold said. "Knowing her, she'll get off the job and into the car and start driving. With the pills in her purse, she can do it."

Nancy/Sarah said hopefully, "I think in Lexington Nancy can get along very well without the drugs because she has done well without them for a long time. She's not a drug addict today."

"Unless there is special pressure," I said.

And there would be special pressure, that I knew, connected to the Lexington trip. In one way, more pressure than Nancy had known since the hour we met, for now she was completely on her own. I hoped because of the help we had given she could overcome the odds against her without suffering a setback.

Four days later she was on her way to Kentucky in her car, accompanied by her mother. The day they left Ontario, the words that rang in my ears over and over were those of John when he broke down. His frantic plea, "Don't leave! Don't leave me!" His fear and tears, his shaking and moaning. He had felt abandoned, annihilated at the thought I would no longer be near. The Atlantic Ocean and the continent of Europe would soon separate us and the span of the United States would separate him from Diane, Harold and Clint.

With all my heart I hoped Nancy had the strength to survive the separation. Find in the bluegrass country new awareness of her inner self.

Nancy did not know one person in Lexington. She would arrive certain only of seeing a psychiatrist who had promised to treat her, Dr. Kim Larmore.

She phoned the day after she arrived to tell me she and her mother had driven to Cleveland, stayed two nights with her grandmother, then headed south for Lexington. Arriving in the evening they checked into a motel. Harold's friend, the allergist, had found Nancy a furnished apartment and her mother helped her settle in. Later they drove around the city. Nancy then took her mother to the bus stop, watched as the bus headed for California. Her mother had decided not to subject herself to the torment of flying.

Nancy wrote on May 15, giving her address as 1670 Alexandria Drive, Apartment 7, Lexington, Kentucky, 40504:

> Dearest Mrs. Campbell,
> Hi. I've really been busy for the past couple of days, do-ing a lot of work on my furnished apartment. It is about half a mile from Dr. Wilbur's office, a big old house on top of a hill, surrounded by big trees. It has stone walls on both sides of the driveway leading up to the house. Really spooky. (I'll send you a picture as soon as I have it developed.)
> Lexington is beautiful. It's all country, farms and horses. I never saw such green grass or open space or blue skies. All the houses in the residential area are made of red brick, and most have at least two chimneys. They look like mansions. When I drive, I have to be *very careful;* most of the streets are *one way.* I found out the *hard way.* The names of the stores are different, too. There's the "Hinky Dinky Gro-cery," "Kroegers," "A & P" and "Winn Dixie," among others.
> Everyone here tells me I talk with an accent. I didn't want to say anything but they have one, too. There is a part of Lexington that looks like East LA but I guess every city has that. Only this part is called "Cheapside." I got lost in it and didn't like it very much. I have yet to see any Mexicans or Orientals but there are many black people here. Most of Lexington looks very rich, the houses are bigger than most apartment complexes back home. The names of the streets are different, too. Many of them have quaint names like

"Cross Keys Road," "Mockingbird Lane," "Blueberry Road" "Cricklewood Drive." Mine isn't that original but it *is* close to town.

I won't know my phone number until Thursday (that was how I got lost in "Cheapside," trying to find the stupid telephone company). It stays light here until after 9:00. Everything is strange here. I'll get used to it, I guess. I'll never get used to the quiet though.

It really helps me to think of you and the Gaffneys. Believe me, that's all I ever think about. I'm a stranger here so I can't help but think of home. I'm coming home as fast as I can get "well." I hope the progress here is as fast as it was there. I have lost time here, mostly at night. I think, from the clothes, that it must be John, but there have been no signs of any drugs.

I am constantly wondering how you are and hoping very much that everything is o.k. for you. There is a hollow emptyness inside. I miss you more than I can say.

Love,
Nancy,

A second letter from Nancy arrived shortly after:

Papasan [Harold Gaffney] called me today. It really is good to talk to him. He sounds as though he is feeling better than he was when I left. I am very relieved; I love him and it worries me when he doesn't feel well because I learned when I lived with him that by the time you knew he didn't feel well, he was *very* sick. He really is a wonderful person. Both he and Diane are always helping others. I think of all they have done for me and it sometimes overwhelms me. Just as you do. I really am a very lucky person.

Everything here is fine. I hate it but I'll get over this. One of these mornings I'll wake up and just *love* it to death, I'm sure. I'll think it's the only place on earth and I'll wonder why I didn't come here when I was born. Yes, it will be wonderful. . . .

I talked to my grandmother in Cleveland. That was funny, too. She said maybe if everything goes well Thursday at the doctor's, I'll be on my way home Friday. Yeah, sure, I can just see it. "Here, drink this, you'll feel much better." Instant cure! I'm optimistic but not *that* optimistic! I couldn't make her understand that there is a little more to it than that. I finally gave up. But she really is a character.

It's almost the end of the school year, so hang in there! I'll bet you're really looking forward to summer. I hope you enjoy your trip to Europe. I know you'll take joy in the beauty you see. My first appointment with the doctor is the day after tomorrow. I'm a nervous wreck, I sure hope that he can help. He must know what he's doing. I am also going to be meeting with Dr. Wilbur. Now that really makes me nervous. Somehow I keep expecting her to look and act like Joanne Woodward. I'll be so glad when the first session is over.

Good grief, I'm rambling on and on. It's almost 3:00 in the morning, so I guess I'd better try to get some sleep or I'll go around like a zombie tomorrow. I just had to write to you, sort of like talk to you, even if I don't have anything new to say. I just miss you, and wish you were here or I were there. I can't believe I've only been away from you 12 days. Feels like 2 months. You told me one time that I would survive without you. I'm trying, really I am. But I wasn't kidding when I said that I love you more than anyone in the whole world. I don't trust anyone like I trust you. I keep telling myself, "You'll get used to Kentucky, Gooch." One of these days I'll listen to myself. In the meantime, I'll have to settle for writing wacky letters to you, and you'll have to read them!

I love you so very much.

                                Nancy

Nancy's ambivalence was evident. First she said everything was "fine," then in the next sentence, "I hate it but I'll get over this. One of these mornings I'll wake up and just *love* it to death, I'm sure." She was trying to look on the sunny side, hope she could overcome her loneliness and fear. I did not feel too alarmed, at least she was examining her feelings and admitting both the love and the hate.

She also told me unabashedly she loved me more than anyone "in the whole world," that she missed me and wished I were there and she would try to survive without me. I hoped as desperately as she did that she would.

About this time Nancy/Sarah wrote Diane and Harold:

> I thought perhaps it might be time for a progress report. Fortunately, there have been no major crises, for which I am

very grateful. I think the most significant development to date has been Sherry's improvement in vision. It is a gradual process, one which started even before Nancy left for Kentucky. If for some reason her integration process was not meant to be completed at a previous time, I am pleased to see her once again regain use of her sight, for her blindness was a frightening ordeal for her. I think perhaps this is due to the unavoidable interruption of her integration. I am speaking from my own opinion, of course.

John has also been out. He has done some harmless exploring and I am pleased to see that he has not attempted to seek out any drugs. He has discovered a less desirable part of town and is attracted to it, but this is most likely because he is most comfortable in this environment. He has made a friend already, a young boy in the building who likes the things John does (the more acceptable things). He left a note for Nancy saying he needed a mitt, and Nancy got one for him, so he has spent a few pleasurable hours playing catch. I am pleased. I do not anticipate any problems. I think Nancy just needs time. She misses you and Emily very much. She is frightened to be alone and away from your security.

Of course, we all miss those of you who cared for and helped us. Even John shows this in his once-again tough manner that he presents to others. I show this in my need to communicate with you and people who understand and know the others. So we all have our ways.

I will keep in touch and hope you will do the same. Please give my best to Emily and Dr. Johnson. I am hoping that all is well with you.

Sincerely,
Sarah

I received a letter from Nancy, who found a job as security guard at the Lexington airport:

I'm working at the airport full time now, 7 days a week, 8 hours a day. The job is not a hard one, or an exciting one. Haven't met a hijacker yet. I've taken away a few bullets, a few knives and a lot of toy guns. I feel like a heel taking toys from the kids; they scream bloody murder half the time. We even have to confiscate water guns filled with water. Then there is a long, complicated sheet to fill out. Brother!

It has been raining here a lot—I love the sound of it, so pleasant and comforting. But it does get cold (even for me). Will see you soon. For all you have given me, all that I can give in return is my love. Very often, that does not seem enough to me, but it is a part of myself that I have never been able to give before, and that I give to you with joy because you have earned it over and over. I'm not sure you could ever understand what you mean to me. But I know you have a fairly good idea.

I feel so shaky, mom. I know that as usual, everything will turn out o.k., but this one is a really hard hill to climb. I just hope that whatever happens you will always know that I do love you. I *do* think that you are wonderful.

Love,
Nancy

She was telling me how depressed she felt, "this one is a really hard hill to climb." She also was assuring me she loved me in spite of what she must have felt my betrayal in sending her to an alien land and alien therapist.

Then Nancy/Sarah sent a brief note:

Mrs. Campbell—
I want to wish you a wonderful trip to Europe. And to thank you for all the help you have given us with your time and efforts. It has been most valuable. And very much appreciated.

Sincerely,
Sarah
P.S. Know that whatever happens here is for the best, and for a reason. We must all know that and take hope.

I received several letters from Nancy/Jennifer, whom I had believed integrated. But Nancy evidently could not go it alone, she was in need of personalities, both old and new. She must be feeling frightened and alone in Lexington, I thought. Nancy/Jennifer scrawled, showing she had regressed to a child:

Momey John say you dont love us no mor and you dont come for us. i have a calnder i color for you to com. if i keep

collering, you will com like the doktor say. I tri not to cri or
run away so i be good. you dont forget to love me.
Jennifer

Another envelope from her contained the following:

Bos [boss] lady I am
long away plas [place]
Were be you? i look
for mi momey
can you find
her for me,
Plees, i love her.
I get los, you be nice
to me, I remember.
I tri not to cri but
be a good girl.
Jennifer

I thought sadly of Jennifer, who once told us, "I don't trust nobody.
Don't need nobody. Don't make promises to nobody." And then had
added, "Mrs. Campbell is my favorite person." Now she felt completely
abandoned.

Before I left for Europe I received a depressing letter from Nancy/
Sarah:

Dear Mrs. Campbell,
Julie-Renee has not appeared as of this writing although
I expected her one time when Nancy had difficulty with her
vision. Nancy is experiencing the most difficulty—deep
depressions and loneliness. She has not attempted to make
any friends and has even rejected attempts by others. She
hides her pain but cries herself to sleep every night.

I wrote a letter to Nancy, encouraging her not to let John lead her
into drugs. And to give Dr. Larmore a chance to help her. She wrote
back telling me Nancy/John tried to sabotage her therapy and then
wrote of a devastating experience:

Dearest Mrs. Campbell,
Yes, John did try to sabotage my therapy, simply by preventing me from showing up. [John had been coming out

and taking over, going elsewhere.] He has stopped and I
have faithfully resumed therapy at this point. Dr. Larmore
wants to see me on a daily basis and I will try to do that
because he insists that it is necessary. I'm not really in a
position to argue.

Sherry came out to help me earn money. Yesterday she
left me on her job, for some reason I am not aware of. I
suddenly found myself as a "go-go" dancer following lost
time, not knowing how I reached the club or what happened
in the lost hours. I checked my time card and found that I
still had 5 hours to go. I was frightened to be there, dressed
in only a bikini and high heels, among about 40 men. I had
never been there before. I knew my job was to dance and
drink and talk to the men. I was scared to death. I knew only
I was at the Red Lion Lounge, and that this was where
Sherry worked.

There was loud music. It seemed to vibrate from every
wall. I looked up and saw a beautiful woman on a stage,
slipping a see-through white cape off her shoulders. That
was all she had left on but by the pile of clothes on the floor
of the stage, I guessed that there had been more in the
beginning.

I looked away, embarrassed. I was even more embarrassed
to see how little I had on. A skimpy bikini, at least. And high
heels. I felt naked.

I went up to the bar. The men called out to me, offering
to buy me a drink. I kept my eyes straight ahead, and
pretended not to hear. I would have given my eyeteeth for
a full-length bathrobe right then. I asked the bartender
what time it was. 3 A.M. The time cards hung on the wall.
I found my name. 12:00—8:00. Five more hours to go? I
could never do it. But Sherry had left me. What revenge
would she take on me if I walked out? I knew she would
set me up for something worse. Visions swirled through
my head.

The bartender was talking to me.

"Hey, get a move on. You're up!"

"Up?" I followed his eyes. The naked girl was picking up
her clothes. Stepping down off the stage.

As we passed each other she said, "Hurry up! You want
to keep them waiting?"

She gave me a little push. I thought I was going to be sick,
I was so frightened. I really can't dance very well and now

I had to get up on the stage. I couldn't. . . , But something pushed me forward.

I was acutely aware of my bareness. The jukebox music started, a song that was fast and wild. I tripped on the steps going up to the stage, got my balance, managed the last two steps. The men burst into applause, yelling, "ALL RIGHT!" I felt a small courage. I even tried to smile. Tried to dance. The music reeled out too fast, God, it was hot under those lights. Somehow I kept moving.

They whistled and yelled, "Take it all off! Take it OFF, baby! Come on, SHOW US!"

I was shaking like a leaf and having a hard time keeping the tears back. I was afraid to leave because Papasan and you and Diane said to let Sherry keep the job and I didn't know what Sherry would do to me if I left.

I kept smiling, and moving. I thought the song would never end but at last it was over. I stumbled down the stairs, glad to be out from under the lights. Another song started right away. A bikini-clad girl waiting in the wings looked at me in surprise.

"Get back up there," she hissed.

Oh, no, again?

Back up the stairs . . . into the lights. I felt off balance. How could Sherry dance in these spiked high heels? The men didn't yell so much this time. I could hear the murmur of voices as I moved. I don't even think they were watching. I felt relieved but also aware of how awkward I must look. After an eternity the song ended. I walked carefully down the steps, a titter of applause rippled through the room for a second. Another bikini-clad girl brushed past me up to the stage and began to dance, throwing back her long hair. She looked like she was loving every minute of it. The men broke out in cheers and applause. My legs were trembling and I felt perspiration trickle down my neck. The same girl who had ordered me back on the stage was sitting at the table near the stage.

I walked over to her, feeling unsteady. "Bathroom?" I asked. She stared at me like she didn't understand, then said, "Around the corner."

"Thanks." If I could just get that far . . .

I collapsed on the bathroom floor, threw up. When the heaves subsided, the fears came. I thought, I will get through this . . . I will.

"Hey, hon . . . you O.K.?"

I looked up, trying to clear the dizziness. The girl who had stripped just before I went on stood above me. She now wore clothes, thank God. She didn't seem the least embarrassed. I prayed for a quick death.

"You sick or somethin'?"

I couldn't speak so I just nodded.

"I thought so. I could tell when I watched you." I wondered if everyone else knew it, too.

"You comin' down with something?"

I felt dizzy. I nodded.

"You're white as a sheet. You hurt anywhere?"

I shook my head no. Not like you think, I thought.

"You ain't gonna go home, are ya?"

I felt a flicker of hope. "Could I?"

"Look, hon. Two girls already called in sick. Try and stay, O.K.? We're workin' double as it is."

"I . . . I . . . can't dance."

"Can't dance? You gotta be kidding." She reached out and grabbed my shoulders. "You wasn't dancin' out there a few minutes ago, that's for damn sure. But you can dance. You dance like a fuckin' pro. I seen you before. You was made for dancin', girl. Can't dance? Bullshit. Look, we all got bad days. Don't sweat it. You'll be fine."

It was Sherry she had seen dancing "like a fuckin' pro," Sherry who was "made for dancin'." Not poor, scared Nancy.

Then the girl was gone, on again.

I rinsed my face with cool water, steeled what nerves were left and walked onstage to dance. Finally the dancing part was over.

I knew my job also meant sitting with the customers and get them to buy drinks. I wasn't sure if they were allowed to touch. The first guy I sat down with was fingering me all over. I finally slipped away from his table, found another. He was more respectful. He didn't keep saying, "You got a great body" or touch my legs and breasts. We talked about where I lived in California, his job as a construction worker. He said he could tell I didn't belong here, I wasn't that kind of girl. He encouraged me to continue my schooling, get a decent job. I was able to relax for the first time that evening. I knew from Sherry I had to sell a certain number of drinks, get the guys to buy them for me. This guy said his name was Andy.

Andy told me he would buy as many drinks as I needed to fill my quota so he could stay with me and I wouldn't have to go to other tables, which I was afraid to do. All those drinks, even watered down as they were, however, were taking effect. When Andy offered to take me home I thought, I guess it's O.K. He HAD been very nice and I was grateful. I dressed and we left. I gave him the best directions I could to where I was staying but I wasn't too familiar with the street names in this strange city. God, am I one stupid girl! He had no notion of taking me home as we wove in and out of streets I did not recognize. He drove for a long time and I was feeling more and more confused. Still dumb! The signs said, "Cincinnati, Ashland" and there were no more signs to Lexington. I asked nervously, "Hey, is this a joy ride?"

He stared straight ahead and said, "Yep. Now scoot over here next to me." *Dumb no longer!*

I begged him to let me out or take me back. We were in the middle of nowhere. I struggled for control because I knew if Carmen came she would not be able to defend herself. I didn't know how I was going to get out of this one. I asked him if he was going to kill me. He said not if I cooperated.

He then ordered me to do some unspeakable things to him while he was driving. It was dark and there were no cars around. I was terrified but I did what he wanted. He told me some of the things he was going to do to me. He said, "I'm going to rape you. Maybe I will kill you."

Suddenly I saw a lighted gas station, there had been just a pitch-black road for miles. I also realized he had slowed down to forty miles an hour. Another car behind was trying to pass and Andy slowed down even more.

I grabbed for the door handle, opened the door, threw myself out. I rolled to the dirt at the side of the road. I heard the squeal of brakes of the car behind. I stood up, nothing seemed hurt, so I ran for the gas station lights. I was afraid Andy might turn around and come back but he kept going.

I felt no pain but I threw up. I couldn't stop shaking. The people at the gas station, a man and his wife, were very nice, they stayed with me even though they were closing. The man grabbed his gun but the car had sped away. I survived but God knows if I deserved to. I've never done *anything* that crazy in my life. I really set myself up for that one.

I'm paying for it today. My body feels as though every bone has been broken. My feet are so chewed up I can barely walk and my legs, arms, hips and fingers are missing a lot of skin. The skin I do have left is all black and blue and purple. But you can bet I know how very, very lucky I was. I *knew* that man was going to kill me. And I didn't want to die that way. I can't even repeat the filthy things he said he was going to do to me. I've never heard of those things. I stayed awake all night. Talk about paranoid!

I'm going to be a wreck for a while. Dr. Larmore has a place where a few other multiple personalities live and he suggested I move there. So much for independence. I don't want to move but I really don't care any more. I want to survive. I want to live in this world and I'm beginning to wonder if I'm going to have to fight for that privilege. As long as I am so stupid (and fragmented too) my chances are slim. I have no one to blame but myself for what happened last night. I'm going to stick it out here, I *have* to. If I give up I'll just be signing my own death certificate. I don't *really* believe I'm indestructable! My black-and-blue body would attest to that, I'm sure.

I was so pleased to hear from you—I know you are busy since it's near the time you leave for Europe. You know my love and best wishes are always with you, as you are here with me, even though you are so far away. I keep your love safely tucked away in my heart and treasure it above all else. Please, always remember that my love for you has grown each day of my life, and always will. Take care, and be good to yourself.

All my love,

Nancy

I read with horror Nancy's account of her dangerous ride with the strange man she picked up at the Red Lion Lounge. Sherry would have been too street-wise to get in that car, especially in a strange city. Except for the trucker who had knifed her, Sherry also knew her men far better. But at least Nancy had the strength to stay, as she said, rather than letting the far more vulnerable, weaker Nancy/Jennifer or Nancy/Carmen take her place, they would have had no means of escape. The adult personalities were now protecting the children rather than abandoning them to the destructive behavior of adults.

Alarmed because of the danger Nancy put herself in, Harold, Diane and I phoned her, asked to speak to Nancy/Sarah. We told her of our fear. We suggested she speak to Nancy/Sherry, order her to give up her job at the Red Lion Lounge. We suggested Nancy/Sarah also inform Dr. Larmore of the situation and enlist his help.

I also wrote Sherry a strong letter reproving her for leaving Nancy in a dangerous spot, ordering her not to do this again, saying it would end Nancy's chances to get help in Lexington.

Shortly after, we received a tape from Lexington in which first Nancy/Sherry, then Nancy/Sarah, spoke to us long distance, so to speak, about our reprimands.

According to Nancy/Sherry:

> Shit, everybody gets all bent out of shape all of a sudden, man. I was doin' just what I said I was gonna be doin'. I was dancin'. I was tryin' to make the bucks. *Big deal.* I wasn't turnin' tricks and I wasn't strippin'. So I don't know what everyone's all in a uproar about. Really pisses me off, man.
>
> If you wanna think I'm a tramp, then you go ahead, you just think I'm a tramp. No big deal, man. I'm not even workin' at that job any more, 'cuz a fuckin' shrink [Dr. Larmore] got me fired. I said I wasn't goin' to be bringin' no one home or shit like that. I had one guy, man, *one*, his name was Jim. I wasn't acceptin' a cent from him, either. He didn't offer it and I wouldn't ask for it, have took it even if he did give it. It wasn't turnin' tricks, man. We had a relationship goin'. *Big shit!* This is just as much my apartment as it is hers [Nancy's]. Really pisses me off, man.
>
> I got this fucked up letter from Mrs. Campbell. She says, you know, if I wanna be a nothin' that nobody can respect then that's up to me. But that ain't the way I want it and that ain't the way it is. I don't know, man. You guys are just fuckin' with my head.
>
> [The sound of thunder roars over the tape, then Sherry continues:]
>
> Fuckin' lightning and thunder. Rain comin' down. Shit. Man, I don't know what to say. Alls I can tell you is I wasn't doin' shit. You guys think I'm some kind of tramp. That's up to you. But, you know, there ain't no way you can make me believe that.

[The sound of more thunder.] I don't really have a whole lot to say. You know, there ain't much worth sayin' to you. Go ahead and get pissed off. Alls I can say, man, is I try to help her [Nancy] out and everybody gets on my case. You know, like I wasn't gonna work in no fuckin' airport, like a police person, or whatever she was doin' man [Nancy's job at the time]. So I do what I want and that was what I was *good* at. I wasn't usin' no bad judgment. Nancy was the one who got in the car with the guy. I knew how to take care of myself. Can't help it if she's a dipshit. I can't be blamed for that, man.

So, anyway, I just thought I'd say adios. Goodbye, man. I don't want no more letters from ya. Or that Mrs. Campbell, or anyone. I don't care to tell you what I'm doin' 'cuz it ain't none of your business. You're gonna get on my case about it, I'm not even gonna bother. Man, I coulda been makin' good bucks. I coulda paid for her therapy all the way. But if you guys are gonna get in my way, let her do it herself.

That shrink is really fucked. I hate his guts. I hate Nancy's, too. I hate 'em all, man. I'm gonna do my own thing. You guys give me this little pat on the back like I'm doin' real good and I'm sensible, and how you can respect me and all that shit, and what do you do? You turn around and stab me in the back. I don't need it. I really don't.

[A pause, more thunder.] Can you hear that thunder, man? Shakin' the whole goddamn place. Well, I was just tryin' to do the best I could, man. I even came for your therapy or whatever you call it. Tell you one thing, a fuckin' lot more happened in Ontario. I mean it was really good. You were doin' somethin' and it was helpin' us all. And here, man, no one's gonna help no one. Ain't *shit* gonna be done. Nancy's a wreck. Jennifer's back. A lot of good this shrink's doin.' I hate his fuckin' guts. So does John. Nancy don't like him. And all of us hate each other now. That's how good he's gettin' everything together. But if that's the way everyone wants it, man, it makes no difference to me." [A pause] I wish the fuckin' lightning would quit. Makes the whole goddamn house shake, man.

I like it fine here. I ain't got no reason to come home. If that's what you call it. Not even to see George. I'm doin' real fine. I just want you guys off my back. I don't wanna hear from none 'a ya. You just write letters to Nancy and John and whoever, man, and count me out. I don't care about your respect. I don't care about any 'a that shit. Keep it. I don't need it. Anyway, man, it's cool knowin' ya.

There was a long silence as Sherry signed off. Then Nancy/Sarah's lower, far more reflective voice:

Hello, Harold and Diane. This is Sarah. I thought that since this was more or less a community tape I might add my two cents worth. I'll give you something of an updated progress report. Jennifer's back. She was very frightened and unsure of where she was, had that familiar lost feeling. She just came back today. She called Mrs. Campbell and I think she handled it very well. Jennifer calmed down as soon as she talked with her.

I'm a little sorry to see her come because if she gets into bad situations here she's not going to be close to home. But I'll keep an eye on her and do the best I can to prevent anything from happening.

John is also very active. He's been collecting drugs. Not taking them, just collecting them. He's been going down to a bad part of town and has made a few connections. He has the opportunity to deal if he wants. I think, out of everyone, he's having the most difficulty in adjusting. He feels very rejected and somehow cheated because he no longer has Mrs. Campbell. She was the best thing that had happened to him so he's in a rebellious stage. But so far has not done anything really very detrimental, although I don't like to see him go down to that part of town which he refers to as "Cheapside." He is feeling a lot of instability. That is the primary thing giving him the most difficulty.

My thought on this might be that perhaps Mrs. Campbell could make up a list of dos and don'ts for him because he's struggling with right and wrong and how far he can go, before he does something bad. He feels as though he can get the drugs but if he doesn't take them he's not doing something bad. He comes and goes in the middle of the night, he can come at any point and mess Nancy up with her therapy and her job at the airport.

I think it would be a great help to him to know that he doesn't have to make all the decisions because this has always been the difference as to whether or not he was on his own in the streets or being taken care of. He is experiencing a lot of confusion.

He has in the past seen the doctor and has been very obnoxious with him. He doesn't know whether Dr. Larmore is an authority figure for him. They passed insults back and forth. This was not a good example of John. He has been capable of handling himself and taking responsibility, as he proved at home. I think he still has some of that. But in order for it to be easier for him I think he still needs some direction to feel secure, to feel he hasn't lost his parent, Mrs. Campbell. Some of the things she might put on a list are really not important because I think he knows the differ-ence. But she might tell him that he is not permitted to go out late at night. He is not permitted in that section of town. He is not permitted to hold heroin, angel dust and acid, the drugs he's been collecting. He's not permitted to deal with Nancy's therapy. Things like this, and that he might be permitted to go down to the creek, to use Nancy's stationery or some of Nancy's paper, rather, to draw pictures. He will be permitted to walk around town—whatever she feels is best. I believe he will listen to her as he has in the past. He has abided by her decisions and respected her authority.

Here he feels he's been pushed back into the type of environment he left before he met Mrs. Campbell. This is not so. Without her, he does not know where else to go, where else he fits in. He fit into a relationship of mother and son with her, accepted her decisions. But without her here, he feels there are no consequences. I think, in many in-stances in the past, he was testing her. And her consistency proved to him that what she was saying was true. And that's where the respect came.

He needs an authority figure but I don't feel that Dr. Larmore can be that for John and there is no other relation-ship here that can provide authority for him. His basic problem is insecurity. And resentment. I don't view his behavior as particularly detrimental. But I can see that it won't be long before he starts associating with the type of people who live in the bad part of town and he won't be able to stay out of trouble. Because it's all around him and that familiar drive comes back. To be a tough little man. And he's really not. He really fit in better to the role and relation-ship he had with Mrs. Campbell than he ever did on the streets. And he recognizes that. But he feels he has no choice any more. So that's just one suggestion you might mention to her.

Sherry is coming frequently. And I know that you're aware of the job she had. It was not the best place for her to be, she was in a dangerous situation. I recognize she did well at the job, she enjoyed the job and the money was good. But I also recognize that the type of job could lead to nothing but trouble. Those men really were rough. They were not men you would associate with by choice. As I discovered.

She has not, however, been turning tricks. At the point when I talked to you, there was just this one man that she had brought home on two different occasions. She apparently did have some type of relationship going and did not accept money for the sex they had but it was still, in a sense, prostitution because the main purpose was to satisfy him and this went against what Nancy believes in. Sherry took no precautions and that point was a dangerous time. Also, it's possible he had a venereal disease. I will have to get Nancy checked out or I can do it myself if it's difficult for her. I don't think Sherry would take care of this. My point is that Sherry might do this with other men and it might be the beginning of prostitution. The man came from the night club, which is noted for its prostitution.

Sherry is very upset she was terminated from her job because she was very proud of it. But she's going to have to understand that she was endangering all of our lives when she left Nancy at the Red Lion Lounge because Nancy does not have the defenses Sherry has. Nancy is very naive, as you are probably aware. Sherry's very angry, very uncooperative at this point and Nancy is more or less being torn apart because everyone is taking out his anger on her body by doing whatever he wants with it and showing little consideration as to whether it will be helpful. Nancy was devastated to have lost her job at the airport. This is the first time she was ever terminated from a job and this was unfortunate.

John and Sherry have both met the therapist and it hasn't gotten off to a very good start. They have a lot of anger and resentment and it's taken out on the therapist and how he handles it. There's very little communication available to them. John's very defensive. And I imagine that's because the therapist is laying it on pretty heavy.

Nancy is doing as well as I think she can be expected to. She was very dependent upon the support in California and she's feeling a detachment from that and all the emotions that come with it. But she is staying and doing her best, as good as she can. She has an apathy toward the therapy and life here that really concerns me but I think she'll snap out of it. She just needs a little more time to adjust and a little more involvement in what's happening.

She doesn't feel any hope for the therapy but won't admit this to those of you in California because she feels as though she has to live up to something. She is not opening up to Dr. Larmore. Tells him that everything is fine. But she really is drifting. She has very little time because everybody's taking it. This is only the second or third time I've come out since she's been in Kentucky because I don't want to take away the few hours she has left to herself after the others have had their time. She seems to feel that it really doesn't matter any more now that she's moving into this house. She was very proud of her apartment where she had privacy and independence. But in this new place there are other people around and she only has a bedroom. She is not safe here. She really needs some type of supervision.

Two other multiple personalities live here and one lady who takes care of one of the personalities. Nancy hates the house, it's in bad shape, unkept. Very large and empty, not at all welcoming. But she intends to fix up her room. She is giving up one of the things that was good for her, being on her own. I think this is really not possible at this point.

She is discouraged and more or less existing, pretty unhappy. But this is something I expected to happen. It's difficult for her to adjust to change. And certainly her support systems in California were very strong and she relied on them quite heavily. She hasn't made any friends but I think that with time she will. My impression of Dr. Larmore is that he has a lot to offer. The therapy he has established will be adjusted somewhat to fit Nancy's particular situation. At this point, he is taking a noninterference stance, with the exception of talking to the manager at the Red Lion Lounge about Sherry and that took some pressure from Nancy because she really wasn't capable of handling it. Sherry could walk in and get her job back and it was necessary the manager understand that Sherry was only seventeen. When he learned this, he seemed to be somewhat protective of Nancy.

I felt that at first Dr. Larmore was rather apathetic but of course it takes time to get involved in therapy. I allowed for that. Nancy would sit and talk to him like he was a blank wall. Not really thinking about what she said and not really saying much. Right now, though, his primary interest is to help her, understand her, become more knowledgeable about her conditions. In the meantime Nancy is struggling on the outside with coping and therefore she feels he is ineffective. But she has always tended to be impatient.

I think Nancy just needs to give it a little more time. She was geared up for the high level, intense therapy of California where she could see the results of what was happening. Here they're not so obvious and she does not feel she is making any progress. She is also upset that Jennifer and John are back. And also there is another personality. I have no idea who this personality is, or what she's about, but Nancy is totally unable to cope with the idea of a new one. To her this means getting worse. To Dr. Larmore, it means self-expression. And I am not here to say who is right or wrong.

But this other personality has a great deal of energy. Seems to enjoy drinking but does not go for any type of extracurricular activity. She likes being alone and enjoying herself. She has a special language I have observed the past few times that she's come and I can't decode it. I don't think that it's a foreign language, I think it's a self-made-up language. She speaks it very fluently. She also speaks English and most of the time seems happy. I don't know what her function is but I will continue to observe.

Well, I will go for now. I will be in touch and keep you updated. If you have any questions, please feel free to write. And I will answer them. Do not be concerned about anything here. I think everything's going to work out. I hope that everything is well with you. And that you're happy. Please know that I miss you and that I'm thinking of you. And that we all care very much for you. And appreciate all that you've done for us. Thank you.

I felt very upset at the report of Nancy/John gathering up the drugs but had to believe Dr. Larmore would help with Nancy's conflicts. Nancy was upset Nancy/John and Nancy/Jennifer were back and so was I. She obviously needed them desperately, as well as the creation of a new personality. But I was soon to depart for a much-needed vacation in Europe, had to trust Dr. Larmore to handle the situation.

I received two more letters from Nancy. The first read:

There is a void inside of me that comes from missing you and wishing you were near. I can get used to the new city, the different ways, even the darn accent. But not the loneliness. Maybe I'll meet people and make friends but I'll always love you best. I know also that this is good, when I come home our relationship will be even better; you will know me as a whole person and a different person. Hopefully, a better person.

I'm glad you'll have a little more time for yourself, both you and I know what a strain dealing with my problem has been for you. You never quit giving, how you held up was a puzzlement to us all. I think as soon as I get into the therapy here, I'll also start putting everything that has happened together, as best as I can. It might make things easier if I can understand everything. I know it made things easier when you helped me to understand more about the others. I don't know if I can write a book or not, or even if I want to. But if I do decide to write one, I would like for you to co-write it. Certainly you know more about the others than anyone. Especially John, Jennifer and Sherry.

Mrs. Campbell, please take care of yourself and try to take it easy. I miss you and want to know that you are well and happy. And please remember that I love you very, very much. You are an important part of my life, and even long distance can't take that away from me. I will see you again someday, I know it. Please don't forget me, I need to know that you care. Because I care so much for you.

Love,
Nancy

The second letter told how Nancy/John left Nancy/Jennifer at the wheel of Nancy's car when police chased him for speeding well over the limit. When the police caught up with her, signalled her to pull over to the side of the road, she reverted to the behavior she always showed when chased by police. She screamed at the top of her lungs as though they were out to murder her. She could not produce the car license because John had not shown her where it was. The police took her first to jail, then to the psychiatric ward of a general hospital.

Nancy came as Nancy/Jennifer lay on a hospital bed and later wrote of her short stay there:

The light filtered into the windows. I had gotten through the night. The good feelings of my great accomplishment were quickly dashed as I wondered how I was going to get through the day. All night long the screams had never ceased. Didn't those people have to sleep sometime? Maybe things like sleep and bed and rest weren't part of reality in a place like this. This ward certainly had a reality of its own, totally unrelated to the world on the outside. They had put my bed in the hall right next to isolation. The nurse explained to me that was because I was a suicidal risk.

Suicide? Me? What had I done to make them think that? Sleeping pills, booze, jail, tried to hang myself? Now the hospital emergency room. John had done those things, left Jennifer in the car. Another hospital . . . O.K. Another city. Another state.

I didn't remember being brought here. I vaguely remembered a doctor trying to make me talk. But I was so sleepy. What had I said?

I went over to the nurse. She didn't look up.

"Um . . . excuse me. . . . Is there a doctor around? I need to talk to one."

"Honey, your doctor won't be able to see you until Monday."

"Monday!" What was today? Thursday?

"Now you just be a good little girl and don't you go getting yourself all upset."

"But you don't understand! I'm not supposed to be here. My doctor . . . on the outside . . . he doesn't know I'm here. He wouldn't want me here. I *can't* stay!"

"Sorry. Your doctor will be here Monday. You talk to him."

"Please . . . is there a phone around?"

She looked surprised. "Not on the ward. Besides, you don't have those privileges yet. Your doctor will have to decide what level you're on. *Monday.*"

Jesus. Even when they put you in jail, you got one phone call.

I walked across the dayroom, curled up in a chair as far away from that nurse as I could get. Not far enough. A young man was sitting in a chair, tied to it and a big pole in the center of the room, hurling bloodcurdling screams, and fighting to break the bonds that held him. No one paid any attention. I looked up at the wire on the windows.

"Don't be crazy, Gooch. You aren't going to escape." I felt overwhelmed by helplessness. The hot tears poured down my face, as I realized how hopeless it was for me to try and pretend I could fight this world. Well, the world, maybe. My life, never.

Dr. Wilbur and the police brought Nancy from the hospital to her room, after Nancy had called Dr. Larmore, asking for his help. Nancy wrote me:

> The only bad part was that because John left Jennifer at the wheel of my car, the police now want to take away my driver's license. I am going to talk to them and see if I can get it straightened out. I don't want to be trapped without a car.
>
> A boy named Hecky (one of the personalities of another multiple living in the same house) and John have struck up a relationship. One day they decided to be brave and explore the abandoned barn next door, which was forbidden. There had been trouble in that area a couple of days before and the man who lives in the house behind it told police he was going to shoot *anybody* who went near it. The police warned everyone to stay away because the guy was dead serious. Seems he had good reason but I never really got the full story.
>
> The caretaker here told me John and Hecky crawled on their bellies under bushes so they would not be seen to the abandoned barn and slipped inside. They had to prove to each other how brave they were even though both were scared to death! Their "dangerous mission" completed, they returned home for a tough game of poker. It was 9:00 at night. I'd been gone since 1:00. But really, I was O.K. I understood Hecky was lonely for a boy to play with and I'm glad to know John and him get along well. But I have a feeling they will be in one scrape after another.
>
> All else is going O.K. There have been notes hidden all over my room in a special language—can't read them. Dr. Larmore has learned from Sarah that the writer's name is

Andria. So much for progress. Jennifer was gone, John was gone, Sherry was gone. All back. And now Julie-Renee and this Andria. I can accept it all. Somehow it doesn't scare me any more.

Next day. I talked with Dr. Larmore about the driving. No dice. The police have an APB out on my car. If anyone drives it, my license will be suspended for a year. I can't believe how little I'm able to function. I can't hold a job, or keep an apartment, or drive a car. I can't even take classes here now. I have the frightening feeling I'm getting worse. And I don't even know how to fight it. (Sigh!) I'll keep trying, I guess. I think it must all be part of getting well, somehow. The policeman who helped Jennifer came by today. He scared me to death—suddenly there he was in my doorway. I looked and . . . well, he almost had Jennifer again! He was very nice and polite though.

I received a letter from the Gaffneys today. Two, in fact. I am going to write them and reassure them all will be O.K. They are wonderful people. Their close friend, Dorothy Foster, has died of a heart attack, they loved her dearly. It is hardest of all to not be with them now, when I want to comfort them. It is so sad.

I think I'll wrap up my ramblings and mail them off to you. Mostly I just wanted a chance to say hi and tell you that I love you again. Sort of took the long way around it, though. Take care, *please* have a *safe* and wonderful time in Europe.

Love,
Nancy

As I read this sad letter I had the premonition Lexington was definitely not going to be the Shangri-La for Nancy we hoped. Even though she seemed to possess the spirit to stick it out. I could only hope Dr. Larmore would help through the summer. Give her a chance to try to adjust to the loneliness and the new way of life.

It was not all hopeless. Nancy/John had been attending art classes and sent me some of his work. I was surprised by its quality. One was a portrait in pastel chalk of Nancy/Jennifer, himself and me. Another, of Nancy/Jennifer, portrayed her curled up in a chair, a sorrowful, unhappy look on her pretty face. But his note alarmed me, he had regressed in writing to a child:

Mom. This be like my best pitchur. This be you and me and Jennifer together for one mor time when I was happy most. Jennifer too. I'm sorry we did not mak you happy too. You made us happy. It was good to belong to sombody one time. You were a good mom to us. We will remember you for as long as we can. I wish we was better kids for you. I will not hurt you no mor. Bye Mom.

John

Just between us I loved you.

A second letter arrived soon after:

Mom, I will have many pitchers for you when you com back. i lik the chalke ones best. Mom i will be a good boy for you do not wory. I will tak care of jenny like i sad. I love you mom. Plese love me even if Im a bad boy sometimes. I want you to be prode of me because i belong to you. Your son for ever.

John

The day before I left Ontario bound for Europe I received a letter from Nancy/John written in far more mature fashion:

Mom, I can't say I "miss you" 'cause I've got you right with me and it's as good as the real thing. Wouldn't mind a hug, though, specially if it was just for me. I haven't gone sissy or anything, I just figure we're entitled, being related and all that. I've sort of sent hugs once in a while but being as you probably didn't know, it was from your Number 1 kid (and fan), it didn't count as much. So if you could let loose with one of your special letters I'll give you one back that'll cover any distance. Deal? With love and respect,

Your son,
John

I even received a farewell note from Nancy/Sherry:

Hey Mrs. Campbell,
Hear you're going to Europe. Have a blast. Sorry things didn't work out so we would be friends but that's

O.K. It was not so bad while it lasted. No hard feelings,
huh?

Sherry

And a final missive from Nancy. A poem:

I told them once
they turned away
of crosses to bear
of prices to pay

Look at me
at whom I am
hear my fear
understand

It's too late now
They've claimed me firm
a child is born
and in it a worm

And as I grew
they turned away
for they feared the worm
would claim its day

It burrowed deep
as it tried to hide
when it finally rose
it had multiplied

When it spoke
a voice unknown
it shuddered with hate
it uttered a moan

It cried with pain
it laughed with glee
it took what was left . . . .
of what once was me.

I empathized with the fear and pain expressed in Nancy's poem but
hoped she would lose some of it under Dr. Larmore's expert guidance.
At least she would be given the chance to benefit from the knowledge
of the Wilbur Clinic, if she could use it.

I was abroad the entire summer, traveled to a number of countries so it was not practical for anyone to write. Occasionally I sent Nancy a card or short letter, saying I hoped all was going well. I had my own conflicts to contend with. I knew if my husband and I could not somehow narrow the widening emotional gulf between us, it meant the end of our marriage. I banked on Nancy to somehow get through the summer with the help of Dr. Larmore.

THE UNDERGROUND HELL

I returned home late in August after visiting Sweden, France, Germany, Italy and Finland. I enjoyed Florence most, my home away from home. I brought Nancy and each personality a gift, they would expect it.

Before I even unpacked I phoned Diane, eager to hear the latest news of Nancy. Diane told me Nancy was still in Lexington but seemed on the verge of collapse. Diane reported the car incident and Nancy's loss of her driver's license. Without her rented car, I thought, she would be lost in the bluegrass country.

Within two weeks of my return Nancy, forlorn and defeated, called her mother, begged her to drive to Lexington and rescue her. But her mother could not take more time from her restaurant job without jeopardizing it. Diane went instead, retrieved Nancy and drove home. On the way back Nancy/John occasionally took over at the wheel.

On her return Nancy lived at the Gaffneys, knowing her stay might be limited. The Gaffneys were planning to move shortly to their new home in San Antonio del Mar. Nancy would then face living on her own.

I had returned from Europe alone. My husband, who was on sabbatical as a teacher of welding at Mount San Antonio College, planned to remain abroad until February investigating the treatment of metals by different European nations. I had not as yet fully decided to get a divorce but sensed I eventually would. I had dreams of buying a condominium in the adjacent city of Montclair, nearer to where I taught.

Perhaps I had expected the impossible of Nancy. I did not truly judge the depth of her inability to accept emotional and physical separation from us and her mother. She had always lived with her mother, staying for short times with her father, except for the weeks, sometimes months, she had spent at hospitals. Then the Gaffneys' house had been her home for five years.

Dr. Larmore had called Harold to advise that the best treatment for Nancy seemed a continuation of what we were doing. Dr. Larmore said that leaving us had thrown Nancy so off-balance she had been unable to hold a job (Nancy/Sherry deprived her of sleep), often was stoned on drugs (that Nancy/John took), became involved in the automobile accident (caused by Nancy/John) and had to spend a few days in the psychiatric ward (as Nancy/Jennifer came out).

I received a handwritten letter from Dr. Larmore which mentioned two new personalities, Nancy/Andria and Nancy/Laureal. One would prove essential to the eventual freeing of Nancy from her horror-stricken past. Dr. Larmore wrote:

> Dear Mrs. Campbell,
> I have been reviewing in my mind that almost all of the work done here in Kentucky [with Nancy] has been toward (1) the development of rapport, a feeling of safety with myself and (2) teaching them [the multiple personalities], especially thru Laureal and Sarah, that there are common denominators and principles to understanding multiplicity and its treatment. This has been to hopefully give them more hope for the future and to advise them of the necessary steps toward inner communication and cooperation that must precede more definitive adaptation, i.e. the therapy for Andria.
> Your external co-therapist is Sarah. You need to make contact with an inner co-therapist, Laureal, when that is permitted.
> I am enclosing a copy of a bibliography you may find useful, along with a paper.
> > Best wishes,
> > > Kim Larmore

I was happy to hear I now had an inner co-therapist, I could use one. Nancy/Sarah, as external co-therapist, as usual had been the true prophet when she predicted Nancy/John would not integrate in Lexington but return to drugs because Nancy, as she had put it, "needed to escape more in the way Nancy/John did" to overcome her pain at the separation from us. Now a note from Nancy/Sarah reassured:

> Dear Mrs. Campbell,
> I see many positive things happened. The general feeling level inside leads me to believe you are handling each situation in the best possible manner. My only concern is for John and our control of his drug abuse and his associations. I am so very pleased to have you and the Gaffneys working with us again. Thank you.
> > Sarah

We had decided to swing back into action as a team on September 20, to meet again on Thursday nights at the Gaffneys until they left. To become acquainted with, as Dr. Larmore suggested, the new personalities who had come out in Lexington.

I started off reporting, "I had a long talk on the phone with Dr. Larmore. He tells me Laureal listens all the time, like Sarah does. That even if she does not appear, she can hear what I say to her or what anyone says to her."

"That's interesting," Harold commented.

"It seems that, for all intents and purposes, I am again in charge of therapy. When I asked Dr. Larmore what I should do, he told me to ask for Laureal's help. He said she would fill me in about Kentucky and what has happened since. I suppose Andria, who I hope is listening, will agree."

Laureal, who first came out in Kentucky, had stayed within many years, able to observe at all times, as Nancy/Sarah did, and to come and go at will. Nancy described her as seventeen, friendly, considerate in manner, objective, though not to the extent of Sarah.

Diane asked Nancy, "Did Dr. Larmore usually bring Laureal through hypnosis?"

"He would say the key word and count to three," Nancy said. "Because that relaxes *me*. For some reason, Laureal didn't need hypnosis to come."

I said, "Fine. I will put you under hypnosis and if Laureal is willing, she can come. If not, I will understand."

I started, "Zenith, Zero, Nancy. You are going to sleep, Nancy. I am going to count to three and if Laureal wishes to speak to me, I hope she will come when I say 'three.' One, Nancy is sleeping and relaxed. Two, very much relaxed. Three."

At that moment Nancy/Laureal appeared. She said, "Hello, I'm Laureal." She looked like a very poised Nancy.

I greeted her, "Glad to meet you, Laureal."

"Heard a lot about you, Laureal." Harold's reassuring voice.

"We've been waiting to meet you." Diane's greeting.

I explained, "Dr. Larmore said I should consult with you. That you would guide me as to what I should do now. Do you have any suggestions?"

"If you have something specific in mind, Mrs. Campbell, it's a lot easier for me to help you in a way that will benefit you most."

"My personal goals for each person are that he feels good about himself, learns how to deal with the world, becomes responsible for his acts. And lives as happy a life as people can. Do you know of any other goal I should head for?"

"I think they are fine. As we go along, other goals may come up."

"Let's take Nancy first. How could I best tell her how to achieve all this?"

"Her basic problem is that she can't feel good about herself and therefore can't accept us or feel good about us. That would be something to aim for with her."

"And how about Sherry?"

"I think these goals apply to everyone though some of us are stronger than others."

"Who is the strongest?"

"Sherry, I think. She accepts responsibility for herself."

"What about John?"

"His basic goal also is to accept responsibility. And in a roundabout way to achieve other goals. Like painting."

"Jenny seems in a good frame of mind. Is it as good as she looks?" Nancy/Laureal's answer: "Yes."

Diane asked Laureal, "Am I handling Regan okay?"

When I was not there, Diane coped with a raging Nancy/Regan. I suspected her recent outbursts represented Nancy's outlet for her deep fury at the disillusionment she suffered in Kentucky.

Nancy/Laureal said to Diane, "Regan has made progress, she is less destructive. But she's still very angry and unhappy. She needs a way to work out her rage and you could help her."

Diane said, "I've tried to get objects proper for her to tear up so she doesn't destroy what belongs to others. I allow her to beat with her fists on the bed. The last time she saw me she let me hold her and rub her shoulders. I felt she listened to me as she never listened before. And she did *talk* to me, a few words. Something she had never done."

"I think Regan is coming to understand reality," Nancy/Laureal said. "That it is not permissible to tear up other people's possessions. This is unacceptable."

"I've told her she will remain a cannibal if she continues tearing up things, like John's drawings," Diane said. "I just wanted to double-check I was doing the proper thing."

I thought, This almost insane anger of little Nancy/Regan is somehow tied to Nancy's fury as a child at something or someone she felt destroying her. By her acts she pointed to destructive acts committed on her by others.

"I think Regan's most immediate need is to know what's going on," Nancy/Laureal said.

"Does she have *any* understanding?"

"Yes, from the times you talked with her and Dr. Johnson talked with her. As well as Dr. Larmore."

"Have *you* been present, without our knowing it, as we have talked to the others?" I asked.

"Only as an observer."

"But you know what we have done?"

"Yes."

I went on, "Who else should I know? Andria?"

"Andria is the basic personality in the sense *we all come from her*, though we may be the second or third along. She never appeared until recently. But she has a lot of control. And as the others make progress and unity is achieved on the outside—integration occurs—either she will send everybody out and they will learn to share and live united in the world as she joins them, or everyone will go inside. Which is what started to happen originally. She will not be lost inside because she is in control."

"Does she have a choice of these two alternatives?" I asked.

This was an exceedingly important question. If Andria had control, Nancy might never be whole. If Nancy had the greater control, she was more apt to integrate all the personalities.

Nancy/Laureal answered, "I really don't know. Andria has been inside for a *long* time."

"Nobody seems to know about her, of all the people I have met," I said, surprised.

"Right. For the older ones, until they went inside, there was no knowledge of her. But all the young ones, like Regan and Nobody, know her. They are comfortable inside. It is traumatic for them to come out."

When she mentioned "Nobody," a new personality, I thought that in the choice of this name Nancy was indeed telling the world what she thought of herself as child and adult. As Nancy/Laureal warned, Nancy possessed little self-esteem.

I asked, "Do you think it would be a good idea for me to meet tonight the ones I have not met?"

Nancy/Laureal said, "They will come out when Andria feels they are capable of handling what happens on the outside. As things get better, they will start to emerge. You'll have a chance to meet them because

Andria's very much aware of you. She's sending them out slowly. Getting them ready for when she comes. They are like a trial balloon."

I asked, "Then what's happening now is that they are slowly emerging and she will join them on the outside?"

"When they can all achieve the goals you've mentioned."

I felt heartened at her explanation the younger personalities would appear "as things get better." This meant Nancy was more in control.

Harold asked Nancy/Laureal, "Would you like to come out more frequently? Get to know more about the world?"

She said assuredly, "I know about the world. I have no particular need to experience things first-hand."

I corrected an oversight. I said to Nancy/Laureal, "I left out Sarah because everything always seems okay with her. Let me include her now. What can I do for Sarah?"

"One of the primary reasons Andria created Sarah—remember, Andria created all of us—was to help keep things on an even keel. Help with the new understanding you have brought us. Which Sarah is able to provide. This is what Sarah feels best about—that she is able to help."

"So Sarah doesn't need anything except to help in the process?"

"Right."

I said fervently, "Well, I'm certainly willing to let her do it." Thinking, *She has done it all along and very well, indeed.*

Harold asked, "Laureal, do you think Andria is aware of how much we love all of you people?"

"Yes. Very much so."

"How many people now would be listening, do you think?"

"I can tell who is listening and who is not listening and I can block anybody from listening whom you might not want to hear something." She counted off, "John's listening now, so is Jennifer, Andria, Regan and Sarah."

I said, "I do not want to block anyone from listening. I would like to see Jennifer tonight. And I am definitely going to see John. I would like to know if anyone else would like to meet me and talk to me. If so, I would be very happy for them to come. Oh, I also want to see Sherry tonight. Is she listening?"

"No," said Nancy/Laureal.

"I will try to call her then because I have a gift I brought her from Rome."

Diane asked about her special charge these days, "What was the reason for Regan being created?"

"Regan suffered all the injustices that come to children growing up. Many minor things. She had difficulty in reading, during the years between first and third grade. Even the alphabet caused her trouble. She was teased by the other children and felt very bad about it because she wanted to read and it was frustrating to find it so hard."

She went on, "Regan felt angry at herself and with the children who teased her. It wouldn't normally affect someone who was whole. But when you experience it over and over, there was nothing to counterbalance it, to assure her that she wasn't so different, so crippled."

Nancy/Regan was little Nancy, I thought. Replica of Nancy in her early school life except Nancy hid her rage.

I pointed out, "*All* of Regan's experiences seemed to have that frustrating quality."

Nancy/Laureal said, "She has never really played. Or been held tenderly. Or—"

"Felt joy?" I put in.

"Right. Or experienced anything positive."

"That's very sad," I said.

Diane commented, "She can't seem to find an acceptable way to take care of her anger."

"She's striking out now," Nancy/Laureal said. "She's fighting back at long last. She was protected and safe inside. Now she has the courage to show her anger."

I suggested, "I'd like to ask Andria to send out someone she would like me to meet." Then added, to Diane and Harold, "If she chooses not to send anyone, that's okay too. I'll wait a little while. She may be making up her mind."

Suddenly I heard strangulated sounds from the figure on the chair. Then silence. I thought I recognized Nancy/Regan emerging. I asked, "Is this Regan?"

A few more of the weird sounds.

I said, "It's all right. Regan, do you understand we know how angry you are? But we cannot let you destroy things. I'm sorry you feel so bad. Honey, let me help you."

We heard Nancy/Regan panting, she seemed to struggle against crying out. She grabbed a piece of notepaper from the adjacent table, started to tear it up.

I took hold of her hand, said, "People do not go around destroying things. I will have to make you stop. Open your hand, Regan. Open your hand."

Regan whimpered, then burst out, "I hate you! I hate you! I hate you!"

Familiar words to me. I said, "It's okay. You can hate."

Over and over, anger and frustration in her voice: "I hate you, I hate you, I hate you!"

I wondered, Is Nancy as a little girl saying this to her mother, her father, her siblings, her schoolmates, her teacher, a stranger? Or all of them at different times? Because they have hurt her in some way?

"I want you to listen to me, darling," I said to Nancy/Regan.

But she kept up the angry chant: "Hate you, hate you, hate you!"

Suddenly she made a grab for my wristwatch. I warned, "If you break my watch you'll get the spanking of your life. You'll never forget it."

She withdrew her hand. I added, "I don't like to scold you, Regan. I'd rather you sit on my lap. Do you think we could do that?"

She started to whimper but stopped the barrage of "I hate you's." I kept repeating, "It's okay, darling." I held her hands so she could not seize the watch or anything else.

There was silence in the room. I realized I could not give Regan much help at this time, it would take too long, she moved very slowly in thought.

All at once, she was gone. Nancy returned. She asked, "Who's been here?"

I said, "I met Laureal, and Regan just came."

Nancy laughed. "And how do you feel after Regan?"

"I'm okay. She didn't destroy anything."

"It's 9:15." Nancy yawned.

I knew she was tired. I said, "I have three more people to see briefly. I haven't said hello to Sherry, John or Jennifer since the Kentucky trip."

I added, "I wonder if John should be last. With him, I have things to deal with. Though this is a kind of 'say hello to Mrs. Campbell' session. Nothing in depth is really going on. Just 'how do you do.'"

"Ask Sherry to come," Harold urged.

I complied. "Sherry, will you come out? This is Emily Campbell. We haven't talked in a long time."

Nancy sat quietly for a moment, then crossed her legs. Her facial expression hardened. Nancy/Sherry was out.

"Hi, Sherry," I said.

Harold asked, "You aware of what's been going on, Sherry?"

"Yeah." Her brusque, low voice. "I wasn't payin' attention at first but then I started. What d'ya think of that twerp?"

"Regan?" I asked.

"Yeah."

"I think she's probably hurting more than anybody I've ever met in my life."

Nancy/Sherry was silent, perhaps trying to understand the relation between intense rage and hurting.

Harold asked, "What's cookin', Sherry?"

"Not much."

"Did you have any reactions to Kentucky?"

"Yeah, you know, like that shrink. He didn't know his own head."

"You didn't think too much of Dr. Larmore?"

"I don't think much of psychiatrists."

"I understood you once sailed out of his office saying, 'Goodbye shrink.' " Harold laughed.

"Well, I was due at work, man. He was takin' too long." Adding to her complaints, "Do you know what the shrink did when John almost O.D.'d after taking forty pills?"

"He made him throw up and probably saved his life," I said. Diane had described the disastrous details.

"Yeah, but by then so much was in our system that we were really fucked up. We was passin' out. John left and was almost hit by a truck. He just ran right out on the road. And this shrink, Larmore, wouldn't do shit. Jennifer ended up in jail and then in the psychiatric ward for three days."

"John's the one who should have taken all this because he was the one who caused it," I said. "He should not have left Jennifer to drive. I thought he knew better by now."

"You know John." Sherry's sarcasm.

"I'll see you soon, Sherry," I said. "I have a present for you from Rome. I'll bring it next time. This session is just to say hello. Renew our friendship. May I see Jennifer now?"

"Okay with me." She tossed her head as if she could not care less.

In seconds Nancy/Jennifer appeared. I said warmly, "Hi, sweetie. How are you?"

She had regressed to a four-year-old. She said, "Inside everybody is nice, there is no bad things, you don't hate nobody. And it feels good to hab the other people wif you."

"Do they talk on the inside?" I asked.

"Only if they is wif Andria. She's kinda like a babysitter. She watches us."

I said, "Thank you, Jenny. We don't have much time to talk tonight. It's late and I want to talk to John before we leave. We'll see you again soon. Be a good girl."

Nancy/John appeared with a "Hi," as though we had parted only yesterday. I was happy to see my first adopted child, though sad because of his destructive acts in Lexington. Nancy must have felt desperate, indeed, to stop his integration and bring him back, as she did, along with Nancy/Jennifer and Nancy/Sherry. I could not blame him for Nancy's plight.

I said, "Hi, darling. I'll get right down to the point now that you're home. After what's happened in Lexington I'm afraid you'll get into trouble again with Chico and Jim."

He protested, "But that was before, when I wanted to do what Chico said, like take and sell drugs. Now I see Chico and I don't do those things."

"I want Chico out of your life." I spoke with intensity. "It's not just marijuana any more. Chico's not sure you won't turn him over to the police." Diane had reported Nancy/John revealed this in a session with her.

"If he's scared, he ain't all that powerful."

"But he's powerful as far as you are concerned. How about offering me something you could do besides taking dope?"

"I want to see my friends *and* take dope. I do things with my friends. That ain't illegal."

"But it always includes dope. I would like to see Jennifer not having to be left in the lurch when you take dope, like you did in Kentucky. I would like *you* to cut the strings so you don't come every time dope is mentioned."

"That's too strict, man."

At that moment I felt almost everything earned before Kentucky was lost. But I could not give up on Nancy/John. We had both worked too hard to lose the battle.

I said sarcastically, "Apparently nobody else has a mother determined she will not have a doper for a son. Well, I care. You should be earning your own money. It's time you were job-hunting. We'll take this one step at a time, John. Okay?"

He shrugged his slim shoulders. "Okay."

"I'll see you soon, John," I said.

We decided to end the session, it had been a difficult one, what with Nancy/Regan's litany of hate and Nancy/John's threat to keep taking drugs. I wondered if the personalities were exacting revenge on me for abandoning them to the loneliness of Lexington.

One month later, on October 11, at a session Nancy/Laureal appeared briefly once more. I explained that what I experienced with each personality was "not formal therapy." That I had certain beliefs, including the setting of limits and encouraging a sense of responsibility in each person. If the latter occurred he stopped becoming an acting-out vehicle for Nancy. Through his changed behavior her self-esteem rose so she no longer needed him.

Nancy/Laureal said, "I think Andria is trying to help in this ongoing process. At least getting anyone out who appears initially started on it with you so there can be a breakthrough."

I called for Nancy/Jennifer, this day she was sixteen. She told me Nancy/John had taken drugs since returning to Montclair. I felt a mixture of anger and sorrow, though I could understand his despair. As she left she asked, "You still love me?"

"Of course I love you," I said. "I'll *always* love you. I'll tell you a secret. I love you even though at times you're bad. I love you because you're Jenny. It doesn't matter what you do."

"You'll always love me?" As though not believing it.

"I'll *always* love you."

I added, "No matter what John does, I'll *always* love him. It's the things he sometimes does that I don't like because they hurt him. But I love John just because he's John."

Nancy/Jennifer said, "John doesn't talk to Chico any more."

I felt relieved. "That's good."

Worriedly, "Are you still going to adopt John?"

"I already have," I assured her.

"And Nancy?"

"Nancy has her own mother. I don't think she wants to be adopted the way I adopted John."

Nancy/Jennifer looked at me doubtfully. I asked, "You think she could have *two* mothers? Maybe we could consider a dual mothership. Two mommas." I laughed.

We said goodbye to Nancy/Jennifer, I asked to speak to Nancy/ Sherry, eager to catch up with news of her life. She appeared swiftly, told me, "I now keep John from drugs and he rarely sees Chico."

I asked her something I had wanted to know for a long time. "Has Chico held John down and forcibly made him take drugs?"

A shrug of those haughty shoulders. "You know, Chico. His word's law. And he don't ever get high. But he'll say to some of the other kids, 'Let's get John stoned.' "

"Do the kids do whatever Chico wants?"

"Yeah. He's got a gun. And knives. The whole bit, you know. He's also got a large scar on his neck. Wears tank tops a lot. A big guy. Has a tattoo on his arm."

"The full macho routine." I disliked Chico more than ever.

"If the police ever catch up with Chico it's gonna be tough on all these kids doin' his stuff. That guy, man, if he sucks you under you don't know what's happening. He had Nancy under his spell but she cut out before it got *too* bad. She's a little smarter than John."

What destructive fantasy these children live in, I thought, imagining a high on drugs will bring a happier life when realistically it means a living hell, possibly death.

I asked, "Is there anything *good* in that world, Sherry?"

"The way they see it—the drugs. Those kids live for 'em. That's all they got. You ain't nothing without the group."

"So I'm competing with the group when it comes to John?"

"Yeah, but you got a big advantage, man. I thought you had in the first place. John believed you really was his mother and that set him off. Later you just worked into it, you know, like you *were* his mother. His attitude before was 'Screw the world.' "

I asked, "Do you think I have a chance of getting him back into my world after the Kentucky episode?"

"Oh, yeah." Optimistically. "He was in your world, he had a chance to see it, before we went to Kentucky. I think if you see more of him now, if he hung around you two hours at a time, he'd come back into your world."

I said slowly, "The *only* thing I really want from him is that he get out of the drug world. Then he's free to explore just about anything he wants to do. And I won't be sitting on him."

"Well, that dust, you know, it can just blow you away. And Chico, man, like he just wants the kids to stay with it. Some of the kids don't have cars and he'll go and pick 'em up. They'll climb out of windows after the parents go to bed, stuff like that. A lot of 'em are young."

"He's a leech on society. A bloodsucker." I felt angry again.

Nancy/Sherry said, "He runs other operations, too, he's pretty well-off, a big-time dealer."

I asked, "Does he also have a stable of girls?"

"That goes together with the drugs, kind of. You've got the girls hooked too. He tried to get Nancy into that. But she said no."

"Does he know about the other personalities?"

"John told him. Warned Chico sometimes he would look like he was someone else. Chico knows Nancy and he knows me too."

I said thoughtfully, "People don't change suddenly. Underneath all that macho, the real John is always there. He just never lets it show."

Nancy/Sherry advised, "He wants to let it show. He don't really fit in with that gang. They are pretty tough. John's kinda always on the sidelines. Errand boy or something."

"What have you been doing lately?" I asked.

"I ain't really been doin' nothin.' "

"Are you friendly with any girls? Do you have women friends?"

"No, not really." As though this did not worry her.

"Okay. I was just checking because I don't like to think of you not feeling good."

"I'm fine." Cheerfully. "Everything's cool."

I thought how very far Nancy/Sherry had come, she actually was the one who had changed the most up to this point, perhaps she was getting ready to integrate for good.

She said suddenly, "I've seen Andria, or whatever her name is, a couple of times."

"Oh, *have* you?" I was very interested in what Nancy/Andria was like.

"Yeah, in Kentucky. Can't figure her out, she seems different than anybody else. I can't really put the finger on it. In Kentucky she'd write these notes to the shrink. Or she'd sit in a dark room with a candle. Freaky, man. Guru or something."

"It's not so freaky if you can imagine, as I understand it, that she came very early in Nancy's life and has been in a dark quiet place for over twenty years. Light and sound could get to be almost painful."

I thought of persons who were blind, then had surgery. Their ability to see was restored but they had to remain in dim places until their eyes were accustomed to light.

"I kinda got the impression Andria could break or fall apart or crumble," Nancy/Sherry said. "And yet, like the way everyone talks, she seems to be head honcho."

"She's the original person, she says."

"That don't make it her." Sarcastically.

"I have to see John now, Sherry," I said. "You could help me out if, when you know he is trying to bag something, you would dump it."

"I will, man, 'cause I don't go for that dust."

I sighed. "I have kids in my schoolroom singing the praises of a high on angel dust. I curl up inside, wonder what's happening to their heads."

"*All* the kids are takin' it. That's a big thing, man."

"I know. And it scares me more than heroin."

"It's worse, man, 'cause your *brain* ain't the same, you take it, and man, you may not freak out but you ain't the same. It's hard to get back. I mean, *nothin'* compares to it."

I sighed again. "I'm going to have to punish John. I *have* to punish him for taking it."

"He ain't gonna listen to that."

"It means I am competing against drugs. Which is John going to choose—me or the drugs?"

"Well, so far it looks like he's really stickin' with you. I mean, he really *blows* it, shit like that, but the thing that upsets him about blowin' it is you."

"He knows I'm going to be mad."

"And that still counts. He don't care how mad *they* get. You are the one who counts."

I sighed once again, this seemed destined to be an evening of sighs. "I guess it's an important relationship. Here I am, somebody who cares enough about John to be mad at him. That sounds strange but if I didn't care, what would it matter to me what he did? He could just go out and do anything he wants."

Then I asked, as though I had to face him, "Can you leave John?"

"Yeah." Coolly. "Goodbye for now. Good luck." Sarcasm returning.

Within seconds I heard the familiar low, clipped, "Hi." The figure in the chair first stiffened, then assumed a boyish slouch.

I got right to the point, "Hi. Yeah, I *am* mad. You know why?"

" 'Cause I smoked a couple of Thai sticks?"

"That's part of it. You know why else?"

"I didn't go and see Chico again."

"No, I don't mean that. What happens when you smoke the Thai stick? Do you know?"

"What do you mean?"

"What happened after you took the last trip?"

"One of the others came."

"Who?"

"Jennifer, then Nobody."

"And how old is Nobody?"

"Four."

"Can you imagine being four years old and left on a trip? That you don't understand, for such a world is different to you. There's *no way* you can imagine what it is like at four years to be left on somebody's else's trip. Jenny knows this is just another time John has left her. But what about Nobody?"

"I didn't mean nothin'." Very low voice.

"You *never* mean it. You *never* do it on purpose. But you're *always* the one who takes the dope. The only way you can control it so that you don't leave a young person on a bad trip is not to take the dope. That is the *only* way because once you take it, you cannot control what you do. Are you listening to what I'm saying?" I tried to keep calm but the fire within was difficult to control, I had counted so much on his ability to mature.

"Yes." Nancy/John's voice sounded shamed.

"What I'm *really* saying?"

"Yes."

"How worried I am? And upset? First, you disobeyed me, and second, you did something *terrible* to another person." I paused, then said, "John, I *love* you very much. And I will *always* love you. But I *hate* when you take drugs. And I *hate* when you do something destructive to a younger one."

He was silent, stared at me sorrowfully.

"I don't care how *good* you are at times—if you do three hours of chores for Mrs. Gaffney or treat Jenny considerately. That does not relate to the idea that I—DO—NOT—WANT—YOU—TO—TAKE—DRUGS. I wish I could make you understand, John, how strong I feel. There is absolutely nothing you can do to change my feeling about your taking drugs. You cannot take drugs and be a human being in control of your life. You become helpless as soon as you put drugs inside your body. Do you believe that?"

"Yes." Almost inaudible.

I asked him to stand up. I had to drive home the point even more strongly than words, it meant his survival and the survival of Nancy. I struck him three times on his buttocks, not hard but firmly. Not to hurt but humiliate, not to defeat but to make him more thoughtful. I saw tears in his eyes.

"It's alright to cry," I said.

"You're only a part-time mother with full-time rules." Reproachfully, as he sniffed away tears.

"Tell me what you mean by that?"

"You lay down rules."

"Such as?"

"I can't see my friends."

"The dopers, you mean. Chico and Jim. You know the rules I have made that deal with your taking dope, John. I haven't made rules about anything else."

"Why don't you just send me away again?" Despairingly.

To him Kentucky meant I had "sent him away" and the drugs were his revenge. I sighed. "I didn't send you away. The only reason I wanted Nancy to go to Kentucky was that I thought the doctor there could help her."

I pleaded, "I don't want you in that hellhole they call the drug world. I don't want you associating with those people who have no minds and no heart. Who care only about drugs and nothing else. I don't want this to happen to you. That's what we're talking about here. *Always.* I DON'T WANT THAT TO HAPPEN TO YOU."

"I understand that part of it." He sounded sincere.

"I want you to have all the help you need to keep you away from the stuff. You understand?"

"Yeah."

"The next time you think about taking dope, will you remember what I said?" Entreatingly.

"I keep trying." Morosely.

"If we can get you past this problem it will mean a lot to both of us. Call me on the phone, let me know ahead of time, before you get into trouble. If you feel you can't stop yourself, I'll help stop you. I can't read your mind but you can tell me what you're thinking."

I repeated, "You're not allowed to go out and take dope. You're not allowed to see Chico or Jim. Those *are* rules."

"I will do them 'cause you said to." Quietly.

"I can only hope you will." Also quietly.

"Okay. Can I have a cigarette, ma?"

"Sure."

He was accepting me once again as adopted mother, that was all I asked, half the battle won. A cigarette instead of a reefer. I would settle for that.

He smoked, we both sat in silence until he was finished. I sensed this was a most important session for both of us. I was telling him I would not desert him, I cared about him more than ever. I could only hope my spanking had helped him realize he would destroy Nancy if he kept taking drugs. I had to convince the part of Nancy that was John she might die unless Nancy/John stopped taking Thai sticks, angel dust, cocaine, smack or whatever.

When I slapped a child it was never in hate but love and caring. The pain disappeared in a second, the moment was over and there were no scars. The slap was the last resort, when month after month of reasoning failed to stop the destructive act by the personality. Dr. Lauretta Bender, a well-known psychiatrist in New York City, who worked at Bellevue Hospital, was known to slap autistic or schizophrenic children when she wanted them to stop hurting themselves.

I never felt a destructive feeling when I slapped a personality, I felt I had no other way to show them the consequences of refusing to accept responsibility. I resented that I acted in this way even as I did. I was driven by the thought the personality was not going to win over me, I was not going to let Nancy die.

I feel by the slap I violated something valuable in myself, in that I used at times a method I did not approve of. I do not normally favor corporal punishment as a way to deal with aberrant behavior. Today I reprimand myself for the physical means I used to convince the personalities they must not destroy themselves or others. On the other hand, the affectionate touch was also part of my communication with the personalities. I hugged and kissed them at times. I remember when I first touched Nancy/Sherry on the knee as I talked to her, she spun into spontaneous recoil, spit out, "I don't like to be touched!" Love/touch/terror/pain were inextricably connected in her mind.

But I must admit even the expression of hate and violence in the personalities was exciting because it was a challenge. I am not afraid of hate in others because I go on the presumption, even though it sounds naive, that there is a core in everyone connected to the core in me. This core is pure, it has no name. Hate is an overlay. My image is that the core is a white light, it is life itself, the essence of each individual. Even a murderer has that core. When a child is formed, there is no violence, no hate, no disgust, only the ability to love. The violence, the hate, the disgust, are imposed on the child afterwards.

The personalities accepted I spanked with love. In all therapy, the client or patient goes through the process of loving the therapist. What Freud called "transference." The client transfers to the therapist the love (and the hate) he felt as a child toward his mother and father, the source of his first love and hate. Without "transference" in therapy, there can be no change in the client.

It was a necessary step for Nancy to love me first, then hate me as I frustrated her wishes. And then to recognize me as a human being with my own strengths and weaknesses. As she could do this, she would then know she could become close to someone who had weaknesses as well as strengths, and not fear or be disgusted by them. When Nancy professed to love me, this was the love of the child, who as yet has no ability to reason, no judgment. If such godlike adoration persists in adulthood, the person is unable to muster much self-esteem but lives in perpetual need of pleasing a god who can never be pleased. The child asks of himself that he be superhuman.

It is my belief no child has to be grateful to his mother or father—it is a child's right to be raised in a safe environment simply because he is conceived. One of those inalienable rights we speak of at times.

After this session followed others as we worked week after week once more on the need of whatever personality appeared to accept responsibility. Which meant accepting reality over fantasy. Reality might sometimes be grim but fantasy was often fatally destructive.

Sometimes weeks passed, even months, when there was no change in a personality, delaying the thought of integration. Sessions were routine, expected to be, as in raising a child. Like a day-to-day relationship, as I taught and loved and the child listened, learned and, hopefully, allowed himself to love in a more mature way. Love to Nancy in the past obviously meant a threatening danger. She had to learn the feel of a love that was tender and caring, not violent or hurtful.

By the end of the year Nancy/Sherry reported that Nancy/John no longer left the house at night, had given up drugs, looked for a job, spent hours on his art. Nancy/Jennifer, Nancy/Sarah rarely surfaced, which meant she approved of what took place.

We now spent time with a younger group that emerged under the guidance of Nancy/Laureal and Nancy/Andria, the new caretakers. It was significant more caretakers appeared, rather than destroyers. As if Nancy were preparing for the parting of the curtains that would reveal her original trauma, the crime committed against her that caused her to imprison herself so she would never reveal the unspeakable secret.

We all possess what is called a "sixth sense," which arises from a certain accumulation of wisdom and awareness of truth. Reinforced by a strong unconscious desire to surface that truth into consciousness.

Nancy's sixth sense was now growing strong enough to accept the terror that had crucified both her true sexual and aggressive desires, denying free expression to both.

The Kentucky experience, while on the surface a deep trauma for Nancy, led to the emergence of the one personality who would possess the courage to reveal the truth Nancy dared not face.

As we headed into the new year I felt encouraged by what had occurred. I sensed that Nancy/John, Nancy/Sherry and Nancy/Sarah, the older personalities, were ready to fuse. A younger group were emerging. Nancy was finally allowing her earlier years to come out into the open.

I was also delighted at Nancy/Andria's decision to write me even though she would not speak to me personally:

> Mrs. Campbell:
> I am new. My name is Andria. The others all know you. I would like to know you too. I am curious. Who are you? Why are you so important to the others? Please tell me about you.
> Never break my code to any other! It is part of my private domain where few are permitted to enter. If you understand, I will permit you, because the others say you are special.
> I am sorry I could not come when you called me at an earlier time, when you returned from Europe. I was unable to do so. Please do not be discouraged in your discovery of the children you have not met, as Nancy is. Nancy does not realize the great progress we have made. This is partly because she does not understand the changes that are taking place. That will come in time.
> I would like for both of you to know that each and every change that has occurred so far is very necessary to our development. Even those that appear negative. I have anticipated this process that we are experiencing and each step is a reaffirmation to me that we are doing the right thing. That is something I have never believed before.
> Although it is possible that the work you are doing with us appears sometimes slow, I assure you, it is not. Much of our progress is not always evident. To go any faster could jeopardize our strong advantage that comes from having control that enables us to adapt to the changes we must face if we are to be whole. Control is a new experience for almost all of the children. Nancy is gaining some control in learning to observe.
> There will be similar changes in the near future. Not all of them will *appear* positive. This is one reason that Laureal, Sarah and I have stressed with you the control of at least the outside behavior of the children. There must be a very

strong consistency to allow the children a therapeutic environment in which they could function. Left to their own devices now, we would not survive. I am extremely pleased to see each one learn self-control, which is an important step towards integration.

To avoid future confusion and possible disappointment, at least on Nancy's part, I will tell you a little of what I expect to happen. A few more of the children you have worked with will reappear briefly. They will also integrate, although there will be resistances on the part of some of these children to any control that wants them to integrate. Nancy will be remembering more of how these children came to be. Nancy herself will briefly experience lack of self-control.

In the final stage of our development, when total integration is taking place, I expect an attempt to once again sabotage our progress. Perhaps I have already given you causes for discouragement. I hope this is not so. I do wish that this could be easier for all of us, especially you, but this is the only way it is going to happen for us if we are going to succeed in our goal. Which I now see as a certainty if we continue.

The new children you are meeting are not a deterrent. I hope this reassures you somewhat.

Andria

As I read this encouraging letter I realized Nancy was telling me how she felt. Especially in the sentence, "Nancy will be remembering more of how these children came to be." This would be a breakthrough where blocks of memories would surface.

After I had not seen Nancy for a week I received the following letter on February 15, 1980, from Nancy's mother. Nancy as Nancy had attempted suicide. This meant she was now taking responsibility for her deep depression, no longer allocating her morbid feelings and wishes to personalities. Her mother wrote:

Dear Emily,

I went to see Jr. last evening in the Pomona Psychiatric Hospital and we had a very good honest talk. Usually she holds back to "protect" my feelings, but this time she really told me what she is thinking and feeling.

She is so very frightened, not of the hospital she is in, that is simply unpleasant, but of what she must face in the near future.

Jr. told me what you mean to her, therapist, doctor, best friend, teacher and second mother. You are the most important person in the world to her. She told me how it hurt when you yell at her, but she readily admitted she has been a stinker and deserved it.

Before she did what she did to get her where she is, she thought about all she must face in the near future and it was overwhelming to her. She thought she had lost you, she knew she had disappointed you terribly, she was at a point where she felt she deserved for everyone to hate her. She even thought about how I would be hurt by what she intended to do, but her hurt and self-disgust outweighed all else. She said that what she did was the most stupid thing she has ever done, that she is not a suicide person.

Thursday morning she called the Gaffneys while I was there. Harold asked her several times if she wanted to return to their home. In desperation she said yes. Last night she told me, as she has many times before, that she can not take it there anymore. She detests the many trips to Mexico, where, as you know, Harold and Diane are supervising the building of their new home. They take her along when they go, not wanting to leave her alone.

She said she needs peace and quiet right now to "digest" all that is happening to her but she doesn't want solitude. She says she wants "either to come home or go to a psychiatric hospital until I can accept all that is going on inside me right now." I think her request is reasonable.

I am sorry this is so lengthy, but I want you to know what she is thinking and feeling now. I think it is best that she *not* be forced to return to the Gaffneys and also that she not be put through a big ordeal about leaving. Please help her through this. It's very difficult for her to handle alone.

Thank you for everything. I felt badly that I forgot to thank you for calling me Wed. afternoon. You must know how very grateful I am to you. Please call me when you have time.

Sincerely,
Nancy C. Gooch

Nancy left the hospital within a few days, we talked over where she should live. She decided to be on her own. She rented a small apartment in a complex with a swimming pool. We continued our sessions at the Gaffneys as she drove to their home each time, no longer a resident.

That May the Gaffneys moved to their new mansionlike home near Rosarita, Mexico, overlooking the Pacific. Harold seemed reluctant to leave, he was giving up work he found rewarding and productive. He had been active mentally and physically, enjoyed many friends. After he moved he kept writing letters to me suggesting, "Please come down and see us."

Nancy and I started a new era in our relationship. I now saw her either at my condominium where I had moved after the divorce or at her apartment. Clint still wished to be involved, for which I was grateful. I appreciated his support. Nancy liked him, wanted him to remain on our dwindling team. But Clint was soon caught up in his own life, which included caring for a dying wife. He attended sessions when he could but made fewer and fewer appearances.

There was only one word to describe how I felt—the lone member of the group left to treat Nancy—"scared." I thought, How am I going to do this by myself? Nancy had the faith in me little children possess in adults, believing them omnipotent, but this frightened me most. I happen to know I am not omnipotent.

I felt in a quandary, if I did what I was supposed to do right, Nancy would survive. If I did it wrong, she would die. And if I didn't do it at all, she would die.

So there was really no choice. Up to now I had allies, supports, someone was always there. Even if they went out of the room for hours, as they sometimes did, Diane and Harold were on hand if needed.

If not me, who was left to help Nancy? It would be back to a state mental hospital or possibly death by her own hand or a personality. I had to keep the process going within her even though I was overwhelmed at the thought of going it alone, no longer sharing responsibility for her fate.

Many times I wondered if Nancy would end up dead, not only by the suicide attempts of Nancy/Jennifer but acts of the destroyers within. I not only had to be stronger but smarter than they were. I did not know if this were always possible because I dealt with some personalities who had a strength and determination equal to mine.

Yet underneath my fear I also had faith—in myself and Nancy. I have been told my voice is soothing, caring, except when I feel justifiably angry and this helps those in trouble. And if I love, it is forever. I loved Nancy, wished with all my heart to ease her agony.

To the question, "Why did you take on Nancy?" which I am often asked, I answer, "For many reasons." All the above. And other reasons even I do not understand.

Nancy and I, and Clint, when he could make it, continued the regular Thursday night sessions. I saw her in additional sessions when she needed me. We kept no transcripts, I had no tape equipment. Thus there is no record, just our memories. I did not take notes since I was not a professional therapist. Yet I was never alone. I had helpers— Nancy/Sarah, Nancy/Laureal and Nancy/Andria. I had their faith and that was no small support.

There lay ahead two years of fierce passion as Nancy and I fought in what often seemed equal match. Like two Titans in a psychic struggle. My advantage lay in the fact part of Nancy wanted me to win so she could survive.

Now I stood alone with Nancy and her inner beings. There were intensive sessions, some lasting four or five hours, some, even seven or eight. There were moments Nancy hit her head against the wall, so violent her feelings. Or collapsed on the floor, screaming in rage. I would think, At least she is releasing her feelings, able to drop that mask of the "good little girl."

Gone was the order, routine and protection Diane and Harold had provided Nancy twenty-four hours a day for five years. While at the moment I felt it an obstacle to be the lone therapist, the absence of the Gaffneys and, for the most part, Clint, may have shortened the time to revelation of the truth.

But until the ultimate revelation could be made, there ensued hours of work, peeling away the layers within Nancy, as one would an onion. There ensued battle after battle. As the numbers in the room diminished until there were only two of us left, each seemed now to show the will of a tiger.

Clash upon clash, each clash choked with dramatic impact. Nancy's desperation aroused in me an equal amount of will to win. "I *will* win, I will *not* let you destroy yourself," I would feel—a mother defending a child against self-destruction. The scene in the nurse's office where I first met Nancy was merely a preview of things to come between us.

Now I was sole object of her fear and fury. She would try at times to escape me. But she knew in her heart I held out to her not a straitjacket but the straight truth. Truth she could not yet accept because it was too terrifying. Her way of evading the truth had been to run. The terror that struck her early had instilled the habit of flight.

Several clues to that terror were now rising to the surface. One was her antipathy to the taking of a bath. There appeared a new personality, Nancy/J.R. (short for "Junior," representing Nancy, Junior, four years old) who kept begging me to give her a bath.

Nancy forbade this. She warned, "You must not give her a bath." She did not tell me why she felt so adamant nor did I ask, sensing that the idea of placing a small child in a bathtub was deeply threatening. Time and time again Nancy kept me from disrobing Nancy/J.R. when she pleaded that I bathe her.

One of my attempts to persuade Nancy to become aware of the pristine child within was to conduct "guided visualization." I learned this at an education conference as a way of helping students in classroom activities. I would "guide" them verbally into a scene that was safe, beautiful, evoking pleasant imagery so they could feel strengthened, solve problems, release tensions.

Sometimes students would beg, "Can we go to our 'place' today?" The experience helped them become personally involved in the literature I taught and the reading involved. I would tell them, "As you read, visualize pictures in your mind. If you are not a reader it is because you do not make pictures from the printed words."

I tried this on Nancy. I said, "Imagine you are in a beautiful, peaceful wooded area. Tell me what you see." This is akin not to hypnosis, but to psychoanalysis, where the troubled person is asked to verbalize his feelings, talk about his fantasies. Nancy healed a bleeding ulcer temporarily, then an injured arm when guided into imagery.

One day I asked Nancy to visualize she wore a slacks suit and would unzip the trousers, step out of them, look at her body, sense who she was, what she was. She started to obey, then became agitated, refused to go on. She started to scream hysterically, "I can't! I can't!"

I wondered if this terror was connected to the "undressing" she forbade Nancy/J.R. to undergo in order to take a bath. Was Nancy's self-image such an ugly one she could not stand to look at her own body?

It was slow going for both of us yet I felt an emotional calm taking place slowly in her. During the summer of 1981 I received a letter from her that seemed for the first time to release long-forgotten memories of feelings as a little girl when she needed her "mommy" and "daddy."

I wish I could have a drink. Then maybe everything would blur enough to become unrecognizable to my mind and the terror would be replaced by an unmatched calm that slowly fades into limbo and safety. Sometimes out of the corner of my eyes I can glimpse a hand reaching toward me but when I turn to face it, it disappears. Then I hear laughter, as though it is coming from another room. Grownup laughter, secret and forbidden because I don't understand what is funny. Then there is the strangest silence and I have a feeling there is something unfamiliar in the room and I begin to experience the first prick of anxiety.

I would pour a drink and curl up on the couch under mama's shawl. [I had given her a red-and-pink shawl I had knit, six feet long, four feet wide, fringed, to keep her warm. She often felt frozen because of low blood pressure, the feeling of being cold was an internal experience that signified the lack of warmth in her life. I was aware of the small child in her who yearned for a soft blanket, like arms curled around her.] I would close my eyes and will my heart to slow down. Time keeps passing wrong—too slow or too fast, but if I watch the clock it seems normal enough.

When I'm not drinking, everything seems to say I'm waiting for something that will be too horrible to happen. I wonder if that something could be worse than the dreams. When I wake from them I want to run away from everything. I feel like I did when the nightmares were so bad when I was little—wishing mommy or daddy would come and stay in the room until I fell asleep again. I can see the movement at the end of the couch but I'm not going to look or be afraid. What *is* that crawling toward me?

O.K. I am in the bedroom. Middle of the bed. Don't want to be close to the edge. I don't like this one damn bit. It's scaring the hell out of me and I just realized that terror can be hot and cold. Cold in your veins and hot in your chest and face. I have the mirrors in the bedroom covered because my reflection keeps watching me. Swear to God—for a second or two it doesn't match my movements. I have caught a hint of laughter in the eyes and I know there is none in mine. Shit.

I want a drink—just a little tiny bit. I want to sleep until morning and the chance to be busy. I'm glad I have work. I don't want to be alone but it's a long way to morning. If I don't go to bed now I'm going to drink, so good night, pleasant dreams.

Next day: Dreams again last night, each more terrifying than the last. I don't understand why this is happening. I feel as though I'm being punished, which in this case does nothing to ease the guilt. I could hear an echo in everything I said today and it got harder and harder to concentrate. I heard a faint burst of laughter twice today and since I was working alone it was puzzling. I looked and there was no one around but I wasn't surprised. Flashes of the dreams kept coming before my eyes and I felt nauseous every time. I fortified myself with the thought of the bottle at home but then I realized I couldn't have any. Maybe mom will let me have some when I'm with her.

No one inside is hearing the laughter or even seeing the difference in the mirror, but they do get the dreams. They also notice the oddness about the time, but they don't have a clock so I must be influencing them. I've been jumpy all day and perspiring like crazy. The distortion caused by the echo made me feel detached. Sort of talking like through a tunnel. I wish the people inside knew what was going on. The feeling of suspense is getting to me. If I know, then I can do something to stop it. I won't run.

I thought Nancy's nightmares a sign of progress, once she would not even have dared dream of her terror. She was now bringing to semiconsciousness a sense of the torment she had buried. She speaks of a dream in which she "glimpsed a hand reaching toward" her, then the sound of "grownup laughter, secret and forbidden." She has the feeling "there is something familiar in the room" and starts "to experience the first prick of anxiety." Dreams contain the memories we hide from awareness, memories that seem threatening, overwhelming.

In her dream Nancy also talks of waiting "for something that will be too horrible." Then she speaks of "the movement at the end of the couch," asks, "What *is* that crawling toward me?" Adds, "I'm not going to look or be afraid." She stays in the "middle" of the bed, she does not want to be "close to the edge." Whatever is happening, it is "scaring the hell out of me." She describes terror as both "hot and cold." Most important, she says, "I won't run," speaks of "doing something to stop it."

During the next day "flashes of the dream" kept coming before her eyes and she "felt nauseous every time." She expresses the wish "the people inside knew what was going on," adds, "The feeling of suspense is getting to me."

While Nancy was not yet aware of the causes of her terror, her emotions and the thoughts connected to them were rising to the surface in dreams. This meant great progress.

I had known for quite a while Nancy was living out the fears and wishes contained in her nightmares through her multiples. *Nancy* dressed as Sherry in fur jacket, three-inch heels, satin jeans, slipped out of the house in the black of night, hitched rides to the truck stop. *Nancy* picked up the trucker who knifed her and the men who beat her up. *Nancy* indulged in sexual play with four or five men, four or five times a week if she chose, to earn money for *her* drug addiction.

Nancy held the dying Andrew in her arms. *Nancy* screamed obscenities at me, shouting over and over in fury, "I hate you! I hate you!" through Nancy/Regan. *Nancy* spoke the street language of "shit," "fuck" and "cocksucker."

It was all Nancy. The Nancy she had never dared face.

We were closing in on the "why." The new personalities allowed her greater freedom to know. As Nancy in her dreams faced more of the explosive parts of her hidden self, we achieved one vital change. She could now observe the personalities, which she never could before, and through them recall bits and pieces of her past. The personalities were no longer blocked from awareness.

The personalities I had known well and loved, some more than others—Nancy/John, Nancy/Sherry and Nancy/Sarah—occasionally sent notes or letters. In the fall of 1981 Nancy/Sarah wrote of Nancy's nightmares:

> Dear Mrs. Campbell,
> Sorry we haven't been able to get through for a while. To be honest, we are very unsure of what is causing the present circumstance of rebellion. We realize that it stems from a basic emotion, anger or fear, but are puzzled as to why these emotions are being manifested in such a way as the laughter, nightmares and violent, gruesome dreams. It is as though Nancy is telling herself wild stories about animals, people and living things suffering. Often Nancy's parents are the focus. It might be worth exploring with her.
> On a controversial side, we have considered a rather unorthodox technique that has proved beneficial in the past with Nancy. While living with the Gaffneys, we were introduced to "narcohypnosis," the technique of using drugs with hypnosis. The first attempt resulted in Nancy's mem-

ory of Andrew's death, which had been buried deeply. Our thought is modified—perhaps only a half of a glass of beer with the drugs. The added relaxation and reduced resistance combined with hypnosis might produce more productive results. In any event, this suggestion is made with caution and given only for your consideration.

Sent with warmth and love,

Sarah

I had known of the Gaffneys combining drugs and hypnosis but I gathered this experiment did not last long. I preferred the return of haunting memories through the person's own consciousness.

This would be one of Nancy/Sarah's last letters. We were moving toward the moment of truth. It would occur as a result of the trust built up between Nancy, the personalities and me.

Sherry wrote an amazing, for her, letter, just before integrating:

Mom,

Nancy is more clever than us, sure. She knows just how far she can go without paying consequences. She doesn't do dope like John, just slips and takes a drink to "protect" everyone. She doesn't go out and party all night, she just listens to the stereo, chain-smokes or plays solitaire and chalks it up to "insomnia." Everyone feels the same the next day. She doesn't tear up everything in anger, just "clears out some stuff." Pretty smooth. I mean, like *big diff.* Me, John or Regan woulda got our tails warmed good even if we *had* some cool excuses for everything like Nancy. We stopped asking questions about "how far" when we kept banging into that bottom line. We *knew* if we blew it. Not at first, sure, but we learned to tell ourselves while we still had a butt to sit on.

The point is, I don't see Nancy as an adult, and I'm not even trying yet cause I know she's never even been a kid, except for those rare "real" moments. I think responsibility a privilege and ya gotta earn the right to it. Believe it or not I can look back on that time I was with you as something I'm glad I had so that being really grownup *means* something. It's not just an image or status but a trust in yourself that pretending doesn't get. Being a kid ain't nothing to be ashamed of either, if Nancy would just let it happen, and not see it as a plague or something.

All else is super cool. Can't believe the way you guys are making tracks. Go for it. I'm rootin' for you. I luv ya, mom!
Sherry

I had gone through tough times with Nancy/Sherry but felt it all worthwhile when I received this encouraging letter. I never thought she would write "I think responsibility a privilege and ya gotta earn the right to it."

I also received an encouraging letter from Nancy/Andria in December, 1981, a Christmas gift, so to speak:

Dear Mrs. Campbell,
I was wrong to blame you for my feelings of anger and hurt. I must take responsibility for my own actions. Many years before you came into our lives, I made a commitment to myself and the children that at least love itself would never be the cause again for pain. Other pains I, as a child myself, could not protect them from. But in keeping their existence hidden from the world, the world could not love them, and to my thinking, so could never truly hurt them.

But in reality, *someone* had to exist, and so I chose Nancy. My fears were reconfirmed over and over again through the years as I watched her struggle with broken promises and rejections. I wanted to stop her from always reaching out and being hurt but could not. Now perhaps you can. We will meet soon.
All best,
Andria

I was eager to meet her. I sensed somehow she had the key to unlock the past. After all, she was the personality from whom all the others had sprung, she claimed. Perhaps she could reveal the trauma that gave birth to her.

19. Winter, Spring, Summer, 1982

Nancy at times endured a new misery lasting three or four days. The special hurt and pain when a personality integrated. During this period I saw specifically what the word "integration" (or "fused") meant. The purpose it served Nancy and the vanishing personality.

Like the symptoms of a psychotic, the acting-out and words of the multiple personality told Nancy in a covert, cryptic way the fears and terrors she unconsciously buried. At first, the facing of such fears and terrors threw her into a panic.

Nancy/Jennifer was ready to leave, she had started to integrate several times but returned, Nancy still had a need for her. I realized Nancy/Jennifer had truly departed as I saw Nancy relive Nancy/Jennifer's memories and suffering.

For three days and three sleepless nights Nancy was unable to turn off the traumatic memories of Nancy/Jennifer's life. She felt the depressions that made Nancy/Jennifer wish to kill herself. She experienced all the devastating emotions Nancy/Jennifer had endured.

Nancy/Jennifer had told us of Andrew dying in her arms after Zurdo had ordered his death. Nancy was now conscious of her agony at that moment. She felt as Nancy/Jennifer once felt when she watched Andrew given the overdose of a "hot shot," the pure stuff that killed. Nancy lived through the terror of calling for an ambulance, watched the gang members carry Andrew's lifeless body down the steps, out the door of the pad, dump it across the street by the phone booth.

Nancy lived out *her* desperation as she cradled the still body in her arms, felt devastating guilt at not saving the life of the boy she loved. She could have warned him, she knew of the plot to kill him but feared for her own life if she told. Nancy felt panic as she heard the screaming sirens of the approaching ambulance. Terror as she ran across the street, stood in the darkness, watched the white-coated attendants carry away Andrew's slim body. (And was that why she always screamed in agony not only when she heard sirens but at the approach of white-coated men to take her away, believing it meant *her* death because of her guilt?)

I heard Nancy's moans and screams, saw the tears stream down her face as she lived through what happened that night. Further tears when she described street fights with rival gangs, saw young boys she did not know stabbed and beaten, was beaten once herself by a member of another gang.

She also relived the moments of the rape in Echo Park after she lost consciousness. Up to now that horror had been chiefly the pain of Nancy/Jennifer and Nancy/John. Nancy had only been aware of her eye hurting right after the rapist struck her when she first resisted. Now she felt the disgust of his stomping on her chest with his cowboy boots. Of the nauseous odor of his unwashed body, of his forcing part of that body into her. And when she tried to struggle against the violation, as Nancy/John came out, the rapist's further vicious attacks.

She also was aware of her intense rage at being a victim, her desire to fight back, to avenge herself, to kill the one who had brutalized her.

As she emotionally lived these scenes, sometimes, as I have said, banging her head in fury against the wall, I tried to comfort her. I took her in my arms, assured her, "It isn't real any longer, Nancy. You're okay now. You can handle it."

I knew it would take time before she could fully, consciously absorb the terrifying experiences of the past. She now at least seemed to accept the burden of waiting, which lessened each time she could face the thought she might be denying justified anger.

Jennifer had been able to integrate as she became responsible for her behavior and could consider the welfare of others vital to her existence. Nancy/John had integrated but could communicate with me through Nancy. She brought me one of his rare handwritten messages:

> Hey, I can still see ya, and I'm the proudest kid on the block, I'm happy here, mom. I'm not just me, I'm part of everybody, so I figure I belong, sure enough. Best of all, nobody's got bodies so they can't mix me up with a dumb GIRL. I don't gotta prove I'm yours to no one, they know it and believe me, I'll always be your first boy. And mom, your love is just bustin' out all over the place here. It's the best high I ever got.

His last sentence brought tears to my eyes. It made up for all the time I had spent admonishing, threatening John for his self-destructive behavior. In saying he did not want to get mixed up "with a dumb GIRL," Nancy was saying she was a dumb girl, had no way to fight her violators, she needed the strength, the power of a boy, to stand up against terror.

Nancy now faced more of her hidden self, the explosive parts. Even the new personalities were no longer separate but joined in a group under Nancy/Andria as caretaker. We had all worked hard to make this step possible.

In my private life, which continued during the hours I was not helping Nancy or teaching school, I enjoyed my condo, dated, but not often since working with Nancy and teaching occupied so much time. Then I met Lawrence Peterson, manager of a manufacturing plant that made industrial cranes. He also was deeply interested in the study of the human mind, which led to his getting a doctorate degree in psychology from Walden University, Minneapolis in 1986.

He wanted to write about "the odyssey of discovering the self," as well as conduct courses that would show business executives how to help themselves and their staff in developing professionally. He was convinced, as I was, that the suffering of adults was caused by destructive childhood experiences.

I felt grateful to Lawrence for his moral support of my treatment of Nancy, especially at times I felt at a loss. He became interested in Nancy as a person, fascinated by the process of the formation, emergence and then integration of the personalities. He felt sympathy for Nancy and what she had endured. Later, in 1986, he wrote a scholarly paper on multiple personalities as part of his doctoral thesis on "cognitive dissonance." He examined various psychological theories, then cited observations made while watching my work with Nancy.

We were married New Year's Eve, 1981, lived in my condo four years. Recently we bought a home in Ontario, one block from the school Lawrence attended as a boy. His two children, both in high school, have lived with us in recent years.

I considered it a coup when Nancy/Andria finally deigned to come out and meet me. She seemed in her personality somewhere between Nancy/Sarah and Nancy. Her internal image of her appearance was a replica of Nancy/Sherry, the straight, long blond hair, the blue eyes.

I welcomed her, "I'm glad to finally meet you."

"I'm the oldest of the personalities, as you know," she announced. "They all came from me."

"How old was Nancy when you first appeared?" I asked.

"About two years."

"Did anything drastic happen when she was two that would have produced you?"

She stared at me blankly as if I had spoken in Chinese, said nothing.

I tried another tack. "Please talk about anything you choose."

"I stayed with Nancy until she was almost six, then went underground," she said. "I've been a spectator ever since. I came out in Lexington to help her through a very difficult time."

"Dr. Larmore spoke of you," I said. "I gather you were much needed."

"Nancy was at her wits' end," she admitted. "She needed me desperately. Almost the way she did that first time when she was two. She felt utterly alone in the wilderness of Kentucky. Without a friend. Miles from those she loved."

Though Nancy/Andria had twice mentioned the "first time," I decided not to press her about the original crisis but let her speak on. She seemed highly intelligent, sensitive, in control.

She announced quietly, with conviction, "I have chosen who will come out. I am in power now. At first I forbade the children to tell anyone anything. If they slipped, revealed any secret, I quickly pulled them back into my inner circle."

The new formation of personalities, I realized, was indeed no longer separate, disparate, but operated under Nancy/Andria's aegis. She was Nancy's conscience, superego, reservoir of guilt. Caretaker in the sense she guarded against exposure of thoughts, deeds or wishes that would jeopardize Nancy, cause her death.

I learned more of this secret circle Nancy/Andria controlled in a message from Nancy/Laureal, another vigilant caretaker, as Dr. Larmore had noted:

> Andria wishes to take Nancy inside of her circle for the duration of our sessions. Now that Nancy is completely secure in your circle, Andria feels it is time for her to at least acknowledge the circle of the others. This will be a new experience for Nancy—and a *very* important one. Nancy will meet those still left in the circle—including Andria. Andria needs your help in making the decision to do this. This is a very important step. Thank you.

This *was* an extremely important step, it meant Nancy would become aware of what all her personalities were hiding, possess more conscious knowledge of their motives and behavior. Perhaps they would even reveal the murderer of her soul.

In spite of her emotional crippling, Nancy had been able to work and support herself most of the time. In high school she had been a babysitter. Her first well-paid job, at sixteen, was assistant manager at a restaurant, Der Wienerschnitzel. She banked her checks until she earned enough to buy a car. She worked from 5 P.M. until 1 A.M., then slept until time to go to school.

At nineteen, while at the Gaffneys, she worked part-time for a while at Best Products in the jewelry department, selling diamonds sometimes worth $5,000 each. She also worked during this period as peer counselor in the job placement office of the Human Services Department at Chaffey Community College, seeking her degree in associate arts.

When she was twenty-four, she got a job at Bilmar Company, a brokerage firm. In one transaction of certificates of deposit she booked over a million dollars. With the money earned at this firm she rented a small house with a swimming pool in which she lived the last years of her therapy with me. During the times she did not work, which became less frequent and shorter, she received $400 a month disability.

I often thought of Nancy/Sherry, who had finally allowed herself to love me. Most of the time it had been, "You cocksucker, fuck you, get out of our lives." We had worked together six years, on and off. At one time she asked Nancy to find out if George's brothers had concocted the story of his death because he and they did not want him involved with anyone so removed from the world they understood. Nancy checked, learned George was alive and well. Nancy/Sherry had guessed correctly.

Nancy/Sherry and Nancy/John had been the most difficult to convince their only chance to live was to give up trying to destroy themselves. Nancy/John through drugs, Nancy/Sherry through inviting violent men to have sex that might lead to her murder.

Before he went inside, Nancy/John wrote a last letter:

> .Dear Mom,
> I want you feeling good about all of us, I want to be free to use all the talent we have without trying to fight dragons, as we've been doing.
> I may just be selfish. But, darnit, I want the world to see us as a story of success 'cause I worked hard and I'm sort of waiting for the real prize—being whole, beating this thing. And for all of us, maybe the things we're aiming for—the strong things *inside,* will be the "side effects." I do hear ya, mom, so talk to me, please. I'm here to help.
> Love, Your #1 kid,
John

One day I received a moving "Letter to my mother":

Dear Mom,

As I look back I realize that you have been "raising" me as you have your own children. You have strived to instill in me the values that will someday help me to be whole, healthy and happy. I have watched you treat each person, whether toddler or senior citizen, with honesty and respect. You face life head-on; you never just take the easy way out. You treat each human being as if they were special. You are filled with love and show it in so many ways.

Your love takes many forms. It is offered in gifts of the spirit, those intangible treasures that are so often taken for granted. You have taught us to laugh, to see the funny side of life and as we see you live each moment of life to the fullest, we recognize its importance.

Your singing is a source of delight. That sound has made us feel warm and contented and somehow safe, taking solace from its beauty. [I occasionally sang to the little ones to comfort them.]

You have suffered with us, too. Many times you cradled us in your arms as we sobbed out our frustrations, wiping our tears and soothing the hurt away. Willingly, you have shouldered our burdens, listened for hours as we sought comfort, knowing you would take the pain away if you possibly could. Instead, you gave us the only gift you had to offer—yourself and your belief in us. Somehow, we could always find the strength to deal with the rest.

You keep yourself pretty, slim, always attractive. You are popular in your job, well-liked by both your students and fellow teachers. You keep your mind sharp and feel excitement when discovering new experiences. I have always been so proud of you.

I must take a moment to say thank you. For giving me my own life and for letting me be a part of yours . . . For caring through all of the difficult times with me. Most of all, for loving us, especially when we deserved it least and needed it most, and for being constant in that love.

And finally, mom, thank you for just being you. You are the dearest treasure life ever gave me, and I realize how

lucky I am. I hope someday you will know how very much
I love you.

Your daughter
and all your kids

Nancy also started to reward me for my work not only by such letters but by getting more in touch with her anger, her pain, her wish for revenge. She wrote in October, after I asked her to report dreams of the personalities, that Nancy/Andria had dreamed of a tombstone on which was carved the words: "NANCY LYNN GOOCH, BORN JANUARY, 1961, DIED OCTOBER 1982. SHE LIVED HER LIFE IN VAIN."

Nancy's birthday was November 11, 1957, I wondered why she had chosen January, 1961 as date of birth—three years and two months later. Could that have been around the time the first personality was created and thus the time of the original trauma?

Nancy/Laureal reported a dream in which she walked toward an old ivy-covered mansion set in rolling hills. The name on its entrance was "THE GODDAMN SANITARIUM." It could have been any one of the thirteen psychiatric hospitals in which Nancy had felt an enraged prisoner.

The clues to the ancient horror were starting to roll in, if I could only put them together. The personalities now seemed willing, even eager to help.

One of the youngest personalities to appear had an intriguing name. Nancy/Promise was a highly intelligent girl, sometimes six years old, sometimes four.

She had however a gruesome task. She told me her purpose in life was to drain the blood from the personality known as Nancy/The Baby. Obviously this represented Nancy as a baby, unable to raise a finger in defense of herself.

I felt aghast, I had thought Nancy/The Baby had suddenly become so inert because she was integrating, not dying from lack of blood.

I summoned Nancy/Promise to come out. I asked, "Why do you need The Baby's blood?"

She said, as though she thought everyone understood, "I must have blood for the rituals."

"What rituals?" I was mystified, no one had ever mentioned rituals.

"Rituals." Nancy/Promise repeated the word with emphasis.

Nancy/Promise then gave me a letter she had written to a woman named Norah, instructing me, "Please mail this." I gather she wanted me to read it for it bore no last name or address:

> Dear Norah,
> This time is like before. Plese come and get me, Norah, Im just a doormat here and my world is different than theres. i stil promise you i won't cry and i'm not hardly ever hungry. i have to see this lady lots and lots of times and i hate her i get mixed up. She's mad at me most the time cause she says im acting like you but i did try to tell her about the danger but it made her yell a lot.
> I cant get blood from anybody cause that lady will spank me if i get caute. i hate it here, Norah. I love you and i hope you will let me back.
> > Love,
> > Promise

At this time I received a letter from Nancy/Andria revealing her anxiety about both Nancy/Little Nancy and Nancy/The Baby:

> Dear Mrs. Campbell,
> I don't know if it was the switching back and forth like we did, or what was going on, but Nancy told me she

couldn't locate Little Nancy. I went inside to look and I finally found her in what we call the box. Her body was transparent, she appeared very weak. I told her to go outside, hoping the real body might give her strength but she couldn't get out, even when I pushed her.

We could all also hear The Baby crying, but could not find her; not even Little Nancy, who made a weak attempt. As I write this, Nancy tells me the little ones are all fading more and more. Nancy and I are not affected as yet. I don't know if we will be. I don't know what this means but I am feeling nervous. Nancy and I agree this does not feel like integration but we do not know. Neither of us have trouble coming out. I think this has something to do with The Baby, that is just a guess. Something is wrong. I feel it. I'm afraid. I will go inside now and try to find The Baby. If I can make her come, maybe it will help. I do know something important is happening. But what?

Andria

Something important *was* happening, the little ones were disappearing and perhaps we were headed for further understanding of the tragedy in Nancy's life. If we could pick up the clues and make sense of them.

I called out Nancy/Andria a few days later during a session at my home, hoping she was prepared to tell me more about what was happening to Nancy/The Baby. But first I had another question to ask.

"Do you know someone named Norah to whom Promise writes letters?"

Nancy/Andria pursed her lips, as though deep in thought. Then she said, "I may have known a Norah once but I can't remember in what connection."

I explained further, "When Promise wrote Norah she said, 'This time is like before.' I wonder what she meant. I also wonder what she was re-enacting in taking blood from The Baby? And why Promise assured Norah, 'I won't cry.' "

I went on, "And the 'danger' Promise tried to tell me about, she said, but only made me 'yell a lot.' "

Nancy/Andria sank even deeper into thought. Then said slowly, "I don't know about her need to drain blood from The Baby. But I am prepared to tell you about one horrifying experience Nancy endured when she was six years old."

"Please go on." This would be her first important revelation.

"Nancy was in first grade and had to walk several blocks to school. One day she was stopped by a young woman about nineteen who lived four houses down the street with her brother, a man in his early twenties. The young woman invited Nancy into her home, promising milk and cookies."

Nancy/Andria composed herself as though preparing to relate an unholy tale. "This young woman led little Nancy into a bedroom and undressed her, except for her panties. Then she placed her on the bed. Her older brother walked in, wearing only his trousers. He headed for the bed and started to fondle Nancy in places she knew he should not be touching her."

Nancy/Andria looked at me, sadness in her eyes. "Even a six-year-old knew what happened next was not supposed to happen between a grown man and a little girl. He entered private parts of her. There was no sharp pain but she felt terror at the invasion of her body."

She paused, then went on, "After it was all over the sister walked back into the room, dressed Nancy and took her into the kitchen where she gave her the promised milk, cookies and other presents, like hair ribbons and candy. She allowed Nancy to watch her favorite television program, 'Howdy Doody.' "

"How long would Nancy stay?" I asked. "Didn't she have to go to school?"

"They kept her in the house until it was time for her to appear at home after school. They gave her a note explaining her absence from school, saying she was sick, forging her mother's name. They told Nancy to give it to her teacher the next morning."

"How often did this happen?" I felt sick to my stomach.

"About once a week," Nancy/Andria said.

"Why did Nancy keep going into the house?" I asked. "Couldn't she have refused?"

"Nancy felt she was willing to go in and do whatever she had to do with the man because she loved the young woman who fed her, hugged her, kissed her warmly."

"How long did this go on?" I asked grimly.

"About one year. While Nancy was six."

"Did the young man and his sister threaten Nancy if she told anyone?"

"They made her promise she wouldn't tell. The woman said if Nancy did, she wouldn't love her any more. And that no one would believe her because it would be two against one."

Then Nancy/Andria confided, "This man later raped Nancy's older sister, Barbara. Unlike Nancy, Barbara told her mother and father and they brought the man to court. He was sent to prison."

Even animals do not rape their young, I thought, the male is attracted to the female only by her scent, which the younger females lack. I felt a rage at the man and at his sister, the Judas goat, the come-on who provided the cookies, gifts and false affection that bought Nancy's trust and silence.

I thought of how the later rape in Echo Park repeated this earlier violation, the rape that created Nancy/Jennifer and Nancy/John. I also thought of the many personalities who had been born at age six, including Nancy/Regan and Nancy/Lisa, who always demanded milk and cookies, hardly a coincidence.

I saluted the strength it took in Nancy to survive such torture and insult at such an early age, week after week, month after month for a year. I also realized this early rape added terror to the rape in Echo Park when she was fifteen. The latter reawakened the acute fear and rage she felt at six when she was first threatened by what must have seemed a monster-man.

I said to Nancy/Andria, "Thank you for telling me all this. You have helped me immeasurably in understanding Nancy."

"Now she will have to cope with it," Nancy/Andria said. "I have put it on the table, so to speak."

A few days later I received the following letter from Nancy/Andria, which, of course, was Nancy speaking to me:

> There has been a magic in your touch and voice, Mrs. Campbell, which has set a yearning up in all of the children inside for all I had denied them. The real battle began then and I assure you I fought all the harder to keep safe that which was most important to me.
>
> Eventually there came a time when I had to question my beliefs. And when I did, realized that I, too, must someday have the courage to risk myself as my children did. It was a very frightening year of indecision to come to you. But when I did I dared to believe I had done the right thing. I began to let the children go—never pushing them but always finding they chose to go and desired to grow up. Mind

you, I was terrified with each one, but I also experienced a
wonderful freedom somehow. To protect a secret all your
life is a heavy burden. I began to see truth as a freedom in
itself. Eventually, I knew I had to give up everything, as long
as the children belonged to me they would always remain
trapped within. And so, most difficult of all, I left them. I
knew you would take care of them.

Nancy/Andria's words, "To protect a secret all your life is a heavy
burden," summed up Nancy's overwhelming emotional burden. And
when Nancy/Andria spoke of giving up the children so they would no
longer remain "trapped within," Nancy was at last recognizing her need
for emotional freedom. Most important, Nancy/Andria promised in
essence she no longer would fight "to keep safe what was most important
to me." That she was starting "to see truth as a freedom in itself."

Nancy had chosen the name "Promise," chosen it wisely and accu-
rately. Nancy/Promise would help reveal the most deadly promise
Nancy had ever made. An unspoken promise harbored within over the
years, a promise that had been slowly destroying her.

We entered a new year, Clint and I held a session in my home the week after holiday festivities ended. I had one question I wanted to ask Nancy, I had been turning it over in my mind, waiting until we met.

Immediately after we sat down I asked Nancy, "Who is Norah?"

She looked puzzled, said, "I don't know any Norah."

"Have you known any Norah in the past?"

"Not that I remember."

I let the matter drop, perhaps Nancy/Promise could tell me more about Norah if I pressed her. I had another thought about the name "Promise." Perhaps it stood for the promise Nancy made to the first rapist and his sister not to tell anyone of their atrocities.

I called for Nancy/Promise, she appeared at once. I asked, "Who is Norah, the lady to whom you recently wrote a letter asking her to come and get you?"

She looked down at the floor, said, "I'm not allowed to say. If anyone finds out, The Baby will be dead."

She seemed to fall into a trance, uttered an occasional moan. Clint and I sensed some trauma deeply disturbed Nancy/Promise, she appeared under tremendous tension.

Clint placed a small erasable board and crayons of all colors in front of Nancy/Promise—we had discovered that drawing evoked the emotions of the personalities. Nancy/Promise at once came alive, seized a brown crayon, attacked the board.

With the skill of a six-year-old, she sketched a bed and then a female figure with long hair lying on it. As she finished, her eyes enlarged with rage. She threw down the brown crayon, took a black one. She attacked the female figure, completely blacked out the arms, feet, head in wide slashes.

Then, in a blaze of anger she grabbed a red crayon and covered the entire form, as if flames enveloped the body.

Not finished yet, she seized a piece of white paper from the table beside her—we always kept a pad there in case a personality wanted to write or draw. She drew in black a second female figure this time with orange flames emanating from her.

Clint whispered, "Ask her if the figure has a name."

I gave him an approving look, asked Nancy/Promise, "What's her name?"

She raised her head, stared at me, then asked, "Which one?"

I pointed to the second figure. "That one."

She whispered, "Nancy."

I held the first picture before her eyes, "And this one?"

Nancy/Promise was silent, then screamed in terror, "Norah!"

She bolted from the chair, started to run toward the door, slammed into me on the way, announced angrily, "I want to be with Norah."

"Who *is* Norah?" I asked once again in wonder.

She flung at me, "She takes care of me when mama goes away."

I led Nancy/Promise back to the chair. "Tell me more about Norah," I said gently.

She sat down quietly. "Norah did the right thing. Norah said Nancy's mother had bad blood and so did Nancy. Norah took away the bad blood." Then she would say no more.

Over the next few months Nancy/Promise kept trying to collect imaginary blood from Nancy/The Baby. Nancy/Promise, when she came out, informed me, "I'm living in a cave where I protect The Baby. She's weak and pale. There's very little blood in her."

What *was* this all about? Was Norah a relative, a nurse, an imaginary creature? Whoever she was, she sounded mad.

Nancy/Andria wrote me what was for her a startling letter. Gone her cheerful caretaker attitude, in its place raw hatred. She obviously felt the rage I did as she told me of the early rape of Nancy, though far more intensely (this was, of course, Nancy speaking).

> The anger of the past creeps into my guts and grabs hold and squeezes tight. I feel my blood pound in tempo to race the fear to my heart. Damn them all anyway. Damn this whole vicious world! I don't belong in this world. I never did. I watch with mixed emotions as the only world I've ever known crumbles and silently shatters. Shouldn't there be sound as loud as a volcano? Was it so unimportant that not so much as a sigh can be heard for the betrayal as I abandon the world for this empty waste called life?
>
> My circle was my only friend, my confidante. It absorbed my pain and called it its own. It took my children and held them in secret protest against this godforsaken land in which I became one of the lost people. And now I am taken from you, my friend, and told to join this place and conform and live like all others. I can't fight the world again, my friend. They found you and we are exposed in their light, a light

which they turn to just as I have turned to you so many times. I hate them because they destroy, not willing to see. I fear for all that I know and believe, for they will take you away and leave me with the emptiness of nothing.

Goodbye, my circle, my children, my light and my life. I loved you with a fierceness I thought they couldn't destroy. But I've been wrong before. So many times so long ago, I wonder how I could have thought it would ever be different. I feel like I can't hold my head together. It's going to explode and everything is going to smash to smithereens. I want to tear everything apart—to hurt the children—but I still will not be able to satisfy the light. I go inside and its demand never ceases. I give it all I've got and I know it's not enough. I have to get away from here! If only I could escape and know they wouldn't find me. You cannot protect me from the punishment of this place, my friend.

I had forgotten the special anger and fear that I now touch every day. My hate feels so deep for this world! I feel weak and helpless and it makes me want to fight and destroy. Tell me what to do, my friend. Give me your light, the source of strength we've shared for so long. I have to kill the children if they do not fight for my life. I will give all of our lives if the world out there gives me no choice.

Nancy/Andria's mask had fallen, she was no longer the caretaker but an agonized personality, "one of the lost people." She spoke of "not being able to satisfy the light," for "its demands never cease." She confessed her hate made her feel "weak and helpless," increased her need "to fight and destroy." She begged the circle to protect her against the children who wanted to "betray" her.

Nancy had created a wall between parts of herself and the outer world. She had dreamed up her "children," her multiple personalities, to fight for her life. They protected her, did not allow whatever fear, shame and fury she felt to be exposed to outsiders.

Nancy had allowed me to learn about the wall, perhaps she was gaining the strength to permit me to know the deepest truths of her life. I decided to press on gently. Nancy/Andria, at least, was ready, I felt, in spite of her objections to help tear down the wall, reveal the earliest trauma, no matter how agonizing. As several months before she had bravely spoken of the criminal assault on Nancy when she was six.

But for weeks she fought me as I asked why the circular wall was needed any longer. One day she said defiantly, "Stop doing this to me! I must have that wall. It means my very life."

"You no longer need to hide behind it," I said. "I love you, you have to trust me, Andria. We must break down that wall." I repeated this over and over, as though explaining to a retarded child.

Sometimes my husband, Lawrence, would observe a session. I appreciated his interest and support, it added to my strength. He had great patience, deep understanding, an intuitive awareness, as well as a clinical one, of the function of the personalities.

Nancy/Andria fiercely kept resisting my help, often appeared in anguish. She felt I and some of the others within wanted to blast away her wall. But I sensed the treatment was approaching a climax. I also feared she might act as she threatened, over and over: "I intend to kill all the children so they will not reveal the secret." This meant Nancy would die. If one died, all died.

Nancy/Andria became more and more destructive. Believing she was in a state of panic I suggested to Nancy that she live at my home for a while. I thought she needed my full support, she might be working through the agony of the original trauma.

She lost her lucrative job with the brokerage house, they had gone out of business because of changes in the law. She could no longer afford the house with the swimming pool, had to live with her mother. She did have the disability insurance.

At first Nancy/Andria refused my offer, snapped, "I don't have to do what you want. I don't *have* to give up my circle. You can't make me." Her eyes flashed hatred.

It was psychic guerrilla warfare. The intensity of her fury amazed me, as did my own strong insistence she stay with me until we overcame her wish to kill all the children to protect her secret. Nancy/Andria now presented the direct opposite of the image Nancy showed the world— the good little girl who would not harm a fly.

I thought of the violent feelings she held back over the years, the emotional lightning and thunder that had never been released. When her beloved father left home, deserting his little "princess." When Andrew, the young man she loved, died in her arms from a drug overdose ordered by the gang leader Zurdo. When she was raped at six, coerced into silence.

Grudgingly, Nancy/Andria agreed to move in, try to work out her anger at the children and her fear of the wall disappearing. I ordered her to stay in the house, fearful of what she might do on the outside, act suicidally as Nancy/Jennifer did. Nancy/Andria fought me, threatened to run away if I did not stop persecuting her. I hid her clothes, except pajamas, so she could not flee. I was determined to help her reach the truth of the past, no matter how intensely she fought.

Late summer of 1983 we started a session one evening in the living room. It was the fourth week Nancy lived at my home. Wearing slacks, a blouse and sandals (she no longer threatened to flee), she sat in the leather camel-colored chair facing the fireplace. Above it hung the Karl Benjamin abstract, verticle geometric figures in blue, black and red. On the adjacent wall, in color contrast, a reproduction of the more muted brown shades of Andrew Wyeth's shack by the sea, lanterns within.

I sat across from Nancy at one end of the couch, patterned in orange, yellow and brown. At the other end sat Lawrence, temporarily forsaking the writing of his book, *Overcoming Psychological Obstacles to Supervision.* He wanted to sit in on the session, as he occasionally did. In front of us our round, glass-topped coffee table with its walnut base, from Scandinavia, held a box of tissues. In case Nancy/Andria, whom I was about to call out, needed them.

When she appeared I said, "Let's keep trying to look beyond the circular wall and see what's outside that makes you need the wall. You're safe with me, Andria. I won't let anyone harm you."

She stared at me as though I were a stranger. Suddenly she jumped up from the armchair, ran to the wall behind it. She stood against the wall for a moment as though to gain support from it. As Nancy/Jennifer once did with the schoolyard wall when the proctor and I cornered her.

Then Nancy/Andria slipped slowly to the floor, lay there as if trapped. Just as Nancy/Jennifer had looked that first day, terror and pleading in those expressive eyes.

Nancy/Andria began to plead to some unknown torturer, "No! No! No! Please don't. It hurts too much. Stop, please, stop!"

Her mouth twisted in pain, she looked as if a lion were about to attack and devour her. I had never seen such desperate fear in the eyes of another human.

I quickly stood up, walked over to her. I tried to take her in my arms to comfort her. She recoiled with added terror, turned her face to the wall. For the first time in the ten years I had known Nancy, my fear became almost stronger than my faith. I thought I might have driven Nancy/Andria over the wall of sanity.

I was afraid she might not possess the psychic strength to face the horror that had caused Nancy's life to go askew. Then I thought, We have worked harder than anyone could imagine, harder than words could convey. We have covered every phase from infancy on, every emotion known to man. I have to believe Nancy would not permit such pain to be revealed if she did not feel strong enough. All along the way she allowed nothing to be divulged until she was ready.

I lowered myself to the floor beside her. She did not seem to know I was there, she whirled in another world. I tried again to touch her in reassurance, she shrank from me as though to say, *Don't dare touch me.*

All I could do was keep reassuring her, "You are safe, Andria. You are safe here. No one can hurt you."

At the word "hurt" she started to scream. Scream after scream of pure agony. One scream following another like the pealing of a church bell. I thought, Neighbors will call the police, accuse me of child-beating. In the most violent of movies I had never heard screams so full of terror shaded with anguish. As if someone were burning her flesh.

I wondered what I could do, if I reached for her again it might alarm her further, she now interpreted the touch as happening in the tortured past. Needing to do something, I stood up, paced back and forth, hands clenched, wondered, Is she going to come out of this? Who, in the images she sees, in the experience she endures, menaces her so fiercely, causing screams that threaten to shatter the wall? I thought, My God, what am I going to do, what have I started, should I call the medics?

I decided to do nothing, wait until the screams subsided. I walked back to her side.

The screams finally ended, followed by anguished sobs. The mourning of her helplessness at the hands of some unknown torturer. Then, all at once she curled up in the fetal position against the wall. Head between her knees, as though trying to disappear into the void that existed before she was born.

I slipped down beside her, said softly, "It's okay, Andria. It's not really happening. It's something you're remembering, like an old movie. You're here with me. Nobody can hurt you." Said the same words over and over like an automaton. Listened now to soft sobbing, thinking this is Nancy trying to tell of the moment all torture and terror first exploded.

I saw the tears streaming down her fragile face, stood up, walked to the coffee table, pulled several tissues from the box, not daring to look at Lawrence. I walked back to Nancy/Andria, her shoulders had finally stopped shaking. She was once again becoming aware of me, slow return to reality.

I handed her the tissues, she wiped away the tears. I sat beside her once again. Slowly her eyes cleared, she was more the old Nancy/Andria.

I held one of her hands, asked, "Where are you, Andria?"

After a long silence, scarcely able to get out the words, she said, "I'm with Norah."

"What is she doing?"

"She's hurting me."

"Why is she hurting you?"

"Because I'm bad."

I assured her, "You're not a bad girl, Andria. You're mama's girl. Norah was the bad person." I was trying to return her to a reality where she was no longer part of the terrifying scene of years past.

"I'm *not* bad?" Sniffing, looking at me in disbelief.

"No way. You're my girl."

Then she begged, "Please don't send me back there any more, mommy. I don't want to go. It hurts too bad."

"You don't ever have to go back there," I said. "I'll never let this happen again. It happened a long time ago."

The screams, the sobs, the flow of tears were behind her now. She looked spent, exhausted, unable to move, to think.

I asked, "Do you want to go to bed?"

She nodded her head yes. I helped her up from the floor, led her to her room, she fell on the bed, lay on her back, eyes closed.

"Is there anything I can get you, Andria?" I asked.

A whisper. "Nothing."

I pulled the light comforter over her, left the room. Joined my husband who, during Nancy/Andria's sobbing, had silently slipped away, was now in bed, almost asleep. He asked, "Are you all right?"

I said softly, "I'll join you in a few minutes." I felt so tired I sensed I would fall asleep the moment I felt the pillow against my head. In spite of the fact I knew this was an evening I would never forget.

The next morning before I went off to Ontario High I looked in on Nancy, she lay on the bed, eyes closed, just as I had left her. I slipped out silently, when she felt hungry she knew the refrigerator held ample food. That afternoon when I returned she was not as usual in the living room reading one of the romance novels or horror books she brought with her. I opened her bedroom door, she still lay in the same position. She did not appear for dinner, I let her rest on, knowing she needed it.

The next morning she was up early, smiled wanly at me over coffee.

She said, "I seem exhausted. I can't do anything but sleep in small snatches. I have these weird dreams and daydreams."

"Do whatever you feel like," I said. "You're entitled to feel tired."

That evening she, Lawrence and I talked casually. I knew she was still recovering from whatever devastating memories she had just lived through. We all went to bed early.

When I arrived home the third day after Nancy/Andria's breakthrough, I found Nancy reading Stephen King's *The Shining*, knew she felt stronger. After dinner I asked, "Do you feel up to a brief session tonight if I call for Andria?"

"Sure," she said.

Nancy/Andria appeared at once. She seemed composed, alert, recovered from the ordeal.

She and I sat facing each other, she once more on the chair, Lawrence at one end of the couch, me at the other. I asked, "Do you feel okay, Andria? Up to some questions?"

"Ask anything you wish." With the poise Nancy/Andria had originally possessed.

"What happened to Nancy as a child that made you scream so long and so desperately three nights ago? What were you visualizing? Who was hurting you?"

Her eyes looked straight into mine with a candor I had never seen before. As though saying, Out with the horrifying truth.

"It was a religious ritual. In a bathtub."

"Bathtub?" I felt a shock.

"That's where it happened. In the bathtub."

"How old was Nancy?"

"It started when she was two."

"And who exactly was Norah?"

"She was the babysitter. A friend of Nancy's mother. She offered to take care of Nancy in her home down the street while Nancy's mother worked. Norah was divorced and had no children. She sometimes kept Nancy overnight or for the weekend."

"Can you tell me what would happen at Norah's home?"

Nancy/Andria described the scene. "Nancy would be playing in Norah's living room. Norah would come in and pick Nancy up. Nancy would smell the alcohol on her breath and know it was going to happen again. Sometimes it didn't happen but when Nancy smelled the alcohol she knew it would."

Nancy/Andria pictured the assailant. She was under five feet, plump and soft to the touch, meticulously combed long bleached blond hair framing a once-beautiful face, now touched with madness. Her small fingers, their nails long and sharp, flashed two diamond rings.

She started to chant to the child, "You are evil. You are the Devil's spawn."

The child started to struggle, seeking to break free. But the woman clutched her even more tightly. The child panted in silence, she dared not cry out.

The woman took her by the hand, led her into the bedroom, placed her on the starched white spread of the bed. Gently, the woman undressed the child, shoes and stockings, dress, panties. Then she lifted the naked little body from the bed, carried the child into the bathroom.

The tub was lit by a circle of flickering candles. The woman resumed her chant, "You are evil, Nancy, Junior. I will save you from the Devil. I will cleanse you, make you pure and clean."

Still no sound from the terrified child, her body rigid, her eyes wide open, staring at the woman.

Raising the fragile child high in the air, the woman slowly lowered her, traumatized, into the empty bathtub. The child had lived this scene again and again, knew her silence would end the agony sooner.

The woman lifted one of the candles, held it close to the child's small hand, singeing the tips of her fingers, a taste of what the "fires of hell," as she called them, would feel like. Still no outcry from the child, who knew the ritual well.

The woman replaced the candle on the tub. She reached for the wire brush, always on the nearby sink. She took the bottle of Lysol, also on the sink, poured it over the brush. Then clutched the brush tightly.

She stepped close to the tub, reached in until she could touch the child. She then invaded the child's body with the brush until blood streamed out.

At that point in Nancy/Andria's description, my husband fled to the bathroom and threw up. I dared not show my horror lest Nancy/Andria misunderstand, think it directed at her.

I fought to remain calm. I asked, "How long did the ritual last?"

"Nancy didn't know. She lost consciousness."

This had to be the moment Nancy summoned Nancy/Andria, her first personality. When Nancy felt her body mutilated, blood pouring out of her most guarded part, she no longer could consciously bear the attack. She created another personality to help absorb the pain and the terror.

She had been forbidden to scream or protest in any way but she had the power—the only power left to her—to create in her mind the visual image of someone racing to her rescue. This saved her sanity.

Nancy/Andria went on, "When it was over, Norah washed the blood off Nancy and the tub and then from her own hands. Gently she helped Nancy out of the tub. Nancy could hardly walk, Norah had to carry her back to the bedroom. Before she dressed Nancy, Norah gave her a small glass of wine to lessen the pain."

I asked, "Did Nancy ever tell her mother or father about Norah's torture?"

"She didn't dare, Mrs. Peterson. Norah threatened to kill Nancy, her mother and her father if she said one word. Norah also said no one would believe a little girl's imagined attack by a responsible older person. One who was a friend of the little girl's mother."

"How long did the rituals go on?"

"When Nancy was four, Norah moved east. Nancy never saw her again. But there was a ritual almost every week for two years. Starting when Nancy was two."

I asked a question that puzzled me. "Promise tried to leave us and return to Norah. Why would she want to do that?"

Nancy/Andria commented, a wise thought, "Part of Nancy liked the special attention Norah gave her. And when Norah was with Nancy's mother and father she always praised Nancy as a beautiful, well-behaved little girl."

I thought of an eighteen-year-old amphetamine addict in my class who once told me, "I can stand anything but being ignored."

Nancy/Andria explained further, "Promise identified with Norah, the powerful, strong person who inflicted her will on others. Promise was draining blood from The Baby, copying what Norah had done to Nancy. Promise was trying to show you, in her way, what caused Nancy's suffering."

I said to Nancy/Andria, "Thank you for having the courage to be the one to tell us about the original torment."

She now seemed to exude the calm that follows an emotional storm. She said, "I guess I had to face it someday. I couldn't keep it in much longer. The children were all forsaking me, I would have been utterly alone."

I felt a certain triumph in Nancy's gaining the strength to face the cruelty that had crucified her. She had mustered enough faith in her real self to unmask the hidden evil. She had become strong enough to put the tormenting truth on the table, look at it, feel it.

The four weeks with Nancy/Andria had led to the ultimate breakthrough. I had never fought or worked so hard to help someone survive. Nancy's trust in me and in herself won out over her urgent need to hide her pain. To reveal her agony to another human being was like having flesh torn back, exposing bones and blood—her very life at stake—because of Norah's threat to kill her, her mother and father if she dared reveal the assaults.

Nancy/Andria's ability to speak up was the reward of years of work on Nancy's part and mine. Years in which Nancy constantly tested my power and my love. As though asking, *Are you strong enough to bear my fear and my rage? Will you turn away in disgust?*

Nancy/Andria was the last of the warriors and she went down fighting bravely. The instinct for survival in Nancy won out over the wish to die and rid herself of all agony. Nancy/Andria, the gatekeeper, allowed the circular wall to melt, released the crucified children from their psychic cells, nothing more for them to hide.

Before hearing Nancy/Andria's revelations I would have said nothing could shock me. But the atrocities inflicted on a helpless child revolted me to such depths that for the first time in my life I wanted to kill another human being, the maniacal Norah. The rapist neighbor I had wanted to hurt savagely, but not kill.

As Nancy came out, ending this crucial session, she said to me, "I created a circular wall, locked myself and the children inside. It was like my vengeance was bottled in jars and put in a sealed-off cellar."

A poetic, apt way to describe her plight. We all to some degree lock ourselves behind walls, I thought. The false smile can be a wall behind which we hide. Or overwork. Or a psychosomatic illness. Or overeating or starving.

That night as Lawrence and I undressed for bed, I was the one to ask worriedly, "Are you all right?"

"It was unbelievable," he said. "I couldn't take any more. I don't see how you did."

"It was victory, not defeat," I said. "The terror, the brutal acts, the rage in Nancy, all had to come out before she could heal."

"I'll never forget those screams," he said. "As if she were fleeing for her life."

"She was," I said. "Her psychic life."

As I sought sleep, I found myself haunted by the scene of Nancy as a terrorized child of two. Silently pleading with the babysitter not to undress her, expose her naked flesh to the light of the burning candles and the torture of the Lysol-soaked brush. Round and round, blood and blood, scream and scream. And after the screams, a small glass of wine to soothe the pain.

Little Nancy could not know what the ritual meant. She knew only the assault on her body's most sensitive, secret part. And the threat of death if she told a soul.

22.   1984–1986

Nancy now realized she had used her personalities as her saviors at moments of pain she could not bear. They restrained her from screaming to the world, "I've been violated, I've been beaten, I've been betrayed." It is betrayal when an adult assaults a child's body, prevents the child from knowing the free flowering of the emotional spirit.

Now I understood the clues the personalities had provided. Nancy/Jennifer swallowing Lysol to try to kill herself. Nancy's refusal to permit Nancy/J.R. to undress in order to take a bath. Nancy's abhorrence of a hairbrush. Nancy/Andria sitting for hours in a dark room mesmerized by a lighted candle. Nancy/Promise drawing a female figure, then slashing her out with a black crayon as orange flames emanate from another female figure—how Nancy felt after Norah's attack.

To this day when Nancy recalls the scenes with Norah, she starts to bleed, so real and lasting the painful memory. Nancy suffered like our soldiers tortured in Vietnam. Except her torture was inflicted when she was a child, far more vulnerable psychically and physically, no chance to fight off the villains.

After Andria's revelations, Nancy needed time to make peace with new awareness of the abuse. She now had to live through what the personalities endured when they first took over for her. Psychic healing would take place slowly over the months, the years to come, before she could fully acknowledge and accept the terrifying past.

To help her through her agony, at times she asked to sleep overnight at my home. One midnight I was wakened by tortured screams, like the ones Nancy/Andria emitted during the crucial session. I rushed into Nancy's room, heard her pleading, "No! No! No!" followed by the screams. I shook her awake, held her in my arms, said, "It's okay, Nancy. It's okay. You're safe now." At least through her nightmare—a different kind of nightmare, one of which she could easily become conscious—Nancy was finding outlet for her hell turned inward. As she aptly summed up her life: "I was too scared to say a word when I was little. And I've been that scared ever since."

Nancy/Promise changed drastically after Nancy/Andria's revelations. Nancy/Promise gave up her ancient "promise," no longer needing to fulfill Norah's demand for eternal silence, no longer fearing she would die if she told of the abominable abuse. She confessed, "There's a black mass inside that keeps me from feeling warm. I'm always cold." Like Nancy felt in Norah's bathtub. The chill of fear.

The black death, Norah's threat to kill her if she talked. So much is symbolic when there is damage to body and mind that early in life, I thought.

I suggested, "Try to get rid of the mass by throwing it up in the sink." Following through on the symbolism.

I took her to the bathroom, encouraged her in the act of vomiting up her fear, disgust and fury. She announced, as she complied, "I'm doing it to get rid of Norah." She leaned over the sink, coughed, said, "Now the mass is moving up another half inch," indicating her heart. Then, "Now it's an inch nearer my throat." And finally, "Now I'm spitting it out into the sink."

There was work to do with a new personality, the last destroyer, Nancy/Ricky. He wanted to kill Nancy and the others as Nancy/Jennifer had tried to do. Nancy/Ricky had to be helped give up his death wish. At one point he and I engaged in a fight on the floor. I held him down by sitting atop him, insisting, "You *cannot* kill Nancy. You must give up this wish. You have to accept responsibility."

He made a final desperate attempt to kill her by trying to force *her* to integrate into *him*. He wanted to be the only one in power. At this time Nancy was tested at the Voorman Clinic, her I.Q. was 166 and I was not about to let that height of intelligence go down the drain.

One night Nancy wrote of feelings during a battle with Nancy/Ricky in which he was trying by occult means to destroy her:

> Suddenly I saw flashes of light. I felt like they were searing my eyeballs, and something gripped my head, and I felt it was going to crush it. My body seemed to be moving with a will of its own and pulling away from a powerful suction force. I felt I was spinning rapidly. I had a sense of leaving a force and being pulled into another.
>
> I wanted to tell my mom I was in danger and that they, whoever they were, were trying to hurt me. I knew if I kept fighting I would get away and be safe. Every breath was a struggle. I knew somehow that breathing was important and so I fought harder to fill my lungs up. I tried to talk but my mouth felt like it was full of sand. But somehow I gathered enough strength to pull out of it.

While this was description of her fight to survive Nancy/Ricky's attack, it was also repetition of the first attacks by Norah. The "burning" sensation, the feeling of "panic" at the "flashes of light," the awareness someone was "trying to hurt me," and the knowledge of how important just "breathing" was, so she would stay alive. These were the dangerous sensations that had forced little Nancy to create her first personalities.

Nancy/Andria also put into words her memory of this night, which she observed from within, as she wrote me, "Nancy seemed out of it. I could tell she was fighting with every ounce of strength to stay in it and when she started to win the battle, she got this awful pain in her head. I could feel her presence get stronger and stronger. We were all excited inside. We were yelling, 'Come on, Nancy, you can do it!' "

This meant all the other personalities had joined forces with me to fight Ricky, no longer opponents but on the same team. A team searching for truth. I loved the personalities, not as part of Nancy but for themselves. I was intellectually aware they *were* parts of Nancy but emotionally I was aware each was his own person. I could not have been successful without my helpers, especially the parts of Nancy that wished to survive. At times they were even far ahead of me, Nancy had a way of keeping up her courage and mine when I felt momentarily defeated. A saint I am not, there were times of deep despair and the wish to give up.

There was the inspiring moment Nancy/Laureal explained Nancy/Regan to me. She pointed out Nancy/Regan was one of the bearers of Nancy's excessive anger. This was shown in Nancy/Regan's incessant destruction of anything and everything she could lay her hands on, including wallpaper.

Nancy/Laureal wrote me: "Regan has never really played. Or been held tenderly. Or felt joy. Or experienced anything positive." Nancy was telling how she felt as a child who now, through Nancy/Regan, "has the courage to show her anger."

The year 1985 started on a sad note when Harold died on January 31 after complications caused by a malignancy of the colon. Over the years he suffered seventeen progressive amputations on his legs but never lost his will to live or to keep learning more about the human mind.

In the spring of 1985 I was delighted to hear from Nancy/Sarah, absent for a long time:

> Dear Mother,
> In assessing the overall progress we see, we feel very positive. We feel that your therapeutic assistance has been very successful, perhaps to a point that other personalities have never truly reached. If you think back, you will realize the

extent of the abuse and trauma our one collective person has endured. Yet, you have helped create an almost-adult human being who is truly strong and giving to others. We are living in a *reality* that is now devoid of the psychotic symptoms which were once our future.

You have guided someone who has been raped, beaten, stabbed, kidnapped, institutionalized and driven to suicide, into a person who will be able to interact with society on a real level and have a great deal to offer others as she becomes aware of her potential. Although we know you are aware of all these things that have happened, and so we may sound redundant, I say these things as a reminder to you of the great work you have done. All this in hopes that you will not stop with us.

Our thoughts have been with the others we knew in Kentucky, and the hundreds or even thousands we know who exist in this world without hope. They are probably in jails, reform schools, hospitals or permanent institutions. We are most likely talking about highly intelligent, talented, sensitive people who have something valuable to contribute to this world.

Personally, we still have a little ways to go, yet the worst is over. And even if we stopped here, your work would likely put us ahead of many "mentally healthy" people who have not faced an illness in their mind. Even doctors back at Voorman were amazed at our awareness and ability to function and gave you primary credit and support. Your work with us became their guideline and you were always given professional respect by them, which no one else received. From what we have learned, our situation or particular condition takes years and years to "cure." We are very fortunate to have possibly 60 or 70 years left to live a life as a "real" human being. You have natural talents which are rare, and not only in our opinion. It is very important to us that you write your story and share your knowledge before anyone else, because we want it heard in a way that will benefit others. Because you are truly our mother, we have made breakthroughs and had extra experiences that might be difficult to simulate. But the basics were discovered in each of the relationships and the best of the two—you and us— could be utilized together.

As for a total "cure" (integration) by no means have we

given up on this as our goal. We know we need this success
to function completely.

Love,
Sarah

Nancy/Sarah wrote of "integration," nobody had vanished, nobody
died. The personalities were still part of Nancy though they possessed
awareness of separateness, they no longer could take over her body, they
lost all control. Nancy gained the ability to become an artist or an athlete
(like Nancy/John), feel entitled to sexual desire (as Nancy/Sherry did),
know her own integrity and knowledge of self (like Nancy/Sarah).

A dramatic dream of Nancy's, relayed by Nancy/Sarah, revealed
changes occurring in Nancy. She showed greater acceptance of her
frightened and hostile feelings.

> Nancy is walking toward an elementary school. She is
> with another girl, possibly her sister. They sit on a grassy
> slope. They talk for a few minutes, when suddenly a large
> group of people come out from behind a building and start
> walking towards them. The two girls stand up and notice
> that the people are carrying weapons. Nancy turns and tells
> the other girl. The girl just replies very calmly, "I know."
>
> The people come upon the two girls and knock Nancy to
> the ground. Many of them stab her repeatedly. A man with
> heavy boots kicks her in the stomach. A woman with a rock
> begins to smash Nancy's head and face. A boy pushes long
> needles into her body.
>
> Nancy feels terror but no pain. She screams, "Julie-
> Renee!" and looks to see this girl standing above her, watch-
> ing. Nancy is aware that the people do not touch the other
> girl. Nancy whispers, "My mom. Julie-Renee, go to the
> school and get my mother. She will *stop* them. Hurry, Julie-
> Renee; I'm bleeding. I'm going to die!" The girl again
> replies, "I know." But she does not move.
>
> Nancy notices that the blood running in rivers from her
> body runs *around* her friend's feet. Her friend seems sad but
> not really affected by what is happening. Nancy pleads with
> her, "Please, Julie-Renee, make them stop!" The girl turns
> and walks away. Nancy sobs, "Mrs. Peterson! Momma!"
> Then a young girl walks up and pours acid down her throat.
> Nancy dies.

>Julie-Renee leans against a tree, bursts into tears, and Carmen comes. The dream is over.

This dream was highly significant because Nancy was now able, as most of us are, to bring back buried memories in dreams, where the unconscious talks to us in code. No longer did she have to be the catatonic, cataleptic Carmen, she could use the "safety valve" of the mind, as Freud described the unconscious. She no longer needed to deny remembrance of things past that had been too unbearable to consciously endure.

The dream showed the violence of others who knocked her to the ground, stabbed her "repeatedly." A "man with heavy boots" kicks her in the stomach, as the rapist in Echo Park did. A woman with a rock "begins to smash her head and face"—Norah did not attack her head or face but her female identity and body ego, her sense of self. A boy "pushes long needles into her body," how the act of sex with the male neighbor might have felt to her at six. Nancy is aware in the dream of "terror" but no pain—the pain was absorbed by her personalities.

Nancy visualizes herself as dead in her dream. The part of our unconscious of which we may become intellectually aware has no concept of death, according to Freud. We see ourselves live on forever. But there may be depths in the unconscious where the threat of death seems real, as it did with Nancy. Perhaps because the threat to her *was* real so early in life.

Death stalked her daily, stuck to her like her own dark shadow. At the age of two and thereafter, Nancy's nightmare was not a dream. It was based on real assaults. She turned into a baby zombie after Norah's brutality—the dream ends as Nancy/Julie-Renee "leans against a tree, bursts into tears and Carmen [the zombie baby] comes."

As the year 1986 approached, Nancy/Andria wrote, just before she fused:

>Dear Mom,
>More than anything I wanted to say goodbye to you in person but it seems there won't be any time. I should be integrated by morning. I know that I will make it this time because I feel so good inside. In some ways the past two months have been more difficult than ever before, I remember fighting you, and scared as I was, I knew I would die if I gave in. Needless to say, I was wrong. I was set free of fear and anger.

I'll tell you a little secret. When I was four, I used to hide food. I never ate it, I just stored it. I equated it with love. Now I would rather have a hug than a peanut-butter sandwich any day!

Because of your love and guidance, I have been able to go back to my past and change my view of the world and myself. I am a happier person, mom, in control of my life and looking forward to a bright future. I feel "my own person." I tell you all this because the only unfinished business I feel is for you to know how proud I am to be your daughter and how important you are in my life.

I'm ready for integration. I feel funny about leaving when so much is happening but there seems little choice. I hope I can help Nancy from wherever integration is.

I have pride in those who have grown beyond needing you and me. I hope you will not forget to feel the pride in yourself for what you have done for and meant to these children, grown into strong and good people. No one will *ever* be able to take that away from them now. And what you have given will always live on through Nancy. For yourself, I hope that you never lose that caring, sensitive part of you that is truly miraculous. If I had to touch love, I'm glad it was with you. Thank you.

Goodbye,
Andria

It took Nancy one year before she could speak to her mother of the early assaults. I understood her delay, there were times with me when she showed little or no acceptance of reality but I waited, as you do with a child, until she was ready to acknowledge what was fantasy and what had really happened.

When Nancy's mother learned how her daughter had suffered at the hands of Norah and, later, the man down the street, she told me, "Not once did Nancy give me the slightest hint about what she endured. She often cried when it was time for her to go to Norah's home. I thought she simply did not like to be away from me all day. When Nancy told me what had happened, the feelings that raged through me were indescribable. Why did I not have one hint of what was going on? Was I completely blind? Was I so absorbed in all the work I faced each day, both on my job and taking care of a home and family, that I was blinded to what my daughter's life was like?"

She paused, feeling distressed, then went on, "What Nancy went through as a small child will be a shock from which I don't believe I will ever recover. The torture and sexual abuse Norah inflicted on my daughter were beyond any horror movie ever made. That woman did everything she wanted with and to my daughter. She convinced Nancy if she ever told anyone, she would die and so would her father and I."

Then Nancy's mother said to me, gratitude in her voice, "If you had not entered my daughter's life it would have meant either Nancy spending the rest of her natural life in a mental hospital for the hopelessly insane or killing herself. Nancy could never have made it without your total dedication, determination, courage, patience and energy. You went on for years when doctor after doctor gave up. How can I possibly thank you for giving so much for so long?"

She concluded, "It has been overwhelming at times but I realize how very blessed I really am. My daughter is alive. Think of all the parents who have lost their children to drugs, or the missing children that are never found, or the fresh-faced kids that didn't come home from some conflict on the other side of the world."

I understood now where Nancy derived the strength not only to endure what she had suffered but to eventually face the underground terror and conquer it so she no longer needed to rely on secret changelings to protect her from enemies within and without.

This new strength was shown when she appeared on "The Oprah Winfrey Show" during February, 1986 after she and I flew to Chicago. I felt very proud of her, she was poised and perceptive. She looked slim and smart in a wine velvet jacket, beige slacks. I was impressed by her ability to articulate, she talked from the heart and her voice was soft but firm, you could hear every word.

Nancy told the audience, "I was a very quiet child, never complained. I did not know how to cry, especially during the most dangerous times. I have been put in many mental institutions, some for just a few days. I went several times in a straitjacket, as if they believed I was a raving lunatic. They told me, 'We can't take any chances.' "

Asked by Ms. Winfrey when she started to recall the early abuse, Nancy replied, "When my therapist, Emily Peterson, gave me constant feedback as to what I was doing. I learned to observe slowly at first. It was a deep process as I became aware, step by step, of what was happening. Eventually I felt in more control of my life."

She added, "There had been a war going on inside as to who was going to dominate. Who would be the ultimate personality. Meaning who was 'out' and in control for the moment, the day or the night."

Oprah asked me to say a few words. I explained sexual child abuse was usually the cause of multiple personalities. The victim creates the personalities as a defense against unbearable experiences he fears may drive him mad. The personalities also serve to act out his terror, rage and wish for vengeance. Each personality displays different aspects of the core personality—his fear, fury, normal sexual desire. Because Nancy's early assaults hindered her emotional development, her childish wishes were acted out in behavior such as drug addiction or alcoholism, which gave the illusion of temporary respite devoid of danger.

Dr. Bennett G. Braun, president of the International Society for the Study of Multiple Personality, who lives in Chicago, was also on the program. Afterwards he greeted us, spoke to me as a colleague. I was delighted to receive his approval. He gave me a copy of an as-yet-unpublished article. In reading it I was astonished at how often I had acted in the very ways he advised a therapist to do.

My experience as a teacher revealed that a number of students, brave enough to tell us, had been molested by parents or other adults. We all have impulses to commit shameful acts but most of us do not carry them out. Some adults believe you can do anything to a child because he is not fully aware of what is happening to his body and mind. These adults do not realize a child is capable of feeling everything an adult can. The only difference is that a child cannot express his feelings or is afraid to, as Nancy was. Crucify a child early, as Nancy was crucified, and you maim the psychic future.

We live in a violent world, we are a violent society. Violence exists in many American homes. I believe a large percentage of Americans use sex to express violence, impose their will on another person not as an act of love but hate.

One of my favorite plays is Arthur Miller's *The Crucible*. There is intrinsic greatness in John Proctor, the hero wrestling with his conscience and coming out the winner because of his integrity. Another character I admire is Beckett, portrayed in the play of that name by Anouilh, as his integrity also wins over seemingly insurmountable odds.

Part of the heroism in man is his willingness to help others less fortunate. I wondered why Nancy's teachers in the early grades, when she was failing, did not suspect she needed help. Especially when Nancy/Sarah came out for a year and suddenly Nancy's poor grades shot up to A's. Nancy recalls attending a show of paintings where she found several signed with her name though she did not remember creating them. I hope eventually there will be early detection in our schools of emotional disturbances in pupils, including multiple personalities, by counselors and by teachers educated to look for such disturbances.

The history of civilization shows a very slow march toward realization of the vulnerability of children and the recognition of their acute need for love, respect and protection. There seems little awareness that the terror that haunts at two and three years of age may be the terror that haunts at thirty and forty.

When a child's mind and body are violated as Nancy's was, this is far more dangerous to the child's emotional stability than when an adult's mature body and mind are assaulted and there is greater capacity to handle such terror. Nancy could never allow herself to feel anger, had to deny and repress the titanic rage that followed her early abuses.

I helped her face her anger, also made her feel "special." I was there, I cared for her, believed her worthwhile, and she started to feel more self-esteem. But the final cure lay within Nancy, the cure always lies within the self. All I could do was encourage her to use her natural strengths, I knew she had tremendous potential for understanding herself. It showed in her writing and in the sensitive, acute observations of Nancy/Sarah and Nancy/Andria, the helpers. Their perceptiveness and courage both registered within Nancy and emanated from her.

I was delighted when one day Nancy said to me, "I'm tired of walking on eggshells. It's been my way of relieving distress. I'm glad I could trust you to help me find a better way of life."

Today Nancy is in therapy with a woman I admire and respect, Deborah R. Kidwell, who has a master's degree in social work and lives in nearby Claremont. The therapy Nancy now receives would not have been possible without the years of work she and I did. First, the personalities had to fuse. Nancy had to feel she no longer needed them, she could take responsibility for her feelings, control her dangerous impulses.

In her new therapy I expect her to acknowledge more of her justified anger. Accept it as part of her life, go on from there. She will then no longer have to use her energy to hold back anger, for which she has paid a terrific toll emotionally, but will have it available for creative and pleasurable pursuits.

Both Nancy and I dream of starting a clinic for the emotionally deprived. I would like to supervise the therapy and atmosphere, leave the administration to others. I would work out ways, as I did with Nancy, for treatment to be accomplished more effectively, in terms of time and personal energy. You cannot take on too many multiple personalities in a lifetime. The damage done to them is so severe it requires an all-out effort.

I also believe that in the treatment of the multiple personality there has to be both a parent figure and a therapist. Ideally the therapist should not be both, as I tried to be. The therapist should be able to maintain an objective attitude throughout the treatment, not personally involved as a mother substitute. Therapy would progress much faster and in far less complicated form, emotionally speaking, for all involved.

My reward for the years Nancy and I worked together came in a letter thanking me for what she felt I had done for her:

> I know you've heard that I love you from me and "my people" probably a thousand times but the love we give you is the real stuff, the best thing in our lives. I want you to know *why* I love you. I love you first of all as an individual, because you are a person I can respect and admire. I admire your determination and vitality. I wish I had one half of the energy that you do. To me, you are a person who sticks to her principles and beliefs. I see you as a young, alive, beautiful woman who cares enough to give of herself. And I realize now how much better it is that you give of your real self.
>
> I love you because you are there for me, because you didn't go away. I love you because you care enough to do what's right for me, even when I don't agree. I love you for teaching me about life, about being a daughter, and someday about being a mother.
>
> Someday, I promise, I will make you proud of me. Without reservations. And the day that I can also be proud of myself will be the day I teach others, including my children, those qualities in life that I learned from you. Someday there is going to be a "little Emily," your namesake, and she will know what all of this is about. Because I will know how to take care of her. I know that sounds strange, because I can't even take very good care of myself yet, but I have learned enough from you to know that I won't let her into this world until I can.
>
> Not many people get a second chance. In spite of my blowing it at times, still you have kept on loving me, as I guess a real mother would. I wouldn't have expected that from anyone. Please forgive me if I have ever taken you for granted.

I'm not going to be so foolish as to promise: "I WILL NEVER, EVER, EVER IN MY LIFE DO ANYTHING WRONG AS LONG AS I LIVE." But I can promise you I will try my best to do what is right.

I say all this because you are so special to me. Because I love you, and in my eyes, you are the most wonderful human being I know.

All my love,
Nancy

This letter I will treasure always. But more than the thoughts it contains, I will treasure the many memories of the years in which Nancy and I worked together so she could conquer the crippling of her early life. I love her not only for her courage in doing this but in wanting now to help others.

She does not have to *do* anything more, as she says, to make me "proud" of her. I was proud of her the day she, or rather the Jennifer part of her, walked ten miles in the November chill through the rain to thank me for comforting her in the nurse's office.

Nancy led the way to our mutual success in uncovering what she thought the unspeakable so her nightmare at long last lost its power to haunt her.

Epilogue

by Lucy Freeman

This book for me meant entering an exciting new world. A world where I, veteran of years on the psychoanalytic couch, learned of depths of the human mind I never dreamed existed.

I also learned anew the power of our unconscious and how it could come to the rescue of the conscious in times of terror. Emily, through her courage and quiet tenacity, as well as her love for Nancy, helped her make conscious the memories long banished to the depths of her mind, thus freeing her of their torment.

This book also proved once again there is a new peace we may achieve when our unconscious and conscious are in communication. Freud described the goal of therapy as making the unconscious conscious: "Where there is id, let ego be." A strong enough ego allows us to experience our fair share of emotional harmony.

Nancy spent one-third of her life with Emily. Nancy told Emily, "I was like an empty shell when I came to you. You filled me in many ways." She had been drained by her personalities, drained by repression of her natural feelings and drained of energy, used chiefly to deny both the brutality inflicted on her and her overpowering wish for vengeance.

I was struck by the strength of Emily's conviction she could help the stricken Nancy: the indomitable quality of Emily Campbell Peterson in the face of seeming defeat upon defeat. And by the strength of Nancy

Lynn Gooch, who refused to give up during her painful inner journey. Compared to Nancy's life, the lives of most of us seem idyllic.

It was a war from start to finish between Nancy and her personalities who, at the beginning, hated her and Emily. Part of Nancy wanted to defeat Emily, which would make Nancy the loser. Fortunately, part of her also wanted Emily to be the victor so Nancy would live. There were moments, Emily told me, she wanted to say to Nancy, "I give up, you win." But her love for Nancy was too strong for her to throw in the psychic towel.

Dr. Clinton A. Johnson's empathy, his quiet approval of Emily's work and his contributions to the understanding of the multiple personality, were very valuable. Nancy once said to him, "I shudder to think of the way I lived. It's hard to realize some of the things I have done." He reassured her, "Every step we take to understand ourselves is difficult."

I was moved by the courage of Nancy's mother, Nancy Gooch Phipps, whose words in this book tell of her own agony as a child. She helped rescue her daughter by approving Emily's therapy. She also graciously allowed us to interview her and use material from an article she wrote for magazine publication about Nancy, Junior's life.

Not to be underestimated were the roles played by Harold and Diane Gaffney—their ready acceptance of Nancy and the love and steadfastness they offered in the security of their home. Diane drove cross-country to bring Nancy home from the trauma of Lexington. Nancy says of the Gaffneys, "I loved Harold and Diane, though I was closest to Harold, a strange, odd man. I knew he loved me and I appreciated his rather warped sense of humor at times."

The idea of Emily for so many years giving generously of herself in time and dedication without asking one cent amazed me. Emily explained, "My rewards were not money. I had a quest. And I am stubborn when it comes to the quest. I relied not only on my intuition but my increasing knowledge of the human mind. At times I felt like an explorer finding the gold of new awareness. This was my reward."

She said the experience helped her understand conflicts in her life: "I discovered my anger at my father for deserting me when I was three. I had known my anger at my mother. I felt she never gave me the protection I needed and I thought she pushed my father out of the house. Now I realize I was furious at him for not fighting back and staying to care for me."

I saw how very vital it was that Emily helped Nancy overcome her fear of abandonment. The early traumas, fragmenting her world, had intensified her normal fear of being abandoned. She could now face what the traumas meant in all their non-sense. Emily also encouraged Nancy to become aware of her intense childhood hatred. The reliving of hostility and hate toward early childhood figures is a necessary phase of every successful personal psychoanalysis, according to the late Ralph Greenson, M.D., of Los Angeles, internationally famous psychoanalyst, who treated Marilyn Monroe. This is true for the so-called normal person who has not suffered to the extreme degree Nancy did. Nancy's need to relive and thus relieve her fury at those who damaged her as a child, physically and emotionally, was overwhelming.

Certain heartbreaking words by Nancy and the personalities still ring in my ears. I recall the thoughts of Nancy/Sherry as she castigated Emily for wanting the multiples to fuse: "You take away the pain and they ain't nothin'. That's all they know. People treating them like shit. People hurting them." And the words of Nancy when she once cried out to Emily, "Tell me that I'm *real!*" She had felt like papier-mâché, tossed about by the winds of a rage over which she had no control.

One sign of Nancy's freedom has been her ability, for the first time in her life, to let her fingernails grow. She held out her hands, said proudly, "See? I have fingernails at last." She had loathed long fingernails, always bit her nails. Unconsciously, long nails reminded her of Norah's nails, associated with the flow of blood and the burning of her hands by the candle as Norah's hands brought her flesh into contact with the fiery flames. Perhaps Nancy also feared she might use her long nails to rip apart enemies, as Nancy/Regan tried to scratch the wallpaper in her uncontrollable fury. An animal in pain will use his claws to slash and tear at whatever is near in an effort to destroy the cause of his pain.

I saw in full play the use Nancy made of the mental function in all of us which Freud described as the "compulsion to repeat." It is a way of trying to render past terror harmless. Nancy repeated over and over in various distorted ways the theme of her suffering in an effort to relieve it. She told indirectly of the many threats of adults who sexually and violently abused her as a child. By becoming promiscuous and addicted to drugs, she re-enacted the behavior of the emotionally disturbed men and women in her life who possessed their peculiar addictions—religious rituals in which blood was drawn from a violently assaulted two-year-old child, the rape of a six-year-old girl weekly for a year.

I thought of the religious rites of earlier centuries when innocent persons were accused of being "possessed by the devil" and the letting of their "bad blood" supposedly rid them of the devil within. Not too long ago the mentally ill were treated by blood-letting, as though this allowed the "evil" to flow out of them. I wondered if Norah's ancestors, who came from Ireland, had ever taken part in religious rituals. This fantasy of Norah's had to have a basis of reality somewhere in her early life, perhaps she had been violated as a girl in the same fashion.

Nancy/Sarah wrote in one letter, following the revelations of past crimes, "There is no suffering left." But suffering will be part of Nancy's life to some degree, as it is for all of us. No one escapes losses, abandonments, indignities, cruelties. However, thanks to Emily's refusal to let Nancy endure a terror she dared not fathom by herself, today Nancy is no longer victim of assailants unknown. No longer a rag doll without emotions, a "broken doll," as the doctor who sewed the two wrists Nancy/Jennifer had slashed called her.

As I worked on this book I also realized the power of verbalization—the conscious facing of terror that makes it possible to conquer deep fear. Most of us only fantasize our terror but for Nancy the terror had been real. As she could speak of the actual assaults, this had a healing effect. It meant that instead of denying painful reality, she could confront and accept it, limit her defenses to ones that would not harm her. Use her psychic energy for love, creativity, work, friendship, rather than to hold back fear, pain and rage.

Emily told each personality, "Love is the absence of fear. If you live in fear, you cannot love. All your energy goes into protecting yourself. You have no emotional investment left for love. You think only of how you can get power to combat the fear." Nancy's need for power was a key factor, perhaps the most dominant goal, in her life. If only she had possessed the power at two and again at six to fight her assailants, she would have been spared acute hurt and terror. Power to Nancy meant freedom from physical and psychological pain. Power meant the freedom to tell someone of the threats of death made early in life, to end the fear of dying that pervaded her existence: "If you tell anyone, I will kill you." From the babysitter when Nancy was two, to the rapist when she was fifteen.

The wish for power also carried with it the wish to be a boy. It was far too dangerous for Nancy to be a girl. Femininity brought the charge she was "evil," brought the burning of her fingers, then painful scalding in her most secret place, as well as rape by men. But boys were not helpless, they were strong, they could fight and conquer. To try to get power she created Nancy/John, tough, strong-willed, then Nancy/Ricky, who wanted to destroy everyone. In his way, each personality vied for power—Nancy/Sherry through her body, Nancy/Sarah through her intellect.

Only as Nancy faced the early horrors could she give up her consuming wish for power. Nancy's inner landscape had been her unconscious world, one she thought the most powerful. But it was sham power. The unconscious cannot differentiate between fantasy and reality. The only time we are truly powerful is when we are in control of ourselves in a conscious way. The reality is we can control only ourselves. To control someone else is not power but domination.

Thanks to Emily's patience and persistence Nancy can now head toward becoming a whole self, not needing to split into personalities (imprison in her unconscious her sexual and violent fantasies and wishes). Her personalities had served, not wisely but often too well, to come to the rescue of her conscious mind when intense fear and fury overpowered her.

One of the most important truths for me was strong proof of the fact mind and body are one and inseparable. The violent and sexual invasion of Nancy's body affected her psyche. At the age of two, when her body was savagely violated, she had available only the most primitive mental defenses against pain and terror as a means of rescue. Her mind was far from mature but it fought as valiantly as it could to protect her from the more severe disintegration of autism or schizophrenia.

In desperation, without choice, she automatically seized as defense the splitting of herself into different personalities. There may even be a very early stage in the development of our thinking when we lack awareness of ourselves as a separate being. What psychoanalysts call the "symbiotic" stage as we are still merged psychologically with our mothers. Also, each of us uses the stuff of dreams to create "inner personalities." Every figure in a dream no matter how disparate represents a part of ourselves. We create characters in the dark of night that act out memories and desires too dangerous for us to bear in daylight thoughts.

Many times as I wrote away I thought it no wonder the avenue between Nancy's conscious and unconscious thoughts was in gridlock. She had lost, through the early assaults on her integrity, part of her right to be human. She was forced to invest her emotions in the secret changelings who engaged in the dangerous but also protective game of "coming out" and "going inside." This provided a measure of temporary relief from her misery but also led to a wish to die because of her guilt at her own intense violent and sexual wishes.

Most of us are able to sublimate our childhood fears and rages into useful activities, we do not have to protect ourselves from constant fear of death threats by assailants, as Nancy did. In a mild form of the defense that allows us to create different personalities, we may speak as a different person to the various people in our lives. In one voice to a spouse, in another voice to a child, another to our parents, another to our friends, another to our employer, and yet another to a psychoanalyst if we are seeing one. The mark of an emotionally healthy person may be the ability to speak in the same voice to everyone, showing he is his own person consistently, he fears no one.

Nancy's life also proved that "love" to a child is very different from adult or mature love. In a child, the feeling of love has not as yet had time to add dimensions that include trust, tenderness, respect. Love to a child is hungry, greedy, jealous, grasping, murderous, all-possessive. A child learns the feel of mature love from parents in order eventually to love others maturely.

Nancy told Emily, "I have never felt passion." A victim cannot feel passion, he is too terrorized by fear. Nancy had been too afraid of love, of sex. As she put it, "When someone hugged me, I couldn't tell whether I was being embraced or attacked." Norah, the babysitter, had been entrusted to care for Nancy but instead attacked her with violence and wildly distorted sexual obsession. There is strong bond in violence, as well as love, violence at least represents "touch." In Nancy's mind, love/touch/pain/terror were inextricably bound.

Today Nancy no longer needs inner voices, her own soft voice is strong enough. She has accepted her right to be independent, says she has achieved a certain peace within she never dreamed existed. She possesses what she calls "inner deepest awareness." She knows that when psychic wounds run deep, when there have been years of denial of intense fear and fury, the search for truth is slow. She knows too that since nothing can equal the pain of her past, the way ahead will be far easier.

Her hope in allowing her story to be told in starkest detail, is that others may be released from their living nightmares. That what may be learned can be put to use in relieving the agony of those who are similarly mutilated emotionally.

Emily says in her treatment of Nancy she always kept her word: "I felt I could overcome all opposition if I were consistent." She chose a path "I would have wanted someone to take with me if I were in Nancy's shoes. I evolved a philosophy for maximum freedom in exploring a new situation or goal—do not make waves but question, analyze, draw conclusions and trust yourself. I never gave up hope Nancy would learn to trust herself."

It was that hope, plus an almost devout devotion on both their parts, that finally unravelled the mystery of the soul murder of Nancy Lynn Gooch. This led her to know her own self, one to which she could be true. Then, as Polonius said, it "must follow as the night the day" she could "not then be false to any man."

Nancy no longer was driven to be false to herself. A falseness she assigned the personalities to save her life. There was no other choice at the age of two when she felt like the walking dead. But now she was free of the torture of the past. Free to give and receive love that allowed her to feel cherished, no longer used and abused.

She could live in a world of her own making, not that of assailants. Free to leave the terror-stricken orbit in which she had spun in fantasy.

The nightmare was ended.